GOLD
TRIED IN THE FIRE

GOLD
TRIED IN THE FIRE

GREG HINNANT

CREATION
HOUSE
A STRANG COMPANY

GOLD TRIED IN THE FIRE by Greg Hinnant
Published by Creation House
A Strang Company
600 Rinehart Road
Lake Mary, Florida 32746
www.creationhouse.com

Unless otherwise noted, all Scripture quotations are from *The New Scofield Reference Bible* (New York: Oxford University Press, 1967). *The New Scofield Reference Bible* contains introductions, annotations, subject chain references, and some word changes in the King James Version that will help the reader.

Scripture quotations marked AMP are from the Amplified Bible. Old Testament copyright © 1965, 1987 by the Zondervan Corporation. The Amplified New Testament copyright © 1954, 1958, 1987 by the Lockman Foundation. Used by permission.

Scripture quotations marked ASV are from the American Standard Version of the Bible. Public domain.

Scripture quotations marked ESV are from the Holy Bible, English Standard Version, copyright © 2001 by Crossway Bibles, a division of Good News Publishers. Used by permission.

Scripture quotations marked KJV are from the King James Version of the Bible. Public domain.

Scripture quotations marked MLB are from the Modern Language Bible: The New Berkeley Version in Modern English, copyright © 1969 by Zondervan Publishers. Used by permission.

Scripture quotations marked MOFFATT are from *The Bible: A New Translation* by James Moffatt. Copyright © 1954 by Harper & Row, New York.

Scripture quotations marked NAS are from the New American Standard Bible. Copyright © 1960, 1962, 1963, 1968, 1971, 1972, 1973, 1975, 1977, 1995 by the Lockman Foundation. Used by permission. (www.Lockman.org)

AUTHOR'S NOTE: Some Scripture quotations have specific words and/or phrases that I am emphasizing. I have added italics to these verses to show that emphasis.

Cover Designer: Jerry Pomales
Design Director: Bill Johnson

Library of Congress Control Number: 2008923861
International Standard Book Number: 978-1-59979-364-1

First Edition

08 09 10 11 12 — 987654321
Printed in the United States of America

To disciples of Jesus
who want to answer His challenge,
"I counsel thee to buy of me gold tried in the fire,
that thou mayest be rich."
—Revelation 3:18

ACKNOWLEDGMENTS

$\mathcal{I}$ wish to acknowledge the wonderful cooperation, faithful support, and skilled assistance I receive daily from my associates and friends at Greg Hinnant Ministries. God bless them richly!

I also wish to recognize the professional yet personal partnership of the staff of Creation House: Dr. Allen Quain, manager; Jihan Ruano, administrative assistant; Deborah Moss, editor; Candace Ziegler, typesetter; Atalie Anderson, marketing coordinator; Bill Johnson, design director; and Jerry Pomales, cover designer.

Special recognition is most deservingly due Virginia Maxwell, production manager. With uncommon skill and gentle grace, Ginny juggles many book production needs and problems simultaneously, yet makes an author feel she's working on his or her book alone. Thanks, Ginny, for willingly carrying the details of this book the "second mile"! And the third, fourth, and fifth!

CONTENTS

PREFACE

*J*esus challenged the Laodicean Christians, "I counsel thee to buy of me gold tried in the fire, that thou mayest be rich" (Rev. 3:18). Ancient Laodicea was a banking center, and many Christians there were wealthy: "[We are] rich, and increased with goods" (v. 17). They were rich in their "gold," but not Christ's. Their wealth was material and temporal; His was spiritual and eternal. So Jesus' challenge wasn't a call to the gold mining or refining industry. His words were allegorical.

Consider this figurative interpretation of "gold tried in the fire":

- "Buy" refers to a purchase price, but one consisting of a personal, not a monetary, cost. To "buy," they must "pay," not coinage but a yielding or a surrender of their self-will to God's will.
- "Gold" is the item they must buy. Naturally, gold is the world's most desired precious metal and its chief symbol of wealth. Spiritually, it represents the Christian's most desired spiritual possession—spiritual riches, specifically, faith in God and the truth of God. The Bible often compares eternal truth, or God's Word consisting of His knowledge, wisdom, and understanding, to gold (Ps. 19:9–10; Prov. 3:13–14, 8:10). And Peter clearly likens the testing of our faith to the refining of gold (1 Pet. 1:6–7).
- "Tried" means tested, refined, and proved genuine. The difficulties God sends into our lives test, refine, and strengthen our faith; purify our hearts and minds; and enable us to prove the genuineness of God's truth and our genuineness as Christians.
- "Fire" is the strongest purifier. Water and soap wash away a precious metal's exterior impurities, leaving it outwardly clean. But fire exposes and consumes its interior impurities,

leaving it deeply, thoroughly pure. "Fire" speaks of our strongest purifying trials.

Like all His messages to the churches of Asia, Jesus' Laodicean letter calls Christians to become overcomers: "To him that overcometh" (Rev. 3:21). So those who "buy gold tried in the fire" are "overcomers."

Jesus' messages to the churches (Rev. 2–3) are both historical and prophetic. They address not only Christians living at the time (A.D. 95), but also those in the seven periods of this Church Age, the last being symbolized by the materialistically obsessed, morally lukewarm, proudly self-deceived Laodiceans—an unflattering but stunningly accurate depiction of many postmodern Christians. So Jesus' call to the Laodiceans speaks directly to us.

Besides representing the priceless faith in God and truth of God overcomers obtain, "gold" also symbolizes overcomers.

Note these parallels between gold and overcomers.

Gold is one of earth's most precious and noble metals. Overcomers are God's most valuable and honorable servants. Gold is found throughout the creation, in earth's crust and seas. Overcomers are found all over the world, in the "dust" of every continent and "sea" of humanity. Gold is a mark of worldly wealth. Overcomers are spiritually wealthy, or rich in spirit, Bible knowledge, insight, closeness to God, and confidence in Him. Gold is exquisitely beautiful. Overcomers exhibit the beauty of the Lord. Gold is rare. Overcomers are found among God's faithful few. Gold is useful. Overcomers are very useful to God, always accomplishing His will. Gold is malleable, soft enough when truly pure to be impressed and molded by hand. Overcomers are impressionable in the hands of God, who shapes them to His Son's image and their predestined work. Gold is stable, unchanging in its appearance, density, and comparative value. Once taught and proven, overcomers are unchanging in their beliefs, values, and life purpose. Gold is durable—virtually indestructible—unharmed by time, neglect, or weather. Overcomers endure all things, regardless of the season, treatment, or "weather" God sends.

Gold is also an excellent conductor of electrical power. Overcomers' prayers, words, and deeds convey God's life-giving power to spiritually dead people—and they live! Gold is refined in blazing furnaces. Overcomers are refined in fiery trials of faith and patience. Gold overlaid the ark of the covenant, the place where God's presence dwelt among the Israelites. Overcomers abide in God's presence daily and shall see His face eternally. God's earthly throne, the ark's lid or mercy seat, was covered with solid gold. God's heavenly throne will be covered (surrounded) by overcomers enthroned with Him to rule the nations. Gold's chemical symbol (Au) is taken from the Latin word *aurum*, meaning, "shining dawn," a reference to its sun-like shining luster. Wherever overcomers live and work, their lives are a dawning (first light or preview) of the coming kingdom of God on earth. Gold inspired dreams of a false utopia, El Dorado, where gold was as plentiful as sand. Overcomers inspire visions of the only true utopia, New Jerusalem, where pure gold, like clear glass, will be so plentiful it will be used to build the entire city and pave its streets.

Truly, as overcomers "buy" the "gold" of faith and God's truth in fiery tests, they not only possess them, but they also become alloyed with them. Thus they not only *buy* "gold"; they *become* gold.

God confirms this symbolically in Malachi 3:3, where He describes His people as "gold and silver" and Himself as "a refiner" who removes their "dross" (sin and self-will). He further promises to bring a remnant of Jews "through the fire" and "refine them like...gold" in the Tribulation period (Zech. 13:9). And Job said that in his crucible of testing God was refining the "gold" of not only his faith and knowledge but also his *soul*:

> He knoweth the way that I take; when he hath tested *me*, I *[my soul]* shall come forth *as gold*.
>
> —JOB 23:10

Like Job's, our fiery tests produce not only golden faith and golden truth but also golden souls! When ancient refiners could at last see their reflection in the pure molten gold, they knew their refining work was finished. They had pure gold. Similarly, when the heavenly Father sees Himself—His Son's image—in us, He knows our refining is complete. We are His pure gold—overcomers. Thus we conclude that the destiny of overcomers is not only to *buy* but also to *become* "gold tried in the fire."

Jesus challenges us to "buy gold tried in the fire" for one reason: "that thou mayest be rich" (Rev. 3:18), or truly, spiritually, eternally wealthy—not in cash and property, but in God. This book doesn't pretend to be God's Fort Knox, but it does proffer some genuine spiritual gold. Every chapter contains pure ingots of biblical truth and faith. And like their metallic namesake, this "gold" is "fireproof"—if believed and practiced, it will see you through the fieriest tests, anywhere, anytime. And it will make you "fireproof" and "rich" in God! Indeed, these are tested truths for trying times!

Behold this "gold!" Buy it! Become it!

—GREG HINNANT

Chapter One

THE FORWARD-MOVING CHRISTIAN

Joseph ... was a prosperous man ...
—Genesis 39:2

*S*pecially called, anointed, enlightened, believing, fervent, and focused though he was, the apostle Paul's service for Christ was occasionally hindered by Satan. To the Thessalonians he wrote, "We would have come unto you ... *but Satan hindered us*" (1 Thess. 2:18). Sometimes these unwanted blockages were extremely persistent. To the Romans Paul wrote, "I have been *much hindered* from coming to you" (Rom. 15:22).

Like Paul, we are occasionally hindered and sometimes "much hindered" by satanic interference. When we're temporarily prevented from doing God's will, rather than fret and complain we should step back from the frustrating situation and pray for wisdom, grace, and help. Then we should look for areas of our lives, labors, and ministries in which we can move forward. Once identified, we should pursue them heartily, "whatever" they are: "*Whatever ye [are able to] do*, do it heartily, as to the Lord, and not unto men" (Col. 3:23). All evidence indicates that this is the way Joseph thought and lived.

Freshly inspired by a heavenly vision of great future usefulness and honor, Joseph obeyed his father Jacob's call to locate his habitually wayward brothers, evaluate their flocks, and report to his father. But instead of meekly bowing down to him as Joseph's dream rosily predicted, his brothers maliciously rose up and, well, you know the story. (See Genesis 37:12–28.) When Joseph found himself ingloriously chained and sold instead of gloriously promoted and used, suddenly, all his impressive and divinely inspired plans were put on hold—big time!

But thanks to the even bigger grace of God, the young man reacted magnanimously instead of meanly. Soon after his confining enslavement Joseph discovered and developed a liberating attitude. We know this because the first thing we read of him was not, "Joseph thought, 'I can't do anything for God now,' and sank into a deep depression, weeping by night and sleeping by day," but rather, "he was a prosperous man" (Gen. 39:2). This remarkable positivism sprang from God's personal favor, presence, and help. We know this because the Bible twice states, "The LORD was with him" (vv. 2–3). But the original language used here gives additional insight into the secret of Joseph's success, or, from the human perspective, the reason God continued being "with him."

"Prosperous" (Gen. 39:2) is translated from the Hebrew word *tsalach* (saw-lakh'), which means "to push forward, advance, or make progress."[1] Thus we understand that Joseph's "prosperity," which obviously did not lie in his current worldly position, wealth, success, or popularity, lay instead in his *consistently forward-moving attitude and actions, his ability to advance undaunted despite daunting adversities.* When on the road to glory he was suddenly confronted with an imposing Everest of a problem, Joseph apparently halted, prayerfully gathered himself, and pushed forward in the areas of his life that still remained open for progress, namely, his personal fellowship with God and his employment as a household servant to Potiphar, the captain of Pharaoh's royal guard. Thus he became an exemplary *forward-moving man.* It was this, not any flashy, lucrative, or enviable worldly success, that made him "prosperous" in the eyes of the Author of Scripture.

Have we learned and are we practicing this, the great secret to Joseph's prosperity? We will know by the way we react to shut doors, denied requests, disappointed hopes, unanswered prayers, slow-developing visions, or unrelenting and impenitent persecutors. If we say or think, "Well, that's it; our hopes are ruined, we can't do anything now," we haven't learned his secret. If, disappointed, we turn away from God, His ways, and the race set before us, and we become indifferent, indulgent, or lazy, we won't prosper in God. Why? We're failing or refusing to "push forward or advance" in and for the kingdom of God. To the contrary, we'll steadily retreat, sink, and ultimately fail, never seeing the fulfillment of the vision of God's purpose for our lives.

To avoid this dismal swamp of aborted destinies, let's study the diligent ways of forward-moving Christians.

The Ways of Forward-Moving Christians

In youth

In our youth we are usually held back from the most desirable positions, offices, duties, missions, and ministries primarily because of our lack of knowledge, wisdom, and experience. Another reason for this is God's mercy. To keep us from being overstressed and humiliated, He kindly denies us responsibilities that exceed our present capabilities. But wise Christian young people learn that when they cannot lead, they can still learn and so prepare to lead. When they cannot minister, they can still assist ministers and learn the passion, purposes, and ways of true ministry. When they don't have a commanding knowledge of their chosen fields, they can still diligently build their knowledge and observe, study under, and inquire of the masters of those fields.

Therefore, forward-moving Christian youths give themselves to the pursuit of the knowledge of God by waiting upon Him in private prayer and worship, studying His Word, and learning from the wise teachers and experienced mentors He provides. They also redirect their ambition and energies to passing the many tests of faith, patience, loyalty, and courage that fill their days in "Potiphar's house." Thus they answer God's call to not foolishly waste but to wisely use their youth: "Remember now thy Creator in the days of thy youth" (Eccles. 12:1). They also study voraciously the vocation, profession, or ministry to which God has called them and persistently practice the skills He has given them, just as Joseph continued to practice his gift of interpretation even while in Potiphar's prison. (See Genesis 40:1–23.)

They've not arrived yet, but they're on their way. Their vision hasn't visualized yet, but, like Joseph, they're persistently preparing for it by faith.

And as they fully accept and "farm" their valley of preparation, they gain one of life's most valuable assets: contentment in the day of small things. Indeed, young Christians who can say with Paul, "I have learned, in whatever state I am, in this to be content" (Phil. 4:11), are already wise, prosperous—forward moving in spiritual growth—and very rich, though their years are few. Why? "Godliness with contentment is *great gain [or immense true wealthiness]*" (1 Tim. 6: 6).

Young man (or woman), are you using or abusing the days of your youth? Forward-moving or stagnant? Preparing or pouting?

In stagnant churches, families, businesses, or other groups

It is a great day when we decide to move forward in our personal obedience even when those closest to us seem determined not to do so. When it slowly dawns on us that others in our family are not interested in Jesus, or many in our church are lukewarm, or our business or professional associates are unconcerned with excellence, it's decision time. Are *we* as wise as the four Samaritan lepers? (See 2 Kings 7:1–20.)

When their psychologically paralyzed peers adopted a "there's nothing we can do" attitude, these physically disadvantaged men said, "Why sit we here until we die?" (v. 3). Then they began quietly but bravely moving forward, probing the Syrian camp to see if God had already made a way to escape. Soon all their fellow citizens, even the most depressed, were delivered from the debilitating and deadly stagnation that had long gripped them. Are you surrounded by negative, apathetic, or indolent people who have accepted failure as inevitable?

If so, I suggest first that you "fret not thyself because of evildoers" (Ps. 37:1). Second, neither condemn nor berate them, but pray for them. Stagnant people are sick people; they need our intercession, not our indignation. Third, if you can, exhort them to rise above their indolence or adversities. Fourth, whatever you do, refuse to succumb to their spirit of stagnancy! Why sit down among them and die—and host your spiritual funeral! Fifth, rise and move on in your personal walk and predestined work with Jesus, steadily seeking His Word and presence and discharging the duties He gives you "heartily, as to the Lord" (Col. 3:23).

If you do so, you'll be stunned at the way the Lord visits, blesses, reinvigorates, and uses you, even while you're still "besieged" by the sad sons of stagnancy. He will pass by them and, as He did Joseph, give you a message or ministry to the "King's house," or His royal people, the church: "And when they were come into the edge of the camp … behold, there was no man [enemy] there [any more] … *and they told it [the good news] to the king's house within*" (2 Kings 7:5–11).

In adversity, when confined, when maligned

When everything is going your way, it's easy to move forward. The inspiration of success, popularity, and prosperity lifts and carries you effortlessly to the next step. But when the stream of life flows hard against you, every step becomes a struggle. When your movements are temporarily limited or halted by confining forces, such as sickness, storms, wars, conflicts, or other crises, or your good name is maligned by envious or vengeful liars, it's easy to lose energy and use these adversities as an excuse to do less—or nothing!

But God is faithful to never leave you without the knowledge of the next step He would have you take. He won't take it for you, but His Spirit will show you clearly what you can do despite all the things you can't do. When Paul and Silas were wrongfully judged, punished, and confined deep inside the city jail of Philippi, it seemed they could do nothing. They couldn't travel, preach, prophesy, teach, or write in the darkness. They couldn't even walk around in their depressing dungeon. (Their feet were bound in "stocks," high-security torture devices constructed to hold prisoners in immobile, and often contorted and painful, positions.) Yet God faithfully illuminated their hearts with the awareness of something they could do—pray, praise, and worship—and they heartily did it, right in the middle of their horrible pit of persecution: "Paul and Silas prayed, and sang praises unto God" (Acts 16:25). So they pushed forward—and God responded by pushing open the doors that had confined them: "Suddenly there was a great earthquake … and immediately all the doors were opened" (v. 26). Thus He released His forward-moving apostles to advance even further in His plan!

Why not follow their example? In your "prison" of seemingly inescapable personal problems, why not push open your doors of confinement by offering God wholehearted obedience, steadfast prayer, and Spirit-filled praise and worship? You may be able to do little else, but if you will do this, God will meet your forward movement by inhabiting your praises and immediately and immensely blessing your soul. And soon He'll release you to go to "Lydia's house," or the next phase of His plan for your life: "And they went out of the prison, and entered into the house of Lydia…" (Acts 16:40).

After sin or failure

Often it's not enemies that dispirit us as much as our own foolish besetting sins and inexcusably persistent failings. As long as we keep shooting ourselves in the foot, Satan doesn't have to shoot at us with his arrows of resistance: "they [agents of the wicked one]…shoot in secret at the perfect. Suddenly do they shoot at him, and fear not" (Ps. 64:4). That is, until we learn to keep moving forward even when we sin, fail, or come short of the best we know. And how do we do so?

Whenever we sin or fail, we quickly do one thing: confess our sins and faults to God without blaming others or excusing ourselves! Then God's forgiveness, and our restoration, is immediate. How do we know this? His Word promises, "If we confess our sins, *he is faithful and just to forgive us our sins, and to cleanse us from all unrighteousness*" (1 John 1:9). The Word further reveals that after He forgives our sins, He forgets them—forever! "Thou hast cast all my sins behind thy back" (Isa. 38:17). (See Isaiah 44:22.) So we should do the same by making a conscious effort to move on, forgiven and washed by faith, with our faithful Forgiver. David and the Israelites did this.

After his sin with Bathsheba led to the death of his infant son, David chose not to indulge in excessive grief. After learning of the child's death, David "arose…and washed, and anointed himself, and changed his apparel, and came into the house of the LORD, and worshiped" (2 Sam. 12:20). Then he promptly went home and received food to restore his strength. After this, he comforted his grieving wife Bathsheba and turned his attention to the duties and needs of his kingdom (vv. 24–31). Why did he react in this manner? David was a forward-moving man of God. Well versed in Scripture, David may have been following a lesson learned from the Pentateuch.

After the Israelites were punished for murmuring in the wilderness (Num. 21:4–6), they fully and frankly confessed their sins to God and Moses: "The people came to Moses, and said, We have sinned; for we have spoken against the Lord and against thee.... And Moses prayed for the people [to be forgiven]" (v. 7). As they beheld the brazen serpent on the pole, a type of Christ on the cross, they were miraculously healed and instantly restored to full fellowship with God (vv. 8–9). Then, and most significantly, the next verse states, "And the children of Israel *set forward...*" (v. 10).

If David and the Israelites "set forward" after their sins and failings, we should too. So refuse to indulge in anger, self-pity, self-condemnation, or depression when you fail God! As David did, quickly confess your sins to God, be washed and cleansed in Jesus' blood, and rise to walk on with God. Draw near the Lord and permit Him to re-anoint you with His Spirit and reassure you with His presence in prayer and worship. Restore your spiritual strength by feeding meditatively on portions of His Word. Then readdress the duties, needs, and problems of your personal "kingdom," or sphere of authority and influence, without delay. And the angels will write of you, as they did of the Israelites, "And he [or she] *set forward...*"

While suffering

On his first apostolic mission Paul survived a vicious stoning at Lystra (Acts 14:19). If ever a servant of God needed an extended sabbatical by the balmy Mediterranean, it was Paul. Can you imagine the physical pain, disillusionment, and embarrassment he felt—stoned in front of his own congregation, shamefully defeated before the very students to whom he taught the victorious life? But Paul didn't take offense with Jesus over his offensive mistreatment. He knew well why he had been stoned. The demonic "rulers of the darkness of this world" (Eph. 6:12) had, through disbelieving Jews from Antioch in Pisidia, stirred the Lystrans to stone Paul because he was a prolific light-bearer (Matt. 5:14–16). Nor did Paul panic. He realized that God's permission of this vicious attack did not mean He had withdrawn His wider protection. Paul's "hedge" of guardian angels was still in place. (See Job 1:10; Psalm 91:11–12.) So what did Paul do?

He pressed forward! He advanced! He picked up his cruel "cross," went straight back into Lystra, and, while surely taking some rest, continued steadily ministering God's Word to God's people. First, he ministered in Derbe: "The next day he departed with Barnabas to Derbe. And…they…preached the gospel to that city, and…taught many" (Acts 14:20–21). Then, amazingly, he returned later to Lystra and the other cites of Galatia in which he had ministered before his stoning: "They returned again to Lystra, and to Iconium, and Antioch, confirming the souls of the disciples, and exhorting them to continue in the faith" (vv. 21–22). Why did he press on? He knew that while his need of an extended physical recuperation was great, God's grace and the saints' urgent need for spiritual edification were even greater. So he pursued his ministry, trusting God to supply supernatural strength and protection while he recovered from the painful and disfiguring effects of stoning. Not only in Lystra but also everywhere he went, Paul was a "prosperous" man, a New Testament incarnation of the Old Testament term *tsalach*—"to push forward, to advance" in the face of all odds. His example is a stirring challenge to all light-bearers in these increasingly dark End Times.

Are we pushing forward our walk and works with Jesus today despite our crosses? Are we advancing despite our cruel adversities?

In our latter years

Like our youth, our latter years present us with some unique hindrances. Sometimes our "golden years" seem, well, less than gilded. Why? We feel frustrated that we cannot do now what we once could. And that's true: the flesh *is* weak. But that doesn't mean we can't do anything.

When our flesh is weak, the Spirit within us may remain strong and well able to perform significant spiritual works. For instance, we can spend extra time in intercession, which, as I describe in chapter eighteen, is *the* most important work any Christian can pursue at any age and is Christ's current heavenly ministry: "He ever liveth to make intercession" (Heb. 7:25). We can support God's work with the monies we have accrued during the years. The gospel can't grow without giving. We can pass along our wisdom to those who are younger, less experienced, less knowledgeable, and less discerning. Every Joshua needs a Moses and every Ruth a Naomi. And we can assist, counsel, and mentor them as they begin moving into their callings and ministries. When aging, the apostle Paul this did for his beloved ministerial protégés Timothy and Titus and for others. By thus blessing them, we will receive an even greater blessing. Why? As Jesus said, "It is *more blessed to give* than to receive" (Acts 20:35). Any older Christian who practices these things is a forward-moving saint—and young in spirit!

Are we moaning about our aging process or moving forward despite it? Are we allowing our bodily limitations to chain our spirit?

~

To balance our understanding, we must also recognize that there is a wrong kind of forward movement. It occurs when rather than accepting our God-ordained limitations, we press against them.

For instance, when God checks us, rather than waiting on Him we insist on going ahead anyway in defiance of His warning. When people don't cooperate with us, we try to force them to move forward by coercive statements or actions. When the time is not ripe for a particular work or ministry, we try to sow and reap a harvest anyway, out of season. When hemmed in by laws, regulations, or codes, we try to circumvent them by trickery or schemes. All this apparent progression is actually regression. And it's self-deceiving: we think we're going forward when we're really going backward. Why? Anything we do prematurely or improperly in human willfulness will have to be undone, and then done again properly in God's time and way.

This was probably the inspiration for this famous prayer:

> God, give us grace to accept with serenity the things that cannot
> be changed, courage to change the things that should be changed,
> and the wisdom to distinguish the one from the other.[2]
> —REINHOLD NIEBUHR

That's just what we need. We need God's "grace" to serenely accept that if He sovereignly permits a hindrance, we'll have to live with it for now and go around it as best we can. We need His "wisdom" to recognize the things we can press forward. And we need His "courage" to move ahead with these things despite discouraging difficulties. Many personal experiences and observations have convinced me that, whatever our challenges, there are always areas of our lives in which we can advance.

For example, we can always pursue God's presence more in private prayer and worship. We can always go further in the devotional and systematic study of God's Word, life's most noble pursuit and our souls' most nourishing food. We can always go further in working out the reality of our salvation in daily trials; every new day, circumstance, and difficulty bring new opportunities to advance as "doers of the word" (James 1:22). We can always take the next step in our present duties, domestic, occupational, or ministerial. We can always move forward in walking in love by exercising understanding, patience, forbearance, and forgiveness for the people God puts before us. And we can always progress by taking rest at night or by taking half-days, full days, or weekends off for rest and recreation, as needed, so that by recovering strength we will be ready to work or minister again with more energy. So never succumb when the lying thought comes, "Look what's happened! You *can't* do anything now!"

Instead, take a step back and prayerfully ask God what you *can* do: "Lord, what wilt thou have me to do?" (Acts 9:6). Then do it. And keep doing it. Push it forward as often and far as you can. That will make you a biblically "prosperous," or forward-moving, Christian, spiritually rich with "gold tried in the fire," like Joseph, Paul, and all the other overcomers who have pushed forward and advanced God's will despite the presence of great hindrances in their lives.

It will make you like John Bunyan, who wrote the inspiring allegory *The Pilgrim's Progress*, despite being imprisoned twelve years in the uninspiring, depressing, and unhealthy atmosphere of Bedford Jail. It will make you like Martin Luther, who translated the New Testament into the German language despite being hidden in Wartburg Castle as a fugitive from the pope and the Holy Roman emperor. It will make you like William Tyndale, who continued prolifically translating the Scriptures into English, despite having to flee his beloved England and take refuge in Belgium. And it will make you like the apostle John, who, when over ninety years of age and exiled by the Romans to the lonely volcanic island of Patmos, faithfully advanced his personal fellowship with Jesus, abided "in the Spirit on the Lord's day" (Rev. 1:10), and received the greatest prophecy ever given, the Book of Revelation. And that's not all.

Becoming a forward-moving Christian will make you a prime builder of God's kingdom. And one day Jesus will summon all His kingdom builders to help Him rule this earth a thousand years:

Well done, thou good servant; because thou hast been faithful in a very little, have thou authority over ten cities.

—LUKE 19:17

So look beyond your dark devilish hindrance to your bright divine destiny. The best is yet to be!

Chapter Two

THE BEST IS YET TO BE!

Thou hast kept the good [best] wine unto now [the last].

—JOHN 2:10

hroughout its pages the Bible reveals God's *modus operandi*, or usual methods of operation. One of His more recognizable ways is this: He saves the best for the last. After the good and the bad stand down, the best stands up.

The divine One deliberately lets slick impostors, cool deceivers, and crass self-servers run their courses first. Then, when these devilish decoys have all had their say, way, and day, He sends forth His true divine servants to do His will in His way and day.

For example, when Israel's Messianic hopes were running high, the Lord let two popular false leaders, Theudas and Judas of Galilee, run their courses and gather followings in Israel. Then, after their demises, He sent His true chosen leader and *Christos*, Jesus of Nazareth, on His Messianic mission of mercy (Acts 5:35–39).

The Lord also often suffers long with His people's worldliness and waywardness and their shepherds' repeated failures. Then, when their sin and self-will have fully played out, He executes necessary judgments, pours out His Spirit anew, and raises chosen shepherds to lead His sheep into the lush, green pastures of steadfast obedience, spiritual growth, and glorious fulfillment.

For instance, after enduring the long, dismal rulership of King Saul and a whole generation of spiritual stagnancy, God removed Saul and "chose David, his servant, and...brought him to feed Jacob, his people" (Ps. 78:70–71)—and Israel's best king led the chosen nation into its best season to date, spiritually, economically, and geopolitically.

This pattern of divine action—reserving the best things for the end—is encapsulated in the words of the governor of the marriage feast at Cana: "Thou hast kept the good [best] wine until now [the last]" (John 2:10). Though addressed to that ancient village's latest young bridegroom, the governor's compliments were in a larger sense meant for the heavenly Bridegroom, who was also present and the real producer of the wine the governor judged best. So John confirms that, during His days on earth, Jesus saved the best for the last. He still does.

To further clarify and reconfirm this distinctive divine MO, let's consider this illuminating biblical list of last-but-best things.

SAVING THE BEST FOR THE LAST

Daniel

The Book of Daniel records three crises in Babylon in which its kings urgently called for counsel. In order they were: Nebuchadnezzar's forgotten dream of the great Gentile image (Dan. 2), his dream of a great tree (Dan. 4), and Belshazzar's feast, at which the famous "handwriting on the wall" appeared (Dan. 5). In each instance, Daniel's Spirit-inspired counsel proved far and away the best. Yet in each instance his advice was the last requested: "But at the *last* Daniel came in..." (Dan. 4:8).

Joseph

Like Daniel's, Joseph's was the last counsel offered to his Gentile monarch.

When Pharaoh awoke from his famous bad dreams, startled, he called first for all the magicians and wise men of Egypt: "And it came to pass in the morning that his spirit was troubled; and he sent and called for all the magicians of Egypt, and all the wise men thereof: and Pharaoh told them his dream; but there was none that could interpret them unto Pharaoh" (Gen. 41:8). After they had their say, "Then Pharaoh sent and called Joseph" (v. 14), whose gifted interpretation and wise famine preparedness plan proved to be Pharaoh's best counsel (vv. 25–36). Recognizing this, Pharaoh openly proclaimed Joseph his best counselor, "There is none so discreet and wise as thou art" (v. 39), and promptly gave him the best office in his administration: "Thou shalt be over my house [kingdom], and according unto thy word shall all my people be ruled.... I have set thee over all the land of Egypt" (vv. 40–41).

David

David was the last son born to Jesse and also the last reviewed by the prophet Samuel, who had visited Bethlehem by divine directive to search for Israel's next king among Jesse's sons. (See 1 Samuel 16:1–13.) Yet though he was last in these categories, David was Jesse's best son. So he was chosen over his brethren as Israel's best leader: "And the LORD said, Arise, anoint him; for this is he" (v. 12).

David was also Israel's last soldier to have a chance to respond to Goliath's challenge. (See 1 Samuel 17:1–54.) King Saul and all his men of war, including three of David's seven brothers, had ample opportunities to respond in faith to the surly Philistine champion who defied them twice a day for forty days (vv. 10, 16). Yet they all failed to do so: "When Saul and all Israel heard those words of the Philistine, they were dismayed, and greatly afraid" (v. 11). Therefore, despite being last to arrive in camp, and despite his youth and inexperience, David was clearly Israel's best warrior, because he alone drew near and defeated Goliath when everyone else drew back.

Elijah

On Mount Carmel, Elijah permitted Baal's prophets to call for Baal's intervention first: "Elijah said unto the prophets of Baal, Choose you one bullock for yourselves, and prepare it *first*..." (1 Kings 18:25). (See 1 Kings 18:20–40.) Only after their futile prayers, false prophecies, and frenzied prancing about their altar ended without any response did Elijah draw near God and call for His intervention: "Elijah, the prophet, came near, and said...Hear me, O LORD, hear me..." (vv. 36–37).

The amazing spectacles that followed—God's supernatural visitation by heavenly fire (v. 38), the sudden conviction and turning of His peoples' hearts (v. 39), and the gracious, drought-ending restoration of showers of blessing (vv. 41–45)—proved again that God had reserved His best for the last.

The apostle Paul

By his own admission Paul was the last apostle Jesus called during the church's early years: "After that, he [Jesus] was seen…of all the apostles. And *last of all* he was seen of me also…" (1 Cor. 15:7–8). Yet his epistles and his experiences recorded in the Book of Acts reveal that, in every way, Paul became the best of the original apostles—in Christlikeness of love and character; in intimate, even heavenly fellowship with God; in the knowledge of God's plan for the church; in the effectiveness, extent, and duration of Paul's ministry; and in the number and severity of the sufferings he overcame. That he sincerely thought and described himself as "the least of the apostles" (1 Cor. 15:9) because he had formerly persecuted many Christians only reinforces the fact that, humblest of all, Paul was the greatest of all the apostles. Jesus taught us that the greatest saints are the humblest: "Whosoever, therefore, shall *humble* himself as this little child, the same is *greatest* in the kingdom of heaven" (Matt. 18:4). So God saved His best apostle for the last.

God's creation

In the creation, God made the heavens and the earth and all life forms, botanical and zoological first, before He created mankind. (See Genesis 1:1–31.) Thus He saved His best work—and the only made in His express image—for the last.

Also, over the course of human history God has personally and directly created only two men: the first Adam, who indwelt Eden, and the second, Christ, who was born of a virgin in Bethlehem. (Eve was taken and made from Adam, and the entire human race was procreated from Adam and Eve, not created directly by the hand of God.) So God's last Man, Jesus, is His best.

Additionally, two human races, the unredeemed and the redeemed, have appeared on earth descended from God's two created men. The unredeemed are the lost, the natural race descended from Adam. They are born in sin, unaccepting of the Savior, and, tragically, bound for hell. The redeemed are Adam's children who by receiving Christ have experienced spiritual regeneration. They are born not only of the flesh but also of the Spirit and, triumphantly, are bound for eternal life in the new world. This last or redeemed human race is clearly the best.

Bible prophecies further reveal that after God destroys this present earth, which is tainted by the corrosive effects of sin, He will create another, which Peter describes as "a new earth, in which dwelleth righteousness [only]" (2 Pet. 3:13). The apostle John records, "And I saw a new heaven and a new earth; for the first heaven and the first earth were passed away..." (Rev. 21:1). This new and final earth—the eternal home of the redeemed—will be the best earth.

The Bible also reveals that there are two Jerusalems. One is temporary, and the other is permanent. One is embattled, and the other is exalted. One is cyclically in bondage and war, and the other is continually free and filled with peace. Paul writes, "The present Jerusalem...she is in slavery [bondage to the law, sin, and judgment] with her children. But the Jerusalem above is free [redeemed from all sin and wrath]" (Gal. 4:25–26, NAS). Of this latter and celestial capital city the apostle John writes, "And I, John, saw the holy city, new Jerusalem, coming down from God out of heaven, prepared as a bride adorned for her husband" (Rev. 21:2). As precious as present-day Jerusalem is, the perpetual *city of peace* is incomparably better. Though last, it's best.

The Cushite

Two messengers, Ahimaaz and the Cushite, ran to bring David news of the outcome of the battle of Mount Ephraim, each keenly aware of David's anxiety over Absalom's personal condition. (See 2 Samuel 18:19–32.)

First to run, and faster, Ahimaaz arrived and spoke initially to the king. When asked, "Is the young man, Absalom, safe?" Ahimaaz replied, "I saw a great tumult, but I knew not what it was" (v. 29). But this message wasn't true. Ahimaaz lied, apparently fearing David's reaction, when he said he didn't know of Absalom's condition, for the record reveals that Joab had already told him plainly, "The king's son is dead" (v. 20). After Ahimaaz finished his ministry of falsehood, the Cushite arrived with the full, albeit heavy, truth: "[May] the enemies of my lord, the king, and all who rise against thee to do thee harm, be as that young man is" (v. 32).

So God's best messenger, who declared the whole counsel of God, spoke last.

Jesus' miracles

Of all Christ's miracles—healing sicknesses, cleansing lepers, opening blind eyes, restoring hearing and speech, expelling demons—the greatest were His resurrections of the dead. And of His resurrections, the raising of Lazarus was the greatest.

Jesus had revived others before Lazarus (Jairus's daughter, a widow's son in Nain), but they had been expired for hours, not days, and none had been buried or entombed. To the contrary, Lazarus had been dead and buried for *four days* when Jesus raised him. So while He had revived others, only Lazarus was fully resurrected. At Bethany, Jesus demonstrated His power not only over death but also over the grave. This set apart Lazarus' rising as Jesus' greatest resuscitation, and therefore His greatest miracle. (John's Gospel intimates this by noting that it was the news of Lazarus' astounding return from the tomb that drew the huge crowds at Jesus' triumphal entry of Jerusalem; see John 12:17–18.)

Appropriately, then, the raising of Lazarus was Jesus' last miracle, occurring just before His final weeklong visit to Jerusalem. Why? He wanted His last miracle to be His best.

The last kingdom

This conquest-weary earth has seen the rise of many dominions, or spheres of political authority—patriarchal (tribal), barbaric, monarchial, papist, dictatorial, totalitarian, and, yes, now democratic. And one more, the kingdom of antichrist, is yet to rise. All these realms have, or will, ingloriously fail and fall and ultimately give place to the thousand-year kingdom of Jesus Christ.

From every viewpoint and in every category—in truth, worship, righteousness, compassion, justice, peace, law, order, productivity, and duration—this last-rising state will excel its predecessors. So this last dominion will be the best. Unlike its forerunners, the kingdom of Jesus Christ will only rise and never fail or fall: "The God of heaven [shall] set up a kingdom, which shall *never be destroyed...it shall stand forever*" (Dan. 2:44).

Israel's kings

Of all the great kings in Israel's history, none are its greatest. David, Solomon, Jehoshaphat, Hezekiah, and Josiah—these first honorable heads of the Israeli state were but shadows. The last, David's greater son and the Lion of the tribe of Judah, will be the real substance. This King of kings, Jesus to us, will in His millennial glory be addressed, "Wonderful, Counselor, The Mighty God, The Everlasting Father, The Prince of Peace" (Isa. 9:6). And, as stated above, "Of the increase of his government and peace there shall be no end…" (v. 7). So God has saved Israel's best king for the last.

Israel's prophets

Christ openly declared that the last in the long line of Israel's ancient prophets, John the Baptist, was its best: "For I say unto you, Among those that are born of women there is *not a greater prophet than John the Baptist*" (Luke 7:28). But this best-as-last principle didn't end there. The same is true of Israel's modern seers.

Present-day (or modern, national) Israel has yet to be converted en masse to faith in its true Messiah, Jesus. But the Bible foretells that this will occur in the first half of the Tribulation period, immediately after the rapture of the true church and body of Christ. (See Romans 11:25–26; Revelation 7:1–8.) Converted Israel's greatest inspired spokesmen will be its last, the "two witnesses" of the second half of the Tribulation period, known as the Great Tribulation. "And I will give power unto *my two witnesses*, and they shall prophesy…" (Rev. 11:3). Their singular divine inspiration, courage, protection, and spiritual gifts will be so great that they will do what no other Jewish prophet has done—stand alone against *the whole world*, fully united under and deluded by Satan, for three and a half years (Rev. 11:3–12).

So Israel's last prophets, in both the ancient and modern eras, are its best.

Israel's revivals

Beginning with its renowned Exodus, Israel's long and sad history has been blessed with periodic spiritual renewals, or revivals. But all of these seasons of exceptional divine refreshing will pale in comparison to the last.

In the first half of the tribulation period, God will save millions of Jews and Gentiles from all the nations through the ministry of 144,000 very devoted, single, Jewish men, whom Jesus will personally visit, convert, and commission after the rapture of the church. (See Revelation 7:1–8; 14:1; Joel 2:32; Zechariah 8:20–23.) This ultimate Hebrew revival will end in a massive harvest of souls—the translation to heaven of millions of Jewish and Gentile converts to Christ around the midpoint of the Tribulation period just before, and perhaps prompting, Antichrist's military assault on Israel (Rev. 7:9–17).

So despite Israel's great past revivals, God has reserved its best for the last.

THE BEST IS YET TO BE!

The ways of God are as immutable as God Himself. They never change just as He never changes: "Jesus Christ [His character and His ways], the same yesterday, and today, and forever" (Heb. 13:8). So just as God has saved the best for the last for Israel, He has done the same for the church, for you, and for me.

For the church

God has reserved the church's best days for its last. As in Israel's experience, the church's greatest revival will be its last. Jesus will come *to* His people before He comes *for* His people. He will reform and revive us, and then rapture us. This isn't mere wishful thinking. We have Christ's Word for it.

According to Jesus' prophetic parable of the ten virgins (Matt. 25:1–13), in the last days of the church age a midnight "cry," or sudden alarm, will awaken a sleeping church: "They [virgins] all slumbered and slept. And *at midnight there was a cry made...*" (vv. 5–6). This wake-up call will spark a great "lamp-trimming" revival—a worldwide spiritual movement in which all true Christians arise, repent of their spiritual and moral indifference (slumber), and return to true holiness of life, biblical values, and God's ways of living: "Then all those virgins arose and trimmed their lamps" (v. 7). Why the great stirring? The "cry," and the stimulating events connected with it, have convinced them that Jesus will soon appear and they must prepare themselves spiritually, and quickly: "Behold, the bridegroom cometh; go ye out to meet him" (v. 6). This period of earnest spiritual revival, growth, and testing will continue until the Bridegroom appears and translates all "ready," or prepared, overcoming Christians, to His side: "And . . . the bridegroom came, and *they that were ready* went in with him to the marriage [feast in heaven]; and the door [way of passage from earth to heaven] was shut" (v. 10).

During this last season of the church age, there will be a near fulfillment of Haggai's famous prophecy—the "glory" of the church's "latter house" will exceed that of its "former," or first house (Hag. 2:7–9). The greatness of God's mighty acts, the splendor of His truth, the wonder of His compassion, and the radiance of Christ shining in us, in not only great blessing but great adversity, will reach an all-time high. Amazingly, last-generation disciples will become even more Christlike than their first-generation counterparts. For those who wonder, as Mary did when she learned of her approaching miraculous conception, "How shall this be?" (Luke 1:34), I offer only one answer—the all-sufficient, infinitely capable Spirit of God! "Not by might, nor by power, but *by my Spirit,* saith the Lord of hosts [the house of God shall be rebuilt]" (Zech. 4:6). As the ruined Jewish temple was rebuilt against all odds due to the supernatural power, ability, wisdom, and protection of the mighty Holy Spirit working through the Jewish remnant, so the church will be rebuilt and raised to its amazing final glory by the awesome power of the Holy Spirit working through fully surrendered "remnant" Christians. ("Remnant" Christians are the faithful minority who stand true to God and His Word, ways, and values when the majority do not.) Then God's full plan for the church will finally be completed.

The true body of Christ will be sanctified, unified, and filled with God's enduring love (John 17:21, 23, 26). By steady teaching from God's Word, testing, self-examination, and exhortation, we will grow in holiness until we are like a purified bride, no longer marred by spiritual "blemishes" or "spots" of flesh—habitual sins or consistent faults. Thus the Bible's vision of the bride of Christ, or "purified bride" church, will become a reality (Eph. 5:25–27). And by the sustained, comprehensive work of the fivefold ministry the body of Christ will also become a "perfect man" church (4:11–16).

By "perfect man" church we mean God's people will grow in the faith and knowledge of God until we think, live, and minister collectively just as

Jesus—God's perfect man—did individually. Just as He walked the earth perfectly demonstrating His Father's glorious truth, grace, justice, and power, so we, His people, will walk no more in immaturity but in His fully developed spiritual maturity: "[The ministry will edify and perfect the saints] Till we all come in the unity of the faith, and of the knowledge of the Son of God, unto *a perfect man, unto the measure of the stature of the fullness of Christ*" (Eph. 4:13). Or, "This work must continue until we are all joined together in the same faith and in the same knowledge of the Son of God. We must become like *a mature person, growing until we become like Christ and have his perfection*" (NCV). Or, "This will continue until we all come to such unity in our faith and knowledge of God's Son that we will be *mature in the Lord, measuring up to the full and complete standard of Christ*" (NLT).

So Christ's last church—His true spiritual body and bride—will be His best.

For you and for me

If in all the ways listed above God saves the best for the last, shouldn't we expect Him to do the same for us?

If we abide close to Him—steadily seeking, believing, and obeying Him—shouldn't we expect Him to make our last days our best? Though there are sins and failures in our past, why should we surrender to the pessimism of regret? Though there are perplexities in our present that fill our future with uncertainties, why should we surrender to the internal terrorism of anxiety?

Let us rather commit our past, present, and future into the hands of our unchanging heavenly Father, believing, confessing, yes, *knowing* He has saved His best blessings for our last days. And let us say often to ourselves and to one another...

For the church, for you, for me,
The best is yet to be!

Let this golden hope inspire you to fully be His servant!

Chapter Three

ARE YOU HIS SERVANT?

He chose David his servant...

—PSALM 78:70

So popular is the pursuit of self-interest today that our times may go down in history as the age of self. Unfortunately all the self-serving, self-promoting, and self-centered philosophies surrounding us have influenced Christians more than we would like to admit. Evidence of this is seen in the way we are so often reminded that we are not servants but sons of God.

Positionally, this is absolutely correct. Born-again ones are indeed adopted sons and daughters of God through the redemption that is in Christ Jesus, and I for one don't want to deny or discount this blessed Bible fact. To the contrary, I rejoice in it.

But practically, I have a problem with the way it is sometimes lightly stated and perceived, as if being God's children precludes us also being His servants. Those who think and speak this way fail to remember that our Lord Jesus—the only begotten and consummate child of God—consistently chose to serve His Father's will. And He did so, not only when accomplishing the vital work of redemption on the Cross but also every day He lived on this earth. Why? He wanted to illustrate for us what it means to be a servant of God. Clearly and repeatedly, His actions and words exuded the quintessential spirit of servantship. His every choice was driven by loving, submissive, fully dedicated consideration for His

Father's will, not His own.

Ponder the rich, revealing language of God's prime Servant:

I do nothing of myself; but as my Father hath taught me, I speak
[His words, as He pleases].

—JOHN 8:28

I do always those things that please him.

—JOHN 8:29

Knew ye not that I must be about my Father's [not my own]
business?

—LUKE 2:49

I delight to do thy will, O my God. [Christ's motto]

—PSALM 40:8

I have finished the work which thou gavest me to do.

—JOHN 17:4

If thou be willing, remove this cup . . . nevertheless, not my will,
but thine, be done.

—LUKE 22:42

Doing nothing of Himself, always pleasing the Father, always about
His Father's work, delighting in that work, finishing that work, always putting it first, before His own personal desires—clearly Jesus' own words
define Him as an utterly committed servant of His heavenly Father. John's
Gospel gives great emphasis to this fact. (See John 5:36–37; 6:57; 7:16;
8:26; 10:17; 12:49; 14:31.)

How will we follow Jesus' model if we insist that we are only sons and
not also servants in training? Jesus' example proves forever that *sonship
and servitude are not mutually exclusive, that they may and should coex-
ist in us, just as they did in Jesus, the first Servant-Son of the Christian era.*
As if foreseeing these conflicting modern perspectives, the writer to the
Hebrews gave us his, and God's, definitive opinion:

Though he were a Son, yet learned he obedience [as a servant]
by the things which he suffered.

—HEBREWS 5:8

Obviously, his conclusion was that Jesus was *both* the Son and servant
of God. This opinion reflects that of the great Hebrew prophet Isaiah, who
foresaw Messiah Jesus not only as God's anointed Son but as His suffering servant: "Behold, my *servant* shall deal prudently...by his knowledge
shall my righteous *servant* justify many; for he shall bear their iniquities"
(Isa. 52:13; 53:11). What, then, is a servant of God?

WHAT IS A SERVANT OF GOD?

A servant of God is sent by God, not himself or other people. He (or she)
does nothing of himself—all of his works, missions, and teachings spring
from his Master's heart and will, not his own. He is completely dedicated,
or set apart, to his calling and pursues it faithfully, persistently avoiding
distractions and circumventing hindrances.

No faddist, he does not blindly follow popular societal or religious
patterns of operation. Rather he only follows the still, small voice of the
Spirit that calls him from above—whether none, few, or many walk with
him, and whether he is praised or persecuted.

He works for his Master's approval only, not for the plaudits or com-
mendations of men. To him, success is fully discharging his current duties,
whether visible results are impressive or infinitesimal.

He is no hireling. He sees his work as an indispensable, predestined
calling of eternal importance, not just a preferred profession in a passing world. Consequently, he will work long and hard whether he receives
much prosperity or mere provision for his labors. His real salary is a smile
and a word from above, "Well done!"

He is not self-serving or self-protecting. He is prepared to suffer, if
necessary, to deliver his message, complete his mission, or finish his work.
He is committed to the whole counsel of God, willing to speak the truth
in love to anyone but unwilling to alter the truth to appease anyone—and
spare himself trouble.

Aware that God may change his orders at any time, he waits in God's presence daily for further instructions: "As the eyes of servants look unto the hand of their masters, and as the eyes of a maiden unto the hand of her mistress, so our eyes wait upon the LORD our God" (Ps. 123:2). Thus his fellowship with God is extraordinary.

Attuned by this consistent close fellowship with God, he grows familiar with God's voice and eventually distinguishes it every time He speaks: "I heard the voice of the Lord, saying, Whom shall I send…?" (Isa. 6:8). Therefore, in the words of the late Dr. Judson Cornwall, "inerrant communication with heaven" is established.

Alert, he responds promptly once he is sure God has called: "After he had seen the vision, immediately we endeavored to go…assuredly gathering that the Lord had called us" (Acts 16:10).

Adaptable, he is always ready to change his plans to pursue God's plans, just as Jesus interrupted His travel schedule to minister two days in Sychar because He saw His Father's hand working there (John 4:3–43).

This, and nothing less, is what it means to be a servant of God. Admittedly, this is a very humble calling. Perhaps this is why so many Christians today despise it—we're so proud! And self-serving, like the prodigal son!

THE LESSON OF THE PRODIGAL SON (LUKE 15:11-32)

One day the "younger" of "two sons" (vv. 11–12) chose to stop living close to his loving father—and serving him.

He knew his father had plenty of laborers faithfully serving him—non-related "hired servants" (v. 17) and birth-related son-servants, here represented by the "elder son" (v. 25), whom we find working "in the field" (v. 25), and who testifed "these many years do I *serve* thee" (v. 29). So the younger son reasoned, with all these servants around, why did he also need to serve his father? Besides, he had other plans—to serve, enrich, and indulge himself! So, callously, he ignored his father's need of filial love. Yet, greedily, he claimed and clamored for the benefits of his father's estate: "Father, *give me* the portion of goods that falleth unto *me*" (v. 12). Blindly, he set his heart on temporal, material things, not eternal values: "the…goods" (v. 12). Foolishly, he walked away from his loving, provider-father: "The younger son…gathered all together, and took his journey" (v.

13). Selfishly, he went as far away as possible, "into a *far country* [far from his father, his house, and his servants]" (v. 13). Prodigally, he "wasted his substance" on "riotous living" (v. 14) and "harlots" (v. 30). But one day his orgy of self-serving ended.

A "mighty famine" unexpectedly arose in the "far country" and forced the prodigal to rethink his life values and choices. When he "came to himself" (v. 17), two things gripped his mind: his father and his servants. "How many of my *father's* hired *servants* have bread enough and to spare..." (v. 17). Repentant, he began cherishing what he formerly despised—living with and serving his father. Stirred, he determined to earnestly seek his father's favor and voluntarily serve him again...except this time, not as a son-servant, but as a lowly "hired servant"! "I will arise and go to my father, and will say...*make me as one of thy hired servants*" (vv. 18–19). The words to his prayer are very revealing.

As stated, his father had two kinds of servants, family (son-servants) and non-family ("hired servants"). The latter served for pay alone, had no close relationship to his master, and enjoyed neither the rights nor benefits of sonship. The former had all these blessings, yet served voluntarily; he was drawn by love and respect for his father, not driven by a desire for temporal benefits or gain. Of the two, the son-servant obviously enjoyed more honorable status. That the prodigal was now eagerly willing to become not an honorable son-servant but a lowly "*hired* servant" (v. 19) tells us how radically he was changed. And humbled. And emptied of his own will. And finished with self-serving!

I believe our excessively selfish and materialistic generation is on the cusp of just such a complete reversal of attitude. Many Christians who have proudly used their Christian sonship as an excuse to reject Christian servantship will soon learn the lesson of the prodigal son. God is sending a "mighty famine" to the "far country," or this world that is far from Him. These inescapable adverse circumstances will thoroughly humble and change us. And millions of former despisers of servantship will, like the penitent prodigal, begin desiring it, praying earnestly, "*Lord, make me as one of your hired servants!*" (Ironically, this humble attitude will qualify them to receive, in due time, the very best blessings and benefits of sonship! Note *after* the prodigal's radical change of attitude, his loving father freely and joyfully lavished on him his "best" blessings; v. 22–23. See 1 Timothy 6:17.) Why will they now abandon their self-serving and eagerly learn servantship?

They will realize not only that Jesus was a servant, but also that being a servant of God is *the* most honorable calling.

THE HONOR OF BEING A SERVANT OF GOD

The highest compliment God has given His choicest ministers in Holy Scripture is simply the designation "My servant." That seems to say it all.

It implies that a miraculous divine work has been accomplished in which God's Spirit has converted a lost rebel into a glorious, beautiful, fruitful new creature: a servant of God. The list of honorees so distinguished by heaven is quite long and illustrious. Here are just a few of them:

- Job: "*My servant*, Job, shall pray for you" (Job 42:8)
- Abraham: "For *my servant* Abraham's sake" (Gen. 26:24)
- Moses: "Moses, *my servant*, is dead" (Josh. 1:2; see v. 1)
- David: "I have found David, *my servant*" (Ps. 89:20).
- Isaiah: "As *my servant*, Isaiah, hath walked" (Isa. 20:3)
- Daniel: "O Daniel, *servant* of the living God" (Dan. 6:20)
- Paul: "Paul, *a servant* of Jesus Christ" (Rom. 1:1).
- Peter: "Simon Peter, *a servant* and an apostle of Jesus Christ" (2 Pet. 1:1).

Job, Abraham, Moses, David, Isaiah, Daniel, Paul, Peter—can it get any better than this? We shouldn't be surprised that God honors highly those who serve Him humbly. Jesus plainly promised us, "If any man serve me, him will my Father honor [cite, distinguish, award]" (John 12:26). Why? By consistently serving God's will rather than ours, we honor God. And God's eternal law is, "Them who honor me I will honor" (1 Sam. 2:30).

Now that we're familiar with the honor of God's servants, let's explore their special benefits.

THE BENEFITS OF SERVANTS OF GOD

The benefits of God's servants are, in a word, enviable! God reserves His choicest blessings for His committed servants.

He gives them wise and understanding hearts: "Give...*thy servant* an understanding heart to judge thy people...lo, I have given thee a wise and an understanding heart" (1 Kings 3:9, 12).

He gives them special insight into His Word, a full knowledge of His character, and timely messages: "Speak; for *thy servant* heareth....And the LORD revealed himself to Samuel by the word of the LORD" (1 Sam. 3:10, 21).

He gives them heavy anointings of His Spirit to speak and work for Him with power: "I have found David, *my servant*; with my holy oil have I anointed him" (Ps. 89:20).

He gives them key ministries and missions that serve vital purposes in His worldwide plan: "He chose David *his servant*, and took him...to feed Jacob, his people" (Ps. 78:70–71).

He vigorously labors to establish the family, name, and legacy of those who valorously labor to establish His family, name, and kingdom: "I will build him [Samuel, *my servant*] a sure house" (1 Sam. 2:35).

He delights in them with a special love: "Behold *my servant*...in whom my soul [specially] delighteth" (Isa. 42:1).

He boldly defends them before their bold critics: "Wherefore, then, were ye not afraid to speak against *my servant*, Moses?" (Num. 12:8). And He vindicates them when they've been maligned: "Ye have not spoken of me the thing that is right, as *my servant*, Job" (Job 42:7).

He faithfully delivers them from every trial: "Thy God, whom thou *servest continually*, he will deliver thee" (Dan. 6:16).

He avenges them of their cruel and impenitent persecutors: "They brought those men who had accused Daniel, and they cast them into the den of lions...and the lions had the mastery of them" (Dan. 6:24).

He has reserved a very special place for them, nearest to Him, in the eternal city of New Jerusalem: "And his servants shall serve him; and they shall [be so close that they] see his face" (Rev. 22:3–4).

And, finally, in the new world God's servants will receive His highest reward, His personal mark of distinction. He will engrave His regal name, or distinctive monogram, upon their faces: "And his servants...his name shall be in their foreheads" (Rev. 22:3-4). This will be His official and perpetual seal of approval: *This is My servant who serves and stands for Me, and by whom I stand...forever!*

In light of this, it's decision time. Are *you* His servant? Do you want Him to write "My servant" on your personal record and countenance? Do you want Him to recognize your servantship in His illustrious and immortal Hall of Fame, the exclusive "gold club" of divine servants? Will you serve His will alone? You can't if you're serving your own will or the will of others. God chose David to lead Israel because David's wilderness trials proved one thing beyond the shadow of a doubt: David was God's servant, not his own or Saul's or the people's. This may explain the reason for your present "wilderness" trials of faith, patience, love, loyalty, or endurance. They are giving you the opportunity to demonstrate to the Lord one chief characteristic—you will serve *Him!*

So today, just where you are, begin pursuing divine servantship. Be God's servant, consciously, fully, and exclusively. Though over the course of your life you may serve thousands, or even millions, of people for Jesus' sake, never again think or speak of yourself as the servant of any man: "Be not ye the servants of men" (1 Cor. 7:23). Think of yourself only as God's servant, bought by the precious blood of His Son: "For ye are bought with a price" (1 Cor. 6:20). Speak of yourself as God's servant: "James, a servant of God and of the Lord Jesus Christ" (James 1:1). Pray as God's servant: "Oh...give thy strength unto thy servant" (Ps. 86:16). Worship as God's servant: "O LORD, truly I am thy servant; I am thy servant" (Ps. 116:16). Listen for God to speak to you as His servant: "Speak, LORD; for thy servant heareth" (1 Sam. 3:9).

And continue doing these things, day after day, until you hear the sound of a heavenly trumpet followed by these words:

Well done, thou good and faithful servant!...Enter thou into
the joy of thy Lord!

—MATTHEW 25:21

Meanwhile, remember that as God's servant whatever you meet, recognition or reproach, rewards or resistance, has come straight from the
hand of God.

Chapter Four

GOD, THE GIVER OF ALL THINGS

A man can receive nothing, except it be given him from heaven.
—JOHN 3:27

Wilily, the backslidden Jewish religious leaders came to John the Baptist, hoping to arouse envy in his heart over the meteoric rise of Jesus' ministry and the resulting decline of his. But John the Baptist immediately dashed their evil hopes with his beautifully humble, simple, and spiritual response: "A man can receive nothing, except it be given him from heaven" (John 3:27). Paraphrasing, John said, "Jesus could not have this growing popularity unless the ruler of heaven gave it to Him." Thus he acknowledged God as the giver of all things. Unless God gave the Son of man—or any son or daughter of men—a blessing, He could receive "nothing." Have we contemplated the far-reaching depth and width and height of John's colossal proverb?

It decrees that divine permission always precedes human acquisition. Before we children of Adam can acquire something, God must first "give" it or grant permission for us to acquire it. If He doesn't, we'll never obtain it, no matter how diligently we work, pray, strive, or strategize. Truly *whatever* we have had in the past, or have now or will have in the future, is "given"—authorized in heaven and thus permitted to appear on earth—by God. Before we see it or hold it in our hand, it has been selected, approved, and released from His hand.

Clearly and repeatedly the psalmists assert that God's hand gives us all things:

Thou openest thine hand, and satisfiest the desire of every living thing.

—PSALM 145:16

That which thou givest them they gather; thou openest thine hand, they are filled with good.

—PSALM 104:28

DIVINELY GIVEN THINGS

Consider the enormously wide spectrum of divinely given things to the world, to the church, and to individual Christians.

To the world

God gave the world its greatest gift and only Savior, Jesus: "For God so loved the world, that he *gave* his only begotten Son…that the world through him might be saved" (John 3:16–17). Without this extraordinary endowment, the world would have been destroyed and tossed on the scrap heap of the abyss long before this twenty-first century.

Down through the centuries, God has also given the world many gifted people, such as inventors, geniuses, scientists, and scholars, and their timely discoveries, inventions, and studies that benefited all mankind: "*Every good gift*…is [*given*] from above, and cometh down from the Father of lights" (James 1:17). Additionally, He has given thousands of talented artists, architects, musicians, writers, and entertainers and their creative works of paint, stone, sound, song, book, stage, and screen solely for our enjoyment: "God, who *giveth* us richly *all things* [including wholesome art, literature, and entertainment] to enjoy" (1 Tim. 6:17).

Graciously, He gives sinners all over the world conviction and repentance of sin daily: "If God, perhaps, will *give* them repentance to the acknowledging of the truth" (2 Tim. 2:25). He then gives them saving faith to receive Jesus: "For by grace are ye saved through faith; and that not of yourselves, it is the *gift* of God" (Eph. 2:8). And when Christ enters, He gives them a new, soft heart (nature) responsive to Him: "A new heart also will I *give* you" (Ezek. 36:26).

He gives the various continents and regions of the earth rain: "The Lᴏʀᴅ shall...*give* the rain unto thy land" (Deut. 28:12). And He gives the mix of rain, sunshine, and warmth that produces rich, abundant harvests: "He did good, and *gave* us...fruitful seasons, filling our hearts with food and gladness" (Acts 14:17). He also gives abundant natural resources, such as rivers, lakes, forests, fertile plains, minerals, and precious metals: "The Lᴏʀᴅ thy God bringeth thee into [or *gives* you] a good land, a land of brooks of water...of wheat, and barley...thou shalt not lack anything in it; a land whose stones are iron, and out of whose hills thou mayest dig bronze" (Deut. 8:7–9).

He gives nations their respective homelands: "The land which the Lᴏʀᴅ thy God *giveth* thee" (Exod. 20:12). He providentially determines their present boundaries: "And I will *set [determine, give]* thy bounds" (Exod. 23:31). He gives rulers and governments their authority: "The Most High ruleth in the kingdom of men, and *giveth* it to whomsoever he will" (Dan. 4:17; see also vv. 25, 32).

In peacetime, He gives tranquility within nations: "And I will *give* peace in the land" (Lev. 26:6). And He gives favor and cooperation among nations: "And the Lᴏʀᴅ *gave* them rest round about" (2 Chron. 15:15). In wartime, He gives conquering nations and generals their military victories: "I will *give* Pharaoh Hophra, king of Egypt, into the hand of his enemies...as I *gave* Zedekiah, king of Judah, into the hand of Nebuchadnezzar, king of Babylon" (Jer. 44:30).

Thus the wonderful One gives wondrously all things to the world.

To the church

Besides its original and abiding endowments of Christ and His Spirit, the church's primary presents from above are its gifted fivefold ministers: "And he *gave* some, apostles; and some, prophets; and some, evangelists; and some, pastors and teachers" (Eph. 4:11). Without the spiritual edification and guidance these anointed leaders provide, the church could not grow, mature, minister, overcome her opposition, and fulfill her destiny.

The Lord gives ministers "utterance," or Spirit-anointed messages, for the instruction, correction, and inspiration of His ecclesia: "That utterance may be *given* unto me" (Eph. 6:19). He also gives them open "doors," or opportunities to deliver their messages to His people: "I have *set before [or given]* thee an open door, and no man can shut it" (Rev. 3:8). To prove their faith and keep them humble, He gives all Christians, but especially ministers, difficult situations and people who test them: "And lest I should be exalted above measure...there was *given* unto me a thorn in the flesh, the messenger of Satan to buffet me" (2 Cor. 12:7). To preserve them in their trials, He gives them timely infusions of courage and strength: "The Lord stood with me and strengthened me [*gave* me overcoming strength, courage], that by me the preaching might be fully known" (2 Tim. 4:17). To save them and their ministries to His people, He gives them deliverances from every trial: "The oath which he swore...that he would *grant [give]* unto us that we, being delivered out of the hand of our enemies, might serve him" (Luke 1:73–74). And when His plans require it, He gives chosen ministers special favor with political leaders and heads of state: "[God] *gave* him favor and wisdom in the sight of Pharaoh, king of Egypt" (Acts 7:10).

He gives local churches favor in their communities, cities, or nations so that His gospel and kingdom purposes may expand and prosper: "[The church] praising God, and having [*received from Him] favor* with all the people" (Acts 2:47). And He sometimes gives them *disfavor* to test their commitment and loyalty to Him: "At that time there was a great persecution against the church which was at Jerusalem" (8:1). He gives assemblies new converts and committed disciples, that their congregations may grow numerically, organizationally, and most importantly, spiritually: "And the Lord *added [gave]* to the church daily such as should be saved" (2:47). And He gives them divisions and depletions in their ranks to humble them, test their faith, and purify their motives in His service: "And they were all scattered abroad throughout the regions" (8:1).

So Christ gives richly to His church all things.

To individual Christians

Christ's greatest legacy to individual believers is His Word, the Bible, by which we learn of Him, His ways, His plan for the ages, and with which we feed our souls daily: "I have *given* them thy word" (John 17:14); "The Lord *gave* the word" (Ps. 68:11). To individual Christians who ask, He gives the fullness of the Holy Spirit to enable them to fully understand Scripture, mortify sin, overcome testing, and minister with power: "The Holy Spirit, whom God hath *given* to them that obey him" (Acts 5:32). As we study His Word, God gives us biblical wisdom, knowledge, and understanding: "For the LORD *giveth* wisdom...knowledge, and understanding" (Prov. 2:6).

If we seek Him, He gives us supernatural heart rest: "Come unto me, all ye that labor and are heavy laden, and I will *give* you rest" (Matt. 11:28). If we abide in His presence daily, He gives us the highest human joy daily: "In thy presence is [or *God gives*] fullness of joy" (Ps. 16:11).

He "gives" (or personally appoints) teachers, pastors, and mentors for us according to the level of our current spiritual development, whether it is elementary (novice believers), intermediate (growing disciples), or advanced (established disciples and ministers): "Ministers by whom ye believed, even as the Lord *gave* to every man" (1 Cor. 3:5).

By His unerring Word, discerning pastors, mature elders, anointed prophets, and faithful counselors, He gives us good advice: "I will bless the LORD, who hath *given* me counsel [advice]" (Ps. 16:7). And by them He also gives us timely warnings to keep us in the way of life: "*Give* them warning from me" (Ezek. 3:17).

He gives us spiritual gifts (operations of the Holy Spirit) with which to edify or comfort other believers, usually when they are in extraordinary difficulties: "The manifestation of the Spirit is *given* to every man to profit [edify, comfort, improve the condition of the body of Christ]. For to one is *given*, by the Spirit, the word of wisdom...the word of knowledge" (1 Cor. 12:7–8). If we demonstrate full commitment to Him and faithfulness in our duties, He gives us ministries: "Our Lord, who...counted me faithful, putting me into [or *giving me*] the ministry" (1 Tim. 1:12).

He gives us "grace"—divine favor imparting divine strength or ability—to bear heavy physical, emotional, or spiritual burdens: "My grace [strength and ability *given* you] is sufficient for thee" (2 Cor. 12:9). He gives us wise solutions to perplexing personal dilemmas: "If any of you lack wisdom, let him ask of God, who *giveth* to all men liberally" (James 1:5). He gives us divinely tailored training experiences that prepare us to confidently face and overcome the most difficult trials with divine ease: "It is God who girdeth me with [or *gives* me] strength...He maketh my feet like hinds' feet" (Ps. 18:32–33). He gives us deliverances, or timely, life-saving releases from our trials: "God is faithful, who will...make [*give*] the way to escape" (1 Cor. 10:13).

He gives us new seasons and new beginnings in our lives: "And he changeth [and so *gives*] the times and the seasons" (Dan. 2:21). "And the Lord turned [ended or *gave* release from] the captivity of Job, when he prayed for his friends" (Job 42:10). He will ultimately compensate us for all our losses, if we continue trusting and obeying Him: "The Lord is able to *give* thee much more than this [that you have lost]" (2 Chron. 25:9). In His appointed times and ways, He gives us rich personal rewards for our loyalty, trust, endurance, and loving labors in seasons of adversity: "He is a rewarder of [or *gives* rewards to] them that diligently seek him" (Heb. 11:6).

He gives us faithful spouses: "Whoso findeth a wife findeth a good thing, and obtaineth favor from [or *given* by] the Lord" (Prov. 18:22). He gives us children: "[These are] the children whom God hath graciously *given* thy servant" (Gen. 33:5).

He gives us the "grace"—divine favor imparting skill, favor with people, and success—we need to earn a living, obtain the material necessities of life, and share our blessings with others: "And God is able to [*give* or] make all grace abound toward you, that ye, always having all sufficiency in all things, may abound to every good work" (2 Cor. 9:8). He gives us preference with and assistance from superiors, so we may prosper in our occupations or professions: "Joseph found grace [was *given* preference] in his [ruler and employer's] sight" (Gen. 39:4). He even does this when we're in great adversity: "The Lord...*gave* him favor in the sight of the keeper of the prison" (v. 21). He sometimes gives us (or enables us to earn) extraordinary wealth so that our tithes and offerings may help establish His churches, ministries, charities, covenant, and plan for His people: "The Lord thy God...*giveth* thee power to get wealth, that he may establish his covenant" (Deut. 8:18). He gives us delightful blessings primarily to enjoy: "The living God, who *giveth* us richly all things to enjoy" (1 Tim. 6:17). Sometimes these blessings are the things we desire most as human beings: "Delight thyself also in the Lord, and he shall *give* thee the desires of thine heart" (Ps. 37:4).

He gives us victory in the inevitable conflicts of life: "The horse is prepared for the day of battle, but safety [victory] is from [*given* by] the Lord" (Prov. 21:31). He gives us invisible yet impenetrable angelic protection: "He shall *give* his angels charge over thee, to keep thee in all thy ways" (Ps. 91:11). Thus we alone enjoy truly fail-safe security in these insecure and perilous End Times: "I will both lie down in peace, and sleep; for thou, Lord, only makest me dwell in [or *give* me] safety" (Ps. 4:8). If we overcome our trials of faith, He will one day give us a position of rulership in His thousand-year earthly kingdom: "Fear not, little flock; for it is your Father's good pleasure to *give* you the kingdom" (Luke 12:32).

Thus Christ gives all things to individual Christians.

Let this overwhelming biblical evidence permanently alter your outlook on life and enrich you with this golden bullion of truth: *you* can receive nothing unless it is *given* you from heaven! So from now on, when you are in need, exercise your faith in the following ways.

Look upward, and then look outward. That is, first seek help directly from the Giver of all things: "In everything, by prayer and supplication with thanksgiving, let your requests be made known unto God" (Phil. 4:6). Then, as He gives you wisdom and guidance, patiently inquire, confer, and probe this earthly realm, prayerfully expecting God's help. That help may come directly by the Spirit's revelation to your heart. Or it may come indirectly through people. When help arrives, be sure to acknowledge God as its true Giver: "In all thy ways acknowledge *him*" (Prov. 3:6). If He has helped you through human agents, discern His providential hand behind every person's helping hand and immediately thank *Him*, telling Him that you know *He* gave you the wisdom, favor, or resources that gave you success. Then give due human credit by thanking the people who have helped you. This, too, is pleasing to the Lord.

He always blesses those through whom He blesses us: "I will bless them that bless thee" (Gen. 12:3). When God gave Paul timely support through the Philippian Christians, Paul not only worshiped God but also commended the Philippians: "Notwithstanding, ye have well done, that ye did share with my affliction" (Phil. 4:14). We should do the same.

And when adversity strikes, see God's hand behind every human hand that hinders, harasses, or hates you. Tell the Lord you realize *He* has given you the test, correction, disfavor, or opposition that, when accepted as a test from Him and addressed in obedience to Him, will humble and purify you, strengthen and train you, prove and mature you, and conform you more thoroughly to Christ's image.

Why are these "acknowledge the real Giver" spiritual exercises helpful? They will greatly increase your ability to trust God and detect His hand in all your circumstances, whether advantageous or adverse. They will also enhance your ability to see Him working providentially—through ordinary people and events. That will make you more spiritually minded and discerning, and therefore more useful to Christ in His work in these last days.

And most importantly, they will draw you ever closer to God, the Giver of all things—as many days as He gives you in this world.

Chapter Five

HE NUMBERS OUR DAYS

My times are in thy hand...

—PSALM 31:15

As we have just seen in the previous chapter, God "gives," or sovereignly releases into our lives, everything we have and experience—good, bad, and in between. The length of our lives is no exception.

In these increasingly perilous times, we may be tempted to fear that our lives may be snuffed out at any moment by the seemingly uncontrollable forces of terrorism, pandemics, wars, or natural disasters. But the Bible reveals this reassuring truth: "My times [days, seasons, lifetime] are in thy hand [control]" (Ps. 31:15). This verse declares that every believer's life is entirely in God's hands. The sovereign God of heaven, creator of the universe, and Father of our Lord Jesus Christ—not terrorists, criminals, accidental events, mysterious diseases, or random disasters—personally sets, knows, and controls the exact number of days we will live in this world.

Let's ponder some scriptures that confirm that God numbers our days.

Most eloquently Job asserted that God sets the number of our days: "...seeing his [man's] days are [divinely] *determined*. The *number* of his months are *with thee* [God], thou has *appointed* his bounds [time limits] that he cannot pass" (Job 14:5). This reveals that God "determines" and "appoints" our days and their "number" is "with Him."

Jesus' word of prophecy to Peter confirmed that, indeed, the Spirit of God in Christ already knew the exact day and manner of Peter's death, though it was still distant: "When thou shalt be old [many years from now], thou shalt stretch forth thy hands, and another shall gird thee, and carry thee where thou wouldest not [that is, to execution]" (John 21:18).

Psalm 90:10 reveals that the average predetermined lifespan of a redeemed person is seventy years: "The days of our years are *threescore years and ten.*" But other biblical verses and examples show that our trust in God, obedience to His Word, and pursuance of His call directly affect the length of our lives. At His sovereign discretion, the Lord may fulfill, shorten, or lengthen their number.

Here are the biblical principles or general rules by which God "numbers" our days:

1. *Nominal living.* For nominal obedience to His voice, God promises to "fulfill," or complete the full number of our days, just as He did for the Israelites: "The number of thy days I will *fulfill* [grant in full number]" (Exod. 23:26).

2. *Exceptionally bad living.* For exceptionally bad living, He promises to "shorten," or reduce the number of days He has slated for us: "The years of the wicked shall be *shortened*" (Prov. 10:27). (See 1 Corinthians 11:30.)

   The prematurely terminated lives and aborted ministries of the wicked priests Hophni and Phinehas illustrate this shortening of the lifespan due to sin (1 Sam. 2:12–25, 29–30, 34).

3. *Exceptionally good living.* For exceptionally good living, God promises to "add," or increase the days He has set for us: "My son...let thine heart keep [obey] my commandments; for length of days...shall they *add* to thee" (Prov. 3:1–2). (See Proverbs 9:11; 10:27.) The result is something most of us prefer, longevity: "With *long life* will I satisfy him" (Ps. 91:16).

   When Isaiah unexpectedly informed King Hezekiah that his days were finished, Hezekiah prayed passionately, pleading the case that he had walked "in truth," and with a "perfect [humble, trusting] heart," and had consistently done what was right and good in God's sight. Consequently, for his exceptionally close and godly walk with God, God extended his otherwise completed life by fifteen years: "I will add to thy days fifteen years" (Isa. 38:5).

Before considering the above factors, God determines our life spans based chiefly upon the amount of time He foresees it taking for us to come to know Him and fulfill His plan for our lives. When we come to know Him sufficiently and finish our life works, He takes us home. This simple yet biblical explanation helps us understand some of God's mysterious acts.

For instance, why did God permit Satan to afflict Job severely but not lethally? The reason is Job's days and his powerful ministry and testimony were not finished (Job 4:3–5; 42:16–17). Why did Elisha for years powerfully heal the sick and raise the dead, yet later die of sickness, as if powerless? His days and works were complete and God inexplicably but sovereignly allowed sickness to be the means by which His miracle worker expired. Why did the apostle Paul repeatedly escape from Jewish death plots and even revive after a lethal stoning in Lystra? His days and apostolic work were not completed. Why was Peter released from Herod Agrippa's prison just hours before his scheduled execution—yet years later was not released from a Roman prison but was executed as scheduled? In the first case, his days and ministry were not completed; in the second, they were. Why was the prophet Jeremiah saved from death in Jonathan's cistern by the intervention of Ebed-melech the Ethiopian? His days and prophetic work were not finished. Why were Jairus' daughter, the widow of Nain's son, and Lazarus revived by Christ and, later, Dorcas by Peter? Their days and life missions were not fulfilled.

Conversely, why did God let the bold and righteous prophet John the Baptist suffer cruel and unjust execution at the hands of King Herod Antipas? John's days and life mission—to preach repentance to the Jews, prepare them for the Messiah, identify Him, and speak out against Herod's adulterous and incestuous marriage—were finished. In the tribulation period, why will God's "two witnesses" be suddenly killed by the Antichrist's rabid loyalists, despite having been supernaturally protected for three and a half years? By that time they will have "finished" their prophetic mission and divinely numbered 1,260 days of ministry (Rev. 11:3–7).

We do well to remember, however, that there are exceptions to every rule. So, paradoxically, sometimes the wicked live long and the righteous die young.

The exact life span of Cain, the first murderer, is unknown, but it is certain that he lived much longer than his righteous brother. After slaying Abel, Cain went on to build a record-setting worldly life. He married, fathered a son, Enoch (not the Enoch of Genesis 5), and built the world's first city and civilization in the land of Nod, naming it after his son in a vain attempt to preserve his own name. Die-hard Nazi leader, member of Hitler's inner circle, and one-time deputy fuhrer Rudolph Hess survived the Second World War, living in prison to the ripe old age of ninety-two. The feared premier of the former Soviet Union, Joseph Stalin, arguably the most murderous dictator ever, lived seventy-three years, despite murdering inestimable millions of innocents. The cruel slayer of the children of Bethlehem, Herod the Great, lived to approximately seventy years, despite his bloody ways. And even Fidel Castro, the long-loathed, dictatorial, former leader of Cuba, is presently still alive (c. 2008), though weak, at eighty-one.

Why does God let these evil people live long? He doesn't fully tell us in the Bible. Perhaps He lets the wicked live long to further test the faith, patience, and endurance of the righteous. Perhaps He does so to give the wicked more time and opportunities to repent: "Remember, the Lord's patience gives people time to be saved" (2 Pet. 3:15, NLT). Or perhaps He's giving them time to reap in life some of the cruelty, oppression, and grief they have brought upon others, because "whatsoever a man soweth, that shall he also reap" (Gal. 6:7). Perhaps, since God doesn't view time as we do—"one day is with the Lord as a thousand years, and a thousand years as one day" (2 Pet. 3:8)—He gives them a few extra years to enjoy the grace of life, knowing that the moment they pass, they will suddenly be gripped by torment *forever!* (He is, after all, so good that "He is kind" not only to the good but also "to the unthankful and to the evil" [Luke 6:35].) Is this mercy His equivalent to our custom of giving condemned criminals a final enjoyable moment, a "last meal," before they die? Philosophically and pitifully, the psalmist notes, "Truly, you put them on a slippery path...in an instant they are destroyed, completely swept away by terrors" (Ps. 73:18–19, NLT).

Whether or not such conjecture is correct, this much we know: God expects us to trust that He knows best and that His ways are always higher and better than ours. Or as Paul put it, "We know that God causes all things to work together for good to those who love God, to those who are called according to His purpose" (Rom. 8:28, NAS). With this faith, we neither doubt nor fret when the righteous die young.

God took the zealous missionary David Brainerd home at the youthful age of twenty-nine. He permitted the brilliant and inspired Bible teacher Oswald Chambers to pass at forty-three. He took home the remarkably gifted Bible expositor and pastor Matthew Henry at the age of fifty-two.

Why does He do this? From God's perspective, once our work is done, there's really no reason for us to linger in this corrupt and vexatious world when we could enter and enjoy the peaceful presence of God and company of the saints above. The apostle Paul explained, "To depart and to be with Christ...is far better" (Phil. 1:23). And if He lets us suffer martyrdom, He compensates us. The Bible promises extra rewards in the afterlife for those who lose their lives because of their faithfulness to Jesus, His Word, or His call: "Others were tortured, not accepting deliverance, that they might obtain a better resurrection" (Heb. 11:35).

So when saints pass early, we may think, "Why, Lord?" But He apparently thinks, "Why not?" Their spiritual development is complete and their ministerial works are finished (in His unerring evaluation). Why shouldn't He enjoy their fellowship and employ their services in His heavenly kingdom sooner rather than later? Thus He reasons while considering the number of our days.

While God knows the number of our days, generally speaking we don't. Though extraordinarily close to God, chosen, and inspired, an anonymous psalmist admitted frankly, "My mouth shall show forth thy righteousness...all the day; for *I know not the numbers thereof* [of my own days]" (Ps. 71:15). Jesus added, "It is not for you to know the times or the seasons, which the Father hath put in his own power" (Acts 1:7). Why is this?

Primarily, it is because God wants to teach us who are born again by faith to also "live" by faith: "The just shall *live by his faith*" (Hab. 2:4). It is more important to God that we learn to always trust in His faithful character and care of us, live or die, than that He satisfy our curiosity to know exactly how many days we have left in this world. Many have learned to do just this.

As they stood before King Nebuchadnezzar's blazing furnace in Babylon, Shadrach, Meshach, and Abednego were not sure if they would live another day, but they were sure that God was trustworthy every day. So they confidently told the king God would ultimately deliver them, one way or another, sooner or later, from his despotism: "Our God, whom we serve, is able to deliver us…and he will deliver us out of thine hand, O king" (Dan. 3:17). During his terrible illness, Job was determined not to know when he would pass but to trust God's faithful character, come what may: "Though he slay me, yet will I trust in him [His truthful, faithful, loving, unchanging character]" (Job 13:15). These and many others trusted God without knowing their day of death.

Yet for this rule there is also an exception. In both Testaments we see God occasionally showing His intimate ones that their day of death is drawing near.

For example, the Old Testament states that He advised both Aaron and Moses when their respective days of death arrived, giving each specific instructions as to how to prepare for their departures (Num. 20:23–29; Deut. 32:48–50). He informed Ezekiel one morning that his wife would pass that day, and the prophet noted in his scroll, "At evening my wife died" (Ezek. 24:15–18). When God revealed to Elijah that his last day had come, the word spread so rapidly that not only his understudy, Elisha, but also the sons of the prophets (prophets in training) at both Bethel and Jericho were privy to the secret: "Knowest thou that the Lord will take away thy master from thy head *today*? And he [Elisha] said, Yea, I know it" (2 Kings 2:3, 5).

The New Testament continues this revelation by disclosing that the apostles Peter and Paul each foresaw and foretold that their departures were imminent. Peter wrote, "Knowing that *shortly* I must put off this my tabernacle, even as our Lord Jesus Christ hath shown me" (2 Pet. 1:14). And Paul prophesied, "The time of my departure is *at hand*" (2 Tim. 4:6).

(See Acts 20:25.) And Jesus Himself warned His closest followers three times that His passing was imminent and alluded to it on two other occasions: "From that time forth began Jesus to show unto his disciples, how he must go unto Jerusalem...and be killed" (Matt. 16:21).

This forewarning of one's decease is part of the ministry of the Holy Spirit to God's intimate servants. "He will show you things to come," Jesus promised (John 16:13). And Amos declared, "Surely the Lord GOD will do nothing, but he revealeth his secret unto his servants, the prophets" (Amos 3:7). Why does God sometimes warn abiding Christians that their earthly terminus is near? Apparently, He reveals this to lovingly and fully prepare them, their loved ones, and their associates for their departure.

Long ago one psalmist wondered aloud how many days he had remaining: "How many are the days of thy servant?" (Ps. 119:84). Moses prayed wisely, "Teach us to number [consciously appreciate] our days" (Ps. 90:12). Are we following their lead?

Do we wonder about the number of our days? Do we consciously appreciate each day? Do we realize that one day will be our last, a day of either expiration or translation? Why does God want us to know that He—not malicious criminals, crazed terrorists, strange communicable diseases, or random forces of nature—personally sets, knows, and controls our days on earth? Two reasons are apparent.

First, God wants us to "number" our days, or fully understand how few and precious they are and therefore highly value, wisely use, and fully enjoy them.

Second, He wants us to live without the fear of untimely death. "God hath not given us the spirit of fear" (2 Tim. 1:7). Why? Fear torments—"fear hath [or causes] torment [chronic mental and emotional pain]" (1 John 4:18, KJV)—and God doesn't want us tormented. To the contrary, He wants us to rest deeply in mature love for and trust in Him: "There is no fear [mistrust] in [perfect or mature] love....He that feareth is not made perfect [mature] in love [loving trust in God]" (1 John 4:18). And "we who have believed do enter into rest [of mind]" (Heb. 4:3). The biblical revelations in this chapter provide a firm foundation upon which we can build the mature, loving trust in God that quickly and consistently rejects tormenting fear: "Perfect [mature] love casteth out fear" (1 John 4:18).

David chose this line of complete reliance on God in the most perilous period of his life: "Thou hast known my soul in adversities....*But I trusted in thee, O* LORD; I said, Thou art my [all-knowing, all-powerful, all-controlling] God" (Ps. 31:7, 14). And he specifically trusted that God knew and controlled the number of his days: "*My times* [the seasons and days of my life] are in *thy hand* [personal control]" (Ps. 31:15). Why not follow David's example?

Realize that God has put you on this earth to get to know Him and to fully do His will and that your life span is linked to these two divine objectives. Understand also that your allotted days may be fulfilled, decreased, or increased depending upon how you live, righteously or wickedly, humbly or proudly. Don't be fanatical or judgmental; realize that there are exceptions to these rules, so don't judge others by them, only yourself. And use every day to the fullest, seeking the Lord, faithfully discharging your work or ministry, and serving others for His sake. Be not only content but also *thankful* for every new day as it comes: "*This* is the day which the Lord hath made; *we will rejoice and be glad in it*" (Ps. 118:24).

Then, confidently, say with David, "My times are in thy hand," knowing that nothing and no one can remove you until your days and your works are fulfilled.

Until that day, walk closely with God in the light of His truth—and His love.

Chapter Six

ALL THINGS GROW WITH LOVE

This is my commandment, that ye love one another,
as I have loved you.

—JOHN 15:12

*D*uring a ministry trip a few years ago, God blessed me with especially hospitable and gracious hosts. While they were returning me to the airport, I noticed a small pillow sitting in the back seat of their automobile. On it were embroidered the words, "All things grow with love." Noting my hosts' loving spirit and eagerness to see to my needs, I realized that this proverb was more than poetic. It was personal—their personal motto—and powerful! The more I thought it over, the more it gripped me. Here was some golden truth. Truly, where love is all things grow. Everything we touch and see confirms this.

To thrive, plants need a gardener's loving attention and constant care. To be happy and healthy, animals need not just feeding and watering but also petting and praise. To grow and develop normally, babies need not only milk and cereal but also caressing and "love talk." To grow old with grace, the elderly need the loving care of their devoted children or, if they have none, kind caregivers. Why, even inanimate objects don't grow without love! For their stately beauty to be restored, old houses need renovators driven by a love for architectural and decorative splendor. All these familiar things grow for one reason: someone lavishes love upon them regularly. And they are not alone.

Consider also these things that are grown with TLC, or *tender love and care.*

Things Grown With Love

Children

Children need more than the physical necessities of life, such as nutritious food, clothing, shelter, health care, and education. If they are indeed to become healthy, productive human beings, they also need constant parental training, including instruction, counsel, and, when necessary, discipline. And they need steady intercession. Still all these efforts may fail to produce desired results if one more vital ingredient is missing—passionate, persistent, parental love! If we don't love our children with patient, selfless interest, who will? To lead them, we must love them.

To have a delicious cake, you must put all the ingredients into the mix in proper proportion. If our kids are troubled, perhaps we need to see if we're mixing in enough Christian parental love—sincere affection, unwavering loyalty, and sacrificial labor aimed at seeing their full human development and, ultimately, the joyful fulfillment of their destiny in Christ. Are we consistently kind or curt? Attentive or distracted? Do we listen or only lecture? Do we praise their strengths or just criticize their weaknesses? Do we admit it when we fail them, or do we only blame them when they fail us?

Are we ready to enthusiastically serve our children's eternal welfare daily? This, and nothing less, is love.

Friendships

Sometimes we moan and fret because people don't seem to want to be around us. At times this happens for spiritual reasons: the children of darkness naturally avoid the children of light. But there are other reasons we should consider.

For instance, are we being talkative, kind, and gracious with other people, or are we withdrawn, silent, and apathetic? To build warm relationships, we must relate and respond to others warmly: "A man who has friends must himself be friendly" (Prov. 18:24, NKJV). Friendliness builds friendships; coldness creates isolation. If you want others to care for you, care for them first.

Reach out to bless them in a timely and practical way. And be understanding and ready to quickly forgive and patiently pursue friendliness if they fail to respond immediately. Maybe they haven't yet learned the lesson you are just now learning, namely, that friendliness builds friendships.

Churches

If you want the Lord to add disciples to your local fellowship, consider this: love the people you already have.

Give yourself to help and bless them in every way you can. Congregants, intercede for one another daily, for your leaders, your church body, and its outreaches. This releases the Holy Spirit to cultivate greater love, sweeter fellowship, and stronger unity in your ranks. Leaders, commit yourselves to become extraordinary *givers*. Pastors and teachers, study and prepare rich loaves of Word-bread for your people so their faith will be nourished and grow. Deacons (or board members), by childlike prayer and faith in God's faithfulness, seek God's way to solve every problem your congregation faces and pursue it. Teachers, elders, and mentors, patiently instruct, counsel, and correct all the members of your flock, even the slowest and most hopeless, remembering that even "the least of these my brethren" (Matt. 25:40, 45) are precious to Jesus and that His love through you may yet deliver them.

Every leader should help foster a family spirit. Be accessible, as parents are to their children. Share both spiritual and natural activities: pray and play, minister and mingle, work and walk together. Share bread frequently—fellowship meals and Bible truths. Share victories and defeats; rejoice over others' successes and console them in defeat. Refuse to hold unkind attitudes toward even the most "thorny" members of your church. Instead, pray for their repentance, conquer their offensiveness with patient, kind correction, and quickly mend the misunderstandings and rifts they create.

And if in the exhausting heat of the day you find yourself fed up with all these things, remember Jesus' challenge to Peter and to you: "Lovest thou me?...Feed my sheep" (John 21:15–17). Spiritual leader, if you won't keep loving the sheep for their sake, won't you do it for *His* sake?

Ministries

Would you like your ministry to grow? Do you want it to yield more blessing to the saints and glory to Christ? Then begin "loving" it.

Replace your passiveness with passion. Don't just be dutiful; be delighted about the thing Jesus has given you to do: "I *delight* to do thy will, O my God" (Ps. 40:8). Praise God for giving you your ministry assignment, whether it's large or small, noticed or unnoticed. Diligently practice your ministry gift that you may perfect it: "Neglect not [but practice] the gift that is in thee...that thy profiting may appear to [the blessing of] all" (1 Tim. 4:14–15). And beware of ministerial envy! Don't let your proud, old nature desire another minister's work or gift. Be humble and enthusiastic, heartily building the "tabernacle" of ministry God has called you to build. Give yourself to your work daily, sparing no effort: "Give thyself *wholly*" (v.15). The more you thus "love" it, or lavish attention upon it for Jesus' sake, the more it will grow.

So lovingly build your house of ministry day by day—prayer upon prayer, study upon study, message upon message, mission upon mission, sacrifice upon sacrifice—until God's glory descends upon it as it (He) did the tabernacle and raises it to fulfill His predestined plan...to help bless and prepare the bride of Christ!

Our personal fellowship with Jesus

Sometimes we envy saints who walk very closely with Jesus yet fail to see the reason they do so. It's not because Jesus prefers them, nor is it because their human "stuff" is superior to ours. It's because they've *loved* Him. Or more accurately, they've given themselves to Him in love. In their tests they've consistently chosen to put Him and His will above all other interests and loves. As a result, they now have only one great desire: to be near Him and please Him for the rest of their lives.

Knowing that He said, "If you love me, keep my commandments" (John 14:15), they prayerfully study His Word daily and meditate upon it frequently. Aware that He loves obedience, they set their hearts to obey, or live by, the Word they're learning and to follow His Spirit's guidance. Realizing that He urged us to "watch ye...and pray always" (Luke 21:36), they have times of prayer and have prayer all the time. Conscious of His loving invitation, "Come unto me, all ye that labor and are heavy laden, and I will give you rest" (Matt. 11:28), they seek His face when people, problems, and labors drain their spiritual strength. Remembering His promise, "I will come again" (John 14:3), they earnestly prepare themselves for His appearing. Mindful that He seeks "true worshipers" (John 4:23), they worship Him privately every day. As cooing turtledoves, they softly thank Him, bless His name, sing unto Him, and tell Him often that they love Him.

So, by love, their personal fellowship with Him and His personal delight in them grows. And grows. And grows.

The other side of this spiritual axiom is equally true: without love all things wither and die. Indeed, where there is no affectionate care, the divisive, diminishing, destructive force of apathy takes a heavy toll. Soon all the effects of love described above are reversed.

Children become confused, angry, frustrated, and troubled—not mature but immature adults in the making. Friendships cool, fade, and cease. Churches become carnal, fragmented, and void of the Spirit, and cease radiating light and life to their communities. Ministries become weak and ineffective, and they cease edifying Christ's body. Ministers become dull religious professionals, rather than passionate prophets delivering timely words from the Lord. And our personal relationships with Jesus become meaningless—distant, dry, religious cisterns rather than wells of living water springing up with new life morning by morning. Perhaps this is why the Bible emphasizes walking in love so heavily.

When a scribe, or expert expositor of the Torah, asked Jesus which of its commands was "first" in importance, Jesus took the occasion to sum up the essence of the entire body of Old Testament revelation. With masterful insight, He reduced its 613 precepts to two sweeping yet simple commands, both emphasizing the imperative, "Thou shalt love...":

> And Jesus answered him, The first of all the commandments
> is: Hear, O Israel: The Lord our God is one Lord; and *thou*

shalt love the Lord thy God with all thy heart, and with all thy soul, and with all thy mind, and with all thy strength: this is the first commandment. And the second is this: *Thou shalt love* thy neighbor as thyself. There is no other commandment greater than these.

—Mark 12:29–31

How right He was! The very pillars upon which the Mosaic Law stood, the Ten Commandments, underscored and applauded Jesus' evaluation. The first four commands (or first table) of the Decalogue are based on love for God; the last six (last table), on love for our fellow man (Exod. 20:2–11; 20:12–17). Therefore, Jews couldn't keep the Ten Commandments, much less the whole body of the Law, unless they learned to walk in love!

Linked by inspiration, the New Testament continues the Old Testament's prime thematic emphasis on love.

The synoptic gospels repeatedly assert that every phase of Jesus' public ministry—prayer, missions, teaching, healing, delivering, feeding the hungry, raising the dead—was motivated by His love or "compassion." (See Matthew 9:36-38; 14:14; 15:32; Mark 5:19; 6:34; Luke 7:13.) Jesus' greatest, or "high priestly" prayer, climaxed with His request that His Father manifest His very love in Christians on this earth: "that *the love* with which thou hast loved me may be *in them*" (John 17:26). His loftiest lecture, the Sermon on the Mount, teaches by its inspired arrangement that when we consistently walk in love toward everyone, including our enemies, we are "perfect," or Christ- and God-like: "I say unto you, *Love your enemies*, bless them…do good to them…pray for them…[And so] *Be ye, therefore, perfect*, even as your Father" (Matt. 5:44–48; see vv. 38–48).

Purposely, the apostle Paul listed "love" as the *first* "fruit of the Spirit" (Gal. 5:22–23). And he pleaded with the Ephesians to put away all bitterness, wrath, and malice and to "be kind one to another, tenderhearted, forgiving one another…and *walk in love*" (Eph. 4:32, 5:2). He also taught the Colossians that "love…is the bond of perfectness" (Col. 3:14), or the only bonding agent that creates perfect spiritual unity among Christians. He further declared that love was the "greatest" of all Christian virtues: "The *greatest* of these [virtues] is love" (1 Cor. 13:13, NIV). And he added that if we lack a genuinely loving spirit, all the other gifts and graces of the Spirit will ultimately profit us "nothing" (v. 3).

The apostle John strongly and consistently agreed. He wrote, "Beloved, let us love one another; for love is of God, and everyone that loveth is born of God, and knoweth God" (1 John 4:7). Again John taught, "If we love one another, God dwelleth in us, and His love is perfected [fully developed, matured] in us" (v. 12). After declaring that Christians must "walk in the light, as he [Jesus] is in the light" (1 John 1:7), John somberly warned us that love is spiritual "light," and hatred, spiritual "darkness":

> He that saith he is in the *light*, and hateth [continues harboring malice or hatred toward] his brother, is in *darkness* even unto now. [But] he that loveth his brother abideth in the *light*, and there is no occasion of stumbling in him. But he that hateth his brother is in *darkness*, and walketh in *darkness*, and knoweth not where he goeth, because *darkness* hath blinded his eyes.
>
> —1 JOHN 2:9–11

And most significantly, Jesus' new commandment, which is addressed especially to Christians and recorded twice in John's Gospel for emphasis, orders us to lovingly care for each another:

> A new commandment I give unto you, that ye *love one another*; as I have loved you, that ye also *love one another*. By this shall all men know that ye are my disciples, if ye have *love [exceptional, affectionate, sacrificial devotion]* one to another.
>
> —JOHN 13:34–35

> This is my [personal and distinctive] commandment, that ye *love one another*, as I have loved you.
>
> —JOHN 15:12

These mountainous biblical mandates prove that Jesus and His apostles recognized that *all things grow with love*, and that without love nothing will develop and mature as God intended. So they set the ways of life and death before us: Whatever we love will grow and live. Whatever we refuse to love will wither and die. So go grow something! Love it!

You're likely to become more loving if you fully understand the Ten Commandments' imperatives—and their implications.

Chapter Seven

THE TEN IMPLICATIONS

Thou shalt... thou shalt not...

—EXODUS 20:1–17

*L*ove and live by them, or loath and lambaste them, the Ten Commandments are arguably the most widely known verses in the Bible. (See Exodus 20:1–17.) Every minister has preached them, every church has studied them, and every Sunday school student has recited or memorized them. Why, even atheists, agnostics, and advocates of false religions are familiar with these original directives from the holy mount!

Though they are positive revelations of God's will for mankind, these heavenly injunctions are generally viewed as the "Ten Negatives." Why? Most of them—eight to be exact—are forbiddances, using the phrases, "Thou shalt not..." or "Thou shalt have no..." Only two are positively worded statements: "Remember the Sabbath day, to keep it holy," and "Honor thy father and thy mother" (Exod. 20:8–12). This bent toward naysaying leaves the casual, unredeemed reader of Scripture with a bad taste in his mouth, thinking of God as the "Big No" or the "Grand Negator" and His will as something to be suffered rather than enjoyed. But our Creator is neither a disgruntled parent nor the grumpy spoiler of our natural impulses. To the contrary, His will is our highest good, the very best plan conceivable for us, our families, and our world.

These prevailing misconceptions that the Ten Commandments and their Commander are negative exist for several reasons, such as:

- We lack a right relationship to God through Christ.
- We have not received the fullness of the Holy Spirit, who alone enables us to interpret the Bible accurately.
- We have not read or studied the Bible sufficiently.
- We don't understand that Jesus is the perfect expression of God the Father, that whatever Christ is, God is.
- We disbelieve in God's gracious, generous, loving character because of misconceptions held and taught us by our pastor, church, or denomination.
- Satan relentlessly assails our minds with slanderously inaccurate thoughts about God to keep us from knowing and loving Him.

But these are not the only reasons we tend to misinterpret God's statements in general and the Ten Commandments in particular.

Another is our lack of insight into the Ten Commandments themselves. We tend to consider only what they say and not what they imply. The Bible contains implications, or unwritten truths suggested by written facts, in many of its verses. The Ten Commandments are no exception to this rule. Behind each declaration in the Decalogue there are implications (hints) of vital spiritual truths we should perceive, ponder, and practice.

Let's review again God's universal, inspired, ten-part code for righteous living and identify its key implications.

THE TEN IMPLICATIONS

The first implication

"Thou shalt have no other gods before me" (Exod. 20:3). By saying we should have no other "gods," or dominating loves, before Him, God revealed that He desires first place in our hearts, not second, third, or fourth. To obtain His people's well-deserved devoted affection, He tried to stir their gratitude by reminding them that He—not golden calves, stone icons, or carved and decorated tree trunks—saved them from their long and cruel bondage to Pharaoh in Egypt: "I am the LORD thy God, who have brought thee out of the land of Egypt, out of... bondage" (v. 2). So we see that this first command is more than a staid forbiddance of idolatry. It is God's passionate call for the active, growing love of His people.

Taken together His statements imply:

> *I long for your love! I want the unrivaled first place in your hearts. I want you to be affectionately devoted to Me, the only true God and your only Savior from the bondage of sin, more than to any other purported deity, person, worldly goal, material object, or desire.*

The second implication

"Thou shalt not make unto thee any carved image, or... bow down thyself to [worship] them, nor serve them" (Exod. 20:4–5). While the first commandment addresses our supreme love, the second addresses our worship, or audible, visible, bodily expression of that supreme love.

By forbidding that the Israelites make any "image" of created heavenly or earthly things for the purpose of worship (v. 4), God alludes to the fact that He is an invisible spiritual being. He is our Creator, not a part of the visible, material creation, and infinitely grander than anything on the earth, in the sky, or in space beyond. And He certainly isn't our creation; we can't create Him as men do idols. Therefore, no material, mortal, or man-made thing is to usurp the adoration of the immaterial, immortal, uncreatable One. No part of the creation is to be replicated and loved as much as the Creator. (This does not forbid the creation or appreciation of artistic works of beauty, only images and icons made as objects of religious worship.)

By forbidding His people to "bow down" to false gods, God was hinting that He wanted them, and us, to make bowing down to Him a part of our private (and public) worship, prayer, and communion with Him. The Bible reveals that those who saw the glorified Christ were often unable to keep their feet: "When I saw him, I *fell at his feet...*" (Rev. 1:17). Apparently, they felt it more appropriate to be on their knees or on their face in His presence. We too will assume these positions often when we worship the Father and Son in heaven: "The four and twenty elders *fell down and worshiped* him that liveth forever" (Rev. 5:14). (See

Revelation 4:10; 5:8; 19:4.) Physical prostration does not make worship; better our wills be bent and our knees stiff than vice versa. But the second commandment reveals that bowing before God is one of the expressions of worship that pleases God.

By adding that we should not "serve" false gods, God hints that He wants us to serve Him instead. We should therefore see every act of devotion, labor, charity, or ministry as a way of serving God. Thus the epistle enjoins us, "*Whatever ye do*, do it heartily, *as to the Lord*, and not unto men" (Col. 3:23).

This forbiddance of idol worship also shows most clearly that God doesn't want us to conform to the methods of worship practiced by people who don't know Him. It was for this very thing, the Israelites' abominable conformity to heathen worship, that God eventually destroyed their nation and temple and scattered them to the four winds during the Babylonian captivity.

Summing up, God's second commandment tells us:

> *I want you to understand that I am a spiritual, invisible Being—your Creator, not a part of the material creation or one of your creations. It pleases Me when you bow, kneel, or prostrate yourself before Me, not only in your heart but also with your body. I am blessed by both your audible and demonstrative worship. I want you to serve me in everything you do, whether the act is private or public, sacred or secular, physical or intellectual. And please, don't adopt forms of worship practiced by those who don't know Me.*

The third implication

"Thou shalt not take the name[s] of the LORD thy God in vain" (Exod. 20:7). If God the Creator is above all created things, it follows that His name, His unique and superior character, and His names—or personal designators, such as El-Shaddai, I AM, Jehovah, Ancient of Days, Lord of Hosts, heavenly Father—are also above all names. And not only His, but His Son's: "God also hath...given him [Jesus] a name which is above every name" (Phil. 2:9).

We consider having a "good name"—respected reputation and respectable character to back it—to be our best asset. This creature valuation reflects the abiding thought of our Creator. In God's mind, the best thing He has is His great name. The Logos offers a litany of laudation for His "name," or divine character and reputation.

His name is excellent, or "majestic": "O LORD…how majestic is your name in all the earth!" (Ps. 8:1, NIV). His name is "holy," or set apart or distinguished for purity: "Holy…is his name" (Ps. 111:9). We should give thanks to His name continually: "Let us offer the sacrifice of praise unto God continually…the fruit of our lips giving thanks unto his name" (Heb. 13:15). We should sing praises to His name: "I…sing praises unto thy name" (Ps. 18:49). We should study His name, or character, until we know it: "I will set him on high, because he hath known my name" (Ps. 91:14). We should remember His name and trust in and boast of His great faithfulness: "We will remember ["trust in and boast of," AMP] the name of the LORD our God" (Ps. 20:7). His name is to be constantly exalted, or lifted up as superior: "Oh, magnify the LORD…and let us exalt his name together" (Ps. 34:3).

His name is to be feared, or revered with awe and deep respect: "Unite my heart to fear thy name" (Ps. 86:11). His name is to be loved, or fondly adored: "They who love his name shall dwell therein [in Zion]" (Ps. 69:36). His name will endure, or retain its greatness, throughout eternity: "His name shall endure forever" (Ps. 72:17). His name is to be declared, or taught to His people: "[He looses and sends His servants] to declare the name of the LORD in Zion" (Ps. 102:21). Our help is in His name, or unswervingly loving and faithful character: "Our help is in the name of the LORD" (Ps. 124:8). We should call upon that "name," or character of the Lord, when we're in trouble: "I will…call upon the name of the LORD" (Ps. 116:13). We should live for the glory of His name: "Help us, O God…for the glory of thy name" (Ps. 79:9).

Considering the greatness of God's name, only ignorant ones or foolish rebels think or speak disrespectfully of it: "The foolish people have blasphemed thy name" (Ps. 74:18). To take God's name "in vain," as the third commandment forbids, is to:

1. Speak of Him lightly (disrespectfully)
2. Profess Him insincerely (hypocritically; misrepresenting Him)
3. Denounce Him slanderously or profanely (blaspheming Him)

In the first case, we give no thought or study to the profound meaning of His name. Consequently, we treat it like any other. In the second case, we fail to realize that God's reputation is at stake in the way His people live on earth. Consequently, we imagine we can profess allegiance to His name ("I am a *Christ*-ian") without being responsible to possess the reality of our profession by humbly trusting and obeying God's Word in our daily lives. In the third case, we fail to realize that the way we speak of God matters, that we will give account to Him for every idle word we speak. Also, we wrongly believe that God has a last name beginning with the letter "d"!

Thus the Lord implies the following:

> *I want you to treasure, not trash, My "name"—My divine character, reputation, and personal designators. I want you to take it very seriously when you call yourself by My Son's name. My will is for your daily living to enhance, not diminish, the greatness of My name. And I am pleased when you speak of Me always with the highest respect and honor.*

The fourth implication

"Remember the sabbath day, to keep it holy [set apart for God's purpose] (Exod. 20:8). The purpose of this command is not to respect one day above others but rather to set it aside for a different purpose. God's purpose for our typical weekdays is productive work: "The sun riseth… [and] man goeth forth unto his work and to his labor until the evening" (Ps. 104:22–23). He commanded here, "Six days shalt thou labor and do all thy work" (Exod. 20:9). But His purpose for the Sabbath was different. In a word, it was *rest*.

Definition and context make this clear. The word "Sabbath" is translated from the Hebrew *shabbath* (shab-bawth'), which means "intermission," or "to cease, or desist, or interrupt."[1] In this context, God associated this rest with His own rest that followed His six-day work of creation: "For in six days the LORD made heaven and earth...and *rested* the seventh day" (v. 11). So combined, this information tells us that the term "Sabbath" means an *intermission in one's work week*, or a *cessation from labor to rest*.

Following God's example, then, we should work six days every week and rest, or desist from our labors, one day. This is God's wise, loving plan to meet our mortal needs of physical recuperation and psychological refreshment. It has nothing to do with religiosity and everything to do with restoration: "He maketh me to lie down....He restoreth my soul" (Ps. 23:2–3). The Sabbath rest enables us to experience the highest quality of human life as we walk closely with God in this overburdened sin- and work-weary world. By seeking Christ daily, we are revived by His Spirit and saved from the agitation of sin daily; by resting one day a week, we are further saved from the exhaustion of overwork and the oppression of monotony. This Sabbath principle is one aspect of the "abundant life" Jesus came to give us: "I am come that they might have life, and that they might have it more abundantly" (John 10:10).

The New Testament, however, makes it exceedingly clear that Christians are not bound to keep this seventh-day Sabbath literally. (See Galatians 3:23–25; Colossians 2:16–17.) It reveals that this entire age of grace is a Sabbath from the age of law, and that we now desist from working to earn our salvation because we trust in Jesus' finished work of salvation on the cross: "For we who have believed do enter into rest..." (Heb. 4:3). This *soul rest of faith in Christ* is the true substance that was foreshadowed by the seventh-day Sabbath. Not merely one day a week, but every day we enjoy a Sabbath-rest from the dead works of seeking justification with God by our own works of righteousness.

Nevertheless, although we are not legally bound to keep the letter of the fourth commandment, we honor its spirit (resting one day per week) by keeping the first-day rest of the Lord's Day, though not with invasive and onerous legalistic requirements and penalties. This *voluntary* day of rest and worship was the practice of the early church: "And upon the first day of the week, when the disciples came together..." (Acts 20:7). (See 1 Corinthians 16:2; Revelation 1:10.) It is still the voluntary practice of the majority of Christians worldwide.

So in this commandment the Lord tells us:

I want you to enjoy the highest quality of life as you walk with Me through this world. So break off your labors one day a week and rest. This will help you avoid exhaustion and monotony, and delight instead in the joy of life more abundant.

The fifth implication

"Honor thy father and thy mother" (Exod. 20:12). God never bestows honor arbitrarily or without preexisting merit. If God honors someone, they have done something worthy. If He withholds honor, nothing honorable, and perhaps something dishonorable, has been done.

His command that parents be honored, therefore, is based upon the comprehensive compassionate care parents should give their children in life, especially during their infancy, childhood, and adolescence. Those who passionately and patiently render this care for their children are deserving of respect. Some parents, however, clearly are not worthy of this honor because they persistently and impenitently refuse to nurture, provide, or care for their children. And Providence will not praise pernicious parents!

Don't expect Ahab and Jezebel to be honored in heaven for the way they raised Athaliah, who in adulthood proved to be twice the conniving queen of terror her mother had been. Why? They taught her to worship Baal, hate the faithful children of Jehovah, and abuse her power for selfish ends. Don't expect wicked King Ahaz to be revered for the fatherly example he set for his righteous son, Hezekiah. Why? He was an evil, not a righteous, role model. Hezekiah became an honorable man not because of but *despite* his father's poor parenting!

We too shouldn't expect to be honored by God and our children if our parenting is remiss, or worse, ruinously unrighteous! If we dishonor God by disobeying His Word and disrespecting His righteousness, and if we dishonor our children by neglecting, abusing, abandoning, or misleading them, we should expect to receive exactly what we have sown: dishonor! (This is true, though most children are inclined to love and honor even the worst parents, if they will only be truthful and genuinely sorry for their past failures.) It's time we get serious about becoming worthy parents and commit ourselves to our duty of honoring God by selflessly loving, helping, and guiding our children. Then we won't have to remind our children to honor us, because they will want to honor us! Of the proverbial "virtuous woman," it is written, "Her children rise up, and call her blessed" (Prov. 31:28). Parental honor is reserved for honorable parents!

This fifth commandment contains one more hint. We should honor not only our earthly but also our heavenly "parents"—our heavenly Father, who is our eternal covering, and the Holy Spirit, who comforts us with abiding motherly care. It was God's paternal and maternal instincts that prompted Him in the beginning to create the institution of parenting for our good. If parents are to be honored, so is the God who ordained parenthood—and who every day gives loving parental care to all Adam's children, whether they have good, bad, or no earthly parents. This commandment, therefore, indirectly urges every child of God to look up and express loving respect for God's fatherly firmness, faithfulness, provision, and instruction, and for His Spirit's motherly tenderness, correction, and guidance. Together, these heavenly "parents" have conceived, birthed, fed, formed, taught, disciplined, and matured us, naturally and spiritually, all our lives. And their work goes on every day.

So in this commandment God implies:

> *Parents, I want you to be honorable, so your children will want to honor you. Honor My Word and My righteousness and commit yourself to love, minister to, and provide for your children, as I have done for you. Children, I want you to realize that for all your parents have done for you, they are worthy of your respect and recognition. Married or single Christian, pause and consider how I have lovingly parented you all your life and continue doing so. It blesses me greatly when you express loving gratitude to Me for My ongoing fatherly and motherly labor of love.*

The sixth implication

"Thou shalt not kill" (Exod. 20:13). God here orders, not that we refrain from killing animals or plants when necessary, but that we not kill—specifically *murder*—human beings. "You shall not *murder*" (NIV). Appearing more than forty times in the Old Testament, the Hebrew word used here, *rāsah* (raw-tsakh'), means, "to kill, murder, slay" and is widely translated as "murder."[2] Why the distinction between killing animals and plants and murdering humans?

We are the only part of God's creation that is made in His image (form or likeness). Man is a material facsimile of the spiritual form of God. By using either the term "image" or "likeness" four times in two verses in the creation story, God heavily emphasizes this fact: "And God said, Let us make man in our *image*, after our *likeness*.... So God created man in his own *image*, in the *image* of God created he him..." (Gen. 1:26–27). It is because of our unique similarity to Him that God places such high value on human life and mandates that we not take it. But there are at least three exceptions.

Warfare is obviously excluded by this injunction. God Himself called the Jewish people to war on numerous occasions, usually in defensive actions, though on one prominent occasion (Canaan conquest) they took the offensive. One of God's greatest leaders, Joshua, was a renowned man of war, as was Israel's greatest king, David. And many of Israel's judges, such as Jepthah and Samson, were military or paramilitary leaders. If this commandment orders us not to kill in military combat, and yet God repeatedly ordered His people to war, and even helped them slay their enemies, He is the prime offender of His own command. So this can't refer to justified or necessary military combat.

Self-defense is also an exception. Neither God's ancient law nor our modern civil statutes condemn people who, when defending their persons or loved ones, accidentally kill violent aggressors without malice, forethought, or intent to kill. Jesus taught us to "resist not evil" (Matt. 5:39), and we must always endeavor to do so, as far as is possible. But this is not binding for non-Christians. If death occurs suddenly and unexpectedly under such circumstances of self-defense, it is unintentional, and not a true, premeditated act of "murder."

Capital punishment is another exceptional circumstance. When due process has produced hard evidence that irrefutably convicts a willful, premeditated murderer, God's Word authorizes capital punishment by the state. So vital is this to maintaining societal order in a fallen world that it was the *first* regulation God established after the Flood: "Whoso sheddeth man's blood, by man [human authorities] shall his blood be shed..." (Gen. 9:6). Why? First, it protects human life and thus demonstrates God's high regard for the only creature made in His image: "...for in the image of God made he man." Second, God knew that the institution of just capital punishment would deter excessive murder and help prevent a repeat of the murder-madness that consumed the pre-Flood world (Gen. 6:11, 13). Third, He realized state execution would prevent rash revenge murders by incensed relatives of victims.

The Old Testament law continued this capital punishment order: "...the murderer shall be put to death" (Num. 35:30). The New Testament confirms that this still holds during this church age. While murderers can by grace receive eternal forgiveness and redemption through the cross, their debt to society must still be paid to preserve social justice, deter the proliferation of murder, and minimize revenge slayings. Paul goes further, claiming that the just capital punishment of the state is actually a providential act of divine judgment—*God* is executing the guilty through the agency of the state. He writes, "The authorities are God's servants, sent for your good. But if you are doing wrong, of course you should be afraid, for they have the power to punish you. *They are God's servants, sent for the very purpose of punishing those who do what is wrong*" (Rom. 13:4, NLT). Paul confirmed this when in his own trial he testified that, if *he* had committed a capital crime, *he* would personally submit to capital punishment! "If I were a criminal and had committed some crime which deserved the death penalty, *I should not try to evade sentence of death*" (Acts 25:11, PHILLIPS).

So in His sixth commandment, God implies:

> *Since human beings bear My divine image, I place the highest value on human life. So must you. Respect and protect human life above all other life forms. Except in military combat, self-defense, or capital punishment, never take any person's life, born or unborn, rich or poor, wise or ignorant, redeemed or unredeemed.*

The seventh implication

"Thou shalt not commit adultery" (Exod. 20:14). Adultery is a treacherous violation of marital vows, conjugal rights, and family faithfulness.

To buy a few moments of unsatisfying illicit pleasure, adulterers break their solemn promises to their life-mates, and, if they're Christians, to God, in whose presence (sanctuary) and name they have taken their vows. They also steal the bodily pleasures and intimacies that belong exclusively to another man or woman. Most tragically, they destroy the trust upon which family units are built and without which they cannot survive; when you destroy marital trust, you destroy family trust. So when adulterers bed down, they put down three things that are vital to any orderly, productive society: marriage, family, and human rights.

The resulting damage is ruinous. Individual lifelong covenants of holy love are broken, and, to some degree, the battered universal institution of marriage is further weakened. Families are ripped apart and sent hurtling into the abysmal pit of separation, which is filled with swirling emotional darkness, legal strife, insecurity, and bitterness. If there are children, the children are even bigger losers than their parents. Suddenly, and for no fault of theirs, their spiritual, psychological, and emotional foundation is removed. In a moment all their hopes for a bright future are dashed, as they have one parent taken from them, while the other is severely wounded with financial angst, emotional turmoil, despair, guilt, and loneliness—and left as the antithesis of the perfect parent! With this devastating domestic destruction occurring daily in America, is it any wonder that family life as we have known it is coming apart at the seams and cohabitation has become the new national "family" plan?

It was to prevent just such household pain, chaos, and societal disintegration that God commanded us to reject marital infidelity! Knowing that the family is the foundation of society and marriage is the foundation of the family, His seventh mandate went right to the bedrock of all social order, the covenant of marriage. No limp suggestion, this command has sharp, hidden teeth in it. For the balance of the Bible assures us repeatedly that divine judgment will one day bite those who bite the forbidden apple of adultery: "Marriage is honorable in all, and the bed undefiled, but fornicators and adulterers God will judge" (Heb. 13:4). "Never harm or cheat a Christian brother in this matter by violating his wife, for the Lord avenges all such sins, as we have solemnly warned you before" (1 Thess. 4:6, NLT).

By forbidding adultery, therefore, God suggested:

I want you to highly respect, not disregard or destroy, the institution of marriage. Consider it sacred and necessary to your personal, family, and societal well-being. Never intrude into the holy ground of someone else's marriage or desecrate your own—and reap judgment!

The eighth implication

"Thou shalt not steal" (Exod. 20:15). Ideally, for any society to enjoy peace and progress, its members must not lust for monies or material things—or lift them from others without permission. Theft, robbery, extortion, embezzlement, and fraud are egregious violations of our property rights, the rape of our worldly wealth and goods. And that's not all. They are violations of God's rights.

The Old Testament Scriptures revealed that God owns not just Palestine and its people, but also everyone and everything in the wide world! "The earth is the LORD's, and the fullness thereof; the world, and they who dwell therein" (Ps. 24:1). "Behold, all souls are mine" (Ezek. 18:4). Therefore, to steal is to take not only from a person but also from the true Owner of his person and property, the Lord. Thus we steal from God *indirectly*. (To steal from Him *directly* is to without authorization seize, use, or violate God's "holy," or specially consecrated, things, such as His places of worship, lands, offerings, tithes, covenant people, or anointed servants.)

Furthermore, because every person is made in God's image, to offend or wrong any person is to do damage to the image of God, which they bear. (Whether or not people know God, God knows and loves them, and He is mindful of their human needs and rights.) For this reason, God ordered the Jews not only to make restitution (plus a 20 percent penalty!) but also to offer a trespass offering if they stole or misappropriated anything from anyone, whether by theft, deceit, or lying: "He shall restore that which he took.... And he shall bring his trespass offering unto the LORD..." (Lev. 6:4, 6). (See Leviticus 6:1–7.) The restitution made the offense right with the offended party. And by bringing the sacrificial ram to God's altar, the guilty party acknowledged that his theft was not only against the creature but also against the Creator, whose image the creature bore and whose rights had been violated: "…his trespass offering *unto the* LORD." *The Bible Reader's Companion* notes, "Sins against others also are sins against God. Thus the person who stole or defrauded another had to bring a guilt offering to God as a penalty."[3]

Figuratively, this principle applies not only to property but also to relationships. David acknowledged the principle of the trespass offering when, after stealing Uriah's wife—and life!—he confessed that he had sinned not only against Uriah but against his Owner: "Against thee [God], thee only, have I sinned" (Ps. 51:4).

This is why Jesus taught that when we've offended people, we can't fully enter into the worship of God until we first, by confession (and restitution, if possible), make reconciliation with the person whose rights (or property) we have violated:

> If thou bring thy gift to the altar [of worship], and there rememberest that thy brother hath anything [any injustice or offense] against thee, leave there thy gift… and go thy way; *first be reconciled* to thy brother, and then come and offer thy gift.
>
> —MATTHEW 5:23–24

The New Testament continues the Decalogue's sermon against stealing by urging Christians (especially former thieves) to never rob, steal, defraud, or inappropriately use or hold monies or property rightfully belonging to others: "Let him that stole steal no more" (Eph. 4:28). It adds that, while poverty, financial hardship, or even indentured servantship may be provocations, they are never excuses for stealing: "[Tell] bond servants…not to steal by taking things of small value, but to prove themselves truly loyal and entirely reliable and faithful throughout" (Titus 2:9–10, AMP). It also tells us that Zacchaeus' mind was anxious to make restitution to his Jewish victims and their God when he made his inspired, instantaneous about-face: "Behold, Lord, the half of my goods I give to the poor; and if I have taken anything from any man by false accusation, I restore him fourfold" (Luke 19:8). Lastly, it foretells that in the Tribulation period, one of the four major areas of sin will be stealing: "They did not repent of their murders or their witchcraft or their sexual immorality or their *thefts*" (Rev. 9:21, NLT).

So in this eighth command God implies:

> *I own every human being and everything they own. And every person on earth bears My image. To steal from any person is to steal from Me. To violate human rights is to violate My rights. I want you to respect, not violate, people's property rights—and My rights and image in their lives!*

The ninth implication

"Thou shalt not bear false witness" (Exod. 20:16). Here God forbids lying, or consciously making false or misleading statements to misrepresent the character or actions of ourselves or others. This statement touches not only on social behavior but also on legal action. It condemns not only slander but also false allegations and perjury, or lying under oath: "You shall not give false testimony against your neighbor" (v. 16, NIV).

No minor fault, lying is extremely disgusting to God. In fact, it accounts for two of the seven sins He hates most: "These six things doth the LORD hate; yea, seven are an abomination unto him…a lying tongue…a false witness that speaketh lies" (Prov. 6:16–19). Why does God despise lying so strongly?

It reminds Him of His ancient nemesis, Lucifer, whose vicious lies about God's character caused great loss in heaven. We may infer from the whole of the biblical record that Lucifer lied to the angels just as he lied to Eve in the garden (Gen. 3:5). Lucifer's successful slander campaign cost God the fellowship of one-third of His angelic "friends." It also spoiled, if only for a moment, heaven's previously unbroken bliss. The lies of one disgruntled archangel turned paradise into a war zone and its preexisting peace into pandemonium. Lucifer's foment of falsifications also besmirched, however briefly, God's impeccably holy name. That's why God hates lying. When He sees human slanderers busily at work, He has brief, unpleasant flashbacks of *the* original liar, *the* original lie, and *the* original losses. His loving heart also grieves over the senseless ruin they wreak: "One sinner destroyeth much good" (Eccles. 9:18). And as surely as He created the lake of fire for the original liar, He sets a day of reckoning for every other impenitent liar to join him: "all liars shall have their part in the lake which burneth with fire and brimstone" (Rev. 21:8). Terrible as it is, this is the truth.

So in His ninth command God intimates:

> *I detest lies and liars, just as I do Lucifer. I am grieved when I see slanderers ruin the reputations and friendships of good people. So I want you to respect other people's reputations and relations and speak of them always as you wish to be spoken of—truly, with accuracy, and without careless misstatements or malicious misrepresentations or accusations.*

The tenth implication

"Thou shalt not covet thy neighbor's house; thou shalt not covet thy neighbor's wife, nor his manservant, nor his maidservant, nor his ox, nor his ass, nor anything that is thy neighbor's" (Exod. 20:17). With profound knowledge of fallen human beings, God aimed this arrow at two large targets in our fallen hearts, greed and envy. The first is our lustful desire to have every attractive possession and relationship we see our "neighbor" (fellow human being) enjoying. The second is our inborn subtle dislike of him for having them—the very things we want! James shoots at the same target: "Do ye think that the scripture saith in vain [without cause or incorrectly], The [fallen human] spirit that dwelleth in us lusteth [strongly or persistently desires] to envy?" (James 4:5). That's the bad news.

But the good news is, there is a cure for these twin illnesses: "He gives us more and more grace (power of the Holy Spirit, to meet this evil tendency and all others fully)" (James 4:6, AMP). Freedom comes when we consistently choose for the present to be satisfied with and thankful for *whatever* worldly things God gives us. To move us to take this high road, the New Testament commands, "Give thanks in all circumstances, for this is God's will for you in Christ Jesus" (1 Thess. 5:18, NIV). And if our distress over our "neighbor's" perceived advantages in monies, materials, or marriage seems too great to bear, the Spirit points us up and away to the greatest blessing any person can have—and which every Christian does have—our personal fellowship with the Son of God: "Let your manner of life be without covetousness, and be content with such things as ye have; for [because] he hath said, I will never leave thee, nor forsake thee" (Heb. 13:5). This supreme spiritual consolation—our super-satisfying fellowship with Jesus—is more than enough to cause us to be content, whatever our worldly disadvantages may be at present. If we choose this spiritual viewpoint, keeping the tenth commandment becomes, well, a piece of cake.

So the Great Psychologist's final injunction implies:

> *I want you to be thankful for and content with the possessions and relationships you have, not greedy for and envious over what others have. Remember, you always have Me, in whose presence alone is found the satisfying fullness of human joy.*

So there you have them, the forgotten Ten Implications behind the famous Ten Injunctions. Ponder and practice them—and prosper in your soul-life and calling in Christ!

> Thou shalt meditate therein day and night, that thou mayest observe to do according to all that is written therein; for then thou shalt make thy way prosperous, and then thou shalt have good success.
>
> —JOSHUA 1:8

And under no conditions allow your Christian development and destiny to be cut short.

Chapter Eight

SPIRITUAL ABORTION

Thou shalt not kill [commit murder].

—EXODUS 20:13

A vicious violation of God's sixth commandment, abortion is the deliberate cutting short of an unborn yet living human soul created in the image of God.

Regardless of the United States Supreme Court's landmark decision in the case of *Roe v. Wade* on January 22, 1973, and the noisy justifications of the primarily feminist pro-choice movement, abortion remains at base just what it appears to be: cold-blooded murder. Barring a sweeping, corrective, divine revival in this country, enlightened historians will count abortion the worst and most prevalent American societal sin of the postmodern era. And many will point to its favorable legalization as the final turning point in this nation's tragic, and perhaps terminal, moral and spiritual decline.

After the high court's decision in *Roe v. Wade*, abortion has become a favorite theme resounding in our media, political campaigns, living rooms, and churches. Believers have taken in countless sermons, Bible teachings, testimonies, documentaries, and statistical reports on the subject. As a result, many began taking to the streets to crusade against this savage social sin, staging sit-ins, protests, marches, civil disobedience, and other public demonstrations in the latter years of the twentieth century.

Most notable were the vociferous protests of Operation Rescue that began to gain media attention during the 1980s and 1990s. But we have also seen some disturbed, and in some cases demonic, individuals resort to senseless random violence to try to right the woeful wrongs of abortion clinicians. Meanwhile, the ardent political strategies, legislative initiatives, media ads, and public protests of large numbers of sincere Christians have thus far failed to produce substantive changes in the Supreme Court's precedent-setting position on abortion. It remains today what it was in 1973—governmental sanction of the mass murder of innocents.

So massive has this river of fetal blood become that its current depth and width is staggering. The National Right to Life Committee (NRLC) estimates the total number of recorded abortions since January 22, 1973, to be around 49,915,603 (through 2007).[1] That averages approximately 1,426,160 deaths by abortion per year—a shocking 3,907 per day! The NRLC also estimates that the yearly abortion count has steadily decreased from its all-time high in 1990 to its current level (from 2003 through 2007) of 1,287,000 abortions annually, or 3,500 per day.[2] To put this in perspective, there were about 42,642 traffic deaths on our highways in 2006.[3] That means over *thirty times* more people perished in our abortion clinics in 2006 than on our highways!

We may also set our national acquiescence in fetus extermination beside a much more infamous extermination plan, the Holocaust. The historical consensus is that from November 1938 (post-*Kristallnacht*) through April 1945, Nazi Germany systematically gathered and eliminated 6,000,000 European Jews in its various death camps and gas chambers. (This excludes millions of victims from other people groups also considered undesirables.) During these roughly six and one-third years, an average of almost 947,418 human lives were terminated annually by Hitler's henchmen—or 2,595 per day![4] If the NRLC's figure on the total abortions performed in the United States since 1973 is accurate, this nation has terminated far more innocent lives annually and aggregately than even Hitler's mad regime! And we have had the shocking witness of the Holocaust in full view while doing so! To this day we stand still in silent revulsion and horror at the very mention of the Third Reich's hellish death camps—Auschwitz, Dachau, Buchenwald, and others—yet fail to realize that our quiet and systematic program of government-approved mass murder is an American holocaust!

That the general public has now become content with federally approved feticide is an even more ominous sign of a growing spiritual delusion, namely, the notion fed by pop religion that nations or people may remorselessly sin indefinitely without fear of divine punishment merely because God is so very gracious. To the contrary, unless there is massive repentance in this land, we will one day be visited with judgments as massive as our crimes. Why do I say this? Not merely the Old but also the New Testament assures us that God is still a righteous judge of all injustice: "Be not deceived, God is not mocked, for whatsoever a man [or nation] soweth, that shall he [or it] also reap" (Gal. 6:7).

But calm your righteous indignation for a moment while I tell you about an even *more shocking* sin.

This evil is a church sin, not a societal sin. It is committed only by Christians, never by unbelievers. It is a crime of the body of Christ, not the body politic. The ecclesia will answer for it, not the nation. Millions of born-again believers are guilty of this horrific transgression, including many who justly protest the practice of abortion and decry the Holocaust. While we condemn this nation's abortion rampage with prophetic and prosecutorial zeal, the Judge of all the earth is trying to convict us, His redeemed children, of an even more vicious violation of His will. Many of us have never recognized, much less grieved over, this greater wrong. The sin of which I write is *spiritual abortion,* the deliberate cutting short of God's plan for the life of Jesus born in us at salvation.

To better understand spiritual abortion, let's review the facts on physical abortion. Its circumstances are familiar to us all.

Physical Abortion

A human life—a developing mortal body and eternal soul—is conceived by natural procreation. Mystically, God interacts with this natural process of gestation to providentially "form" each one of us while we are still in our mother's womb. Though not fully explained, this divine working is fully revealed. God informed Jeremiah, "I *formed* thee in the womb" (Jer. 1:5). David worshiped God for forming him in the womb: "For you created my inmost being: you knit me together in my mother's womb" (Ps. 139:13, NIV). It is not surprising, then, that the Bible consistently and repeatedly reveals that human life begins at conception, not consciousness.

It further asserts that the time of our divine calling predates the time of our birth:

> Before thou camest forth out of the womb, I sanctified thee, and I ordained thee a prophet unto the nations.
>
> —JEREMIAH 1:5

> Even before I was born, God chose me and called me by his marvelous grace.
>
> —GALATIANS 1:15, NLT

But before this wondrous new human life can emerge, grow, mature, and fulfill its unique vocation in the cosmos, it is violently cut short, or "aborted," by a surgical procedure, or drug-induced, premature vaginal expulsion, tantamount to murder. However rationalized, a human heartbeat is silenced by a human hand. However justified, the gravest injustice is perpetrated as the most precious human right—the right to life—is criminally denied a soul with neither say nor vote in the matter. Thus, a human fetus never becomes the man or woman God intended it to be. What a shame, what a crime, what an abomination is this physical abortion!

Though fundamentally different, spiritual abortion follows an ominously similar pattern. Let's examine it.

SPIRITUAL ABORTION

Appropriately, three times in John 3, Jesus taught humankind that to be a true Christian, or a child citizen of God's eternal kingdom, we must be, in His own words, "born again." "Marvel not that I said unto thee, Ye must be *born again*" (John 3:7; see vv. 3, 5). Succinctly, He meant that our spirits must experience a sudden, new entrance into eternal life just as our bodies have experienced a sudden, new entrance into earthly life. When we are "born again," the most precious divine gift—the life of Jesus—is implanted or conceived in us by a sudden, supernatural act of God's Spirit. Our hearts, in a sense, become "pregnant" with the very Babe of Bethlehem, and Mary's miraculous pregnancy recurs, not in our internal body but in our innermost being.

Thus Jesus' famous natural conception is a parable of our instantaneous spiritual regeneration:

> The Holy Spirit shall come upon thee, and the power of the Highest shall overshadow thee; therefore also *that holy thing which shall be born of thee shall be called the Son of God.*
> —LUKE 1:35

After this miracle of spiritual regeneration, God wants the newly implanted divine nature to grow and mature within us. Then the wonder of Jesus' life will be increasingly manifested in our daily living and character, and we will go on to fulfill our predestined calling in life. But for this to occur, the new life we have received must first be fully energized or empowered.

The imperative of spiritual empowerment

We receive this vital spiritual empowerment when we receive the initial infilling of the Holy Spirit, referred to by the New Testament as the "baptism with the Holy Spirit." In all four Gospels, John the Baptist identified Jesus as the Baptizer with the Spirit: "He shall baptize you with the Holy Spirit" (Matt. 3:11). (See Mark 1:8; Luke 3:16; John 1:33.) Jesus followed John's notification with His own announcement, given only days before Pentecost, stating that He would soon begin filling His followers with the Holy Spirit: "Ye shall be baptized with the Holy Spirit not many days from now" (Acts 1:5).

In the midst of the dramatic Pentecostal outpouring in the upper room, Peter stood up and, under the full and direct inspiration of the Spirit, affirmed that Jesus had indeed "baptized"—spiritually overwhelmed or filled to overflowing—all present with the Holy Spirit. Furthermore, he asserted that Jesus was personally responsible for *everything* that was seen and heard there—the sound of wind, the visualization of fire, and the manifestation of different languages: "He hath shed forth this, which ye now *see* and *hear*" (Acts 2:33).

Some Christian denominations deny that we need to receive this second work of grace, while others seem to believe that the baptism with the Holy Spirit and its typical accompanying signs and gifts of the Spirit signal one's arrival at the "promised land" of spiritual maturity. Neither view is entirely correct. To deny our need of the Spirit's infilling is to deny the very plan of God for His people, to foolishly assert that we do not need what God in His wisdom planned for us to have. On the other hand, to imagine that merely receiving this one experience automatically makes us thoroughly spiritually mature in our thinking, living, and working is equally inaccurate. To the contrary, the baptism with the Spirit, while it is necessary, only begins the Spirit's deeper, abiding work of purifying us and growing, forming, and maturing the Christ life in us. If we are indeed to thrive in the "promised land" of spiritual maturity, we must both be filled with the Holy Spirit and pursue spiritual development.

The triumph of spiritual development

To become spiritually mature, we must give ourselves completely, not partially, to the God who has saved and empowered us: "give thyself *wholly*" (1 Tim. 4:15). (See Numbers 14:24.) Setting aside worldly interests, our one great goal must be to abide so close to Jesus that we "apprehend," or fully grasp, His plans, not ours, for our lives: "I follow after, if that I may *apprehend* that for which also I am apprehended of Christ Jesus" (Phil. 3:12).

We must carefully feed the Christ life in us with the spiritual milk, meat, bread, and water of God's Word every day: "As newborn babes, desire *the pure milk of the Word*, that ye may grow by it" (1 Pet. 2:2). Just as Jesus "often" spent quality time with His Father in prayer—"Jesus Himself would *often* slip away to the wilderness and pray" (Luke 5:16, NAS)—we too must visit the "secret" place of prayer daily: "When thou prayest, enter into thy room, and when thou hast shut thy door, pray to thy Father, who is in secret; and thy Father, who seeth in secret, shall reward thee openly" (Matt. 6:6). We must also learn to praise and worship the Lord regularly, both in public church meetings and in the privacy of our homes.

When tempted to disobey God's righteousness, we must make the right choices, as Joseph did (Gen. 39:7–10), to avoid harming our souls through sin. When given clear direction by God at the crossroads and crises of life, we must follow His guidance, not our selfish desires: "For as many as are led by the Spirit of God, they are [living as] the [true] sons of God [or as Jesus did]" (Rom. 8:14). We must also consistently obey God's Word in all other divinely arranged "various trials" (James 1:2). We must resolutely refuse to be offended with Jesus over the disappointments, injustices, losses, and delays in our lives, knowing that He permits them to develop, not destroy, our characters. And, abandoning all complaining, we must sacrificially "give thanks" to the Lord in every situation, pleasant and unpleasant: "Thank [God] in everything—no matter what the circumstances may be, be thankful and give thanks; for this is the will of God" (1 Thess. 5:18, AMP). As we do these things, we "work out" our salvation (Phil. 2:12), or produce proof of the Savior's presence, power, and purpose in us. And God's will is accomplished, not aborted, in our lives.

Thus our spiritual trek through this life ends in the triumph of full spiritual development, not the tragedy of spiritual abortion.

The tragedy of spiritual abortion

If we reject the rigors of spiritual development, we unconsciously choose the ruin of spiritual abortion. Instead of giving ourselves to wise diligence, we give way to senseless negligence. How do we "neglect so great salvation" (Heb. 2:3)?

If we choose the way of spiritual negligence, we continue living only for the desires of our old man and ignore those of our new man. We seek temporal worldly goals and selfish pleasures rather than God's eternal goals and pleasure. We content ourselves with a worthless form of religion and forfeit a priceless, satisfying, personal fellowship with Jesus. As a result, we fail to develop spiritually and never fulfill our destiny in Christ. Thus we commit spiritual abortion by cutting short, or *aborting*, the purpose of God for our lives. *We kill the life of Jesus in us by a criminal negligence equivalent to murder.* We don't do it as suddenly and tangibly as an abortion doctor disposes of his victims, but we just as surely take life. By ignoring the divine life given us, that life weakens, withers, and expires. (Strictly speaking, Christ in us never fully dies, because eternal life can't cease to exist. But practically speaking, it dies, because it falls into dormancy.) The outward evidence of this inward decease is that we become "Laodicean" Christians (spiritually luke-warm, like the Christians of ancient Laodicea), inferior, unattractive, and un-Christlike specimens of Christianity, "wretched, and miserable, and [spiritually] poor, and blind, and naked" (Rev. 3:17). Throughout our earthly walk, the divine Babe implanted in us remains silent and motionless—not dead, but as dead: "And he was *like one dead*, inso-much that many said, He is dead" (Mark 9:26).

Therefore, "Christ in you, the hope of glory" (Col. 1:27) never lives and moves and has His being in us in this world as He could and should. And God's hopes of receiving glory (honor) through us are dashed—as are our hopes of receiving rich and numerous eternal rewards from Him for a life of works pleasing to Him. What a tragedy! What a crime! What an abomination spiritual abortion is!

A frank comparison

As horrible and heartbreaking as physical abortion is, spiritual abor-tion is even more horrific and heartless.

Consider this concise contrast. Physical abortion wastes fallen humanity. Spiritual abortion wastes redeemed humanity. Physical abor-tion wastes Adam's seed. Spiritual abortion wastes Christ's seed. Physi-cal abortion is executed by unbelievers. Spiritual abortion is executed by believers. Physical abortion is the work of people living in darkness. Spiri-tual abortion is the work of people having the Light of the world and His Word. Physical abortion robs babies of temporal life, liberty, and happi-ness. Spiritual abortion robs believers of eternal rewards, honors, and joys. Physical abortion creates a guilty conscience. Spiritual abortion creates a grieving Christ. Physical abortion is the murder of a man formed in God's image. Spiritual abortion is the murder of God's image formed in a man. It's Calvary all over again—man puts God to death—but at the hands of Christians, not Jews and Romans.

As stated earlier, the current estimate of abortions performed in the United States daily is 3,500. Though we have no definitive statistic to report, the number of underdeveloped Christians who pass away daily, having never allowed Jesus to fully have His way in them, is probably even higher. The former statistic is earth's scandal; the latter is heaven's. But does it rivet our attention and stir our hearts as it should?

~

May I humbly suggest that it is grossly hypocritical for us to protest so vociferously against the ongoing physical abortion in society while we silently commit, condone, or ignore spiritual abortion daily in our souls and churches? If the apostle Paul were among us today, he would have none of our hypocrisy. How do I know this? His writings reveal that he differentiated between church and societal sins and considered the church's first judicial responsibility to be the examination and correction of its own, not the rebuke and reform of outsiders:

> It is not my business to judge those who are not part of the church. God will judge them. But you must judge the people who are part of the church.
> —1 CORINTHIANS 5:12–13, NCV

By no means am I suggesting we stop detesting and protesting physical abortion. To the contrary, it is vital to God's plan and our prophetic calling that we—the light of the world and salt of the earth—continue our vigorous witness against it. I am, however, proposing that as we direct our zeal toward removing our society's most glaring moral sin, we address even more zealously the massive "beam" lodged in our personal and ecclesiastical eyes—spiritual abortion.

Indeed, may the Spirit of God open our eyes wide to see the heinousness of spiritual abortion as clearly as He does. And from now on may we consider not only the right to life of the unborn but also that of the "first-born"—"that he [Christ] might be the *first-born* among [or of] many [fully developed Christian] brethren" (Rom. 8:29).

And may this happen soon, because the signs of the End Times are upon us.

Chapter Nine

Sodom Revisited: A Sign

The disciples came unto him privately, saying... what shall be the sign of thy coming, and of the end of the age?
—Matthew 24:3

During their final week with Jesus on earth, the disciples drew near Him as He sat teaching on the Mount of Olives, and asked, "What shall be the sign of thy coming, and of the end of the age?" (Matt. 24:3).

Jesus responded in this context by teaching them "signs of the times," or certain infallible spiritual indicators that will mark the arrival of the general season in which He will first translate the church and then initiate seven years of final testing and judgment, known as the tribulation period, throughout the world. After this necessary purging of the existing satanic world order, Jesus will usher in His thousand-year kingdom on earth. Among the "signs" the great Prophet mentioned in His Olivet Discourse are: the coming of popular false Messiahs, deadly wars and pandemics, devastating earthquakes, the persecutions of true Christians, the spiritual cooling and defection of many Christians, and the preaching of the gospel worldwide (vv. 4–14). But in this chapter we wish to concentrate on one high-profile sign Jesus gave us in another context.

According to Luke's Gospel, one of the most obvious signs that we are living in the last days before Christ's appearing is the reemergence of bold, unabashed homosexuality on the world scene—even among the ranks of professing Christians—like that witnessed in Lot's day. Luke records that Jesus said:

> *As it was in the days of Lot;* they did eat, they drank, they bought, they sold, they planted, they built.... *Even thus shall it be* in the day when the Son of man is revealed.
>
> —LUKE 17:28, 30

While Jesus specifies the Sodomites' preoccupation with overindulgence, moneymaking, and other temporal material things (constructing farms, buildings), His reference to "the days of Lot" is an undeniable allusion to the prevailing pernicious sin of Lot's generation, gross immorality, and especially homosexuality. So Jesus is telling us that when we see a culture on earth that replicates the excessive materialism and moral laxity of Sodom's culture, we should begin to earnestly anticipate His coming. Why? God is about to wind things up. This should come as no surprise to biblically informed persons.

The Bible tells of two ancient societies in which homosexuality reached such scandalous heights (or depths). The first and most obvious surfaced among the heathen in Sodom in "the days of Lot." (See Genesis 19:1–11.) The second and less known instance arose among the Israelites in the city of Gibeah during the period of the Judges. (See Judges 19:1–30.) In both of these instances God responded by sending swift, sure, and terminal judgments. (See Genesis 19:12–29; Judges 20:1–48.) The inspired record of these two homosexually indulgent societies points out six striking similarities.

First, on both occasions men gathered spontaneously with the intent of gang raping (supposedly) male visitors, though in the former case their lust was denied and in the latter case it was appeased by the offering of a female victim. Second, that they did so publicly and not privately reveals that they were not cautious but recklessly bold in their sin; this implies that such activity was neither resisted by the authorities nor condemned by the prevailing laws or social standards of the day. Third, that their preferred perversity was homosexual and not heterosexual rape reveals that homosexuality was a prevalent if not dominant sexual preference in each generation. And, since moral shifts in society occur slowly, this suggests that homosexuality had long been accepted in these cultures. Fourth, that these crowds were violent indicates a demonic presence, for demons love to stir up violence. Fifth, that God providentially permitted these sad sagas of sodomy to be described in the nineteenth chapter of their respective biblical books may indicate His intent, however subtly, to connect the two periods and cultures in the Bible reader's mind. Obviously, there is more than a numerical commonality present.

Sixth, and most important, is this ominous similarity: *in each of these generations, unchecked homosexuality brought swift, extinctive judgments on those who practiced or defended it when God's appointed time of judgment arrived.* In the first case, God annihilated the inhabitants of Sodom in a sudden and fiery direct divine intervention. In the second, occurring some seven hundred years later, He permitted the united tribes of Israel to slaughter almost the entire tribe of Benjamin in a single day of battle because they had defended the sodomites and rapists of Gibeah (Judg. 20:35, 46–47).

God's actions are sending us a vital message that we must not fail to understand: when sexual perversion, especially homosexuality, reaches the point of not only being accepted but also of being demanding and demonstrative in our streets, some form of divine judgment is not far away. Some may point out that sodomy has always existed. Yes, it has…but in the closet, not in the congress; behind closed doors, not in open public forums; in pornography, not on parade. God's responses to the aggressive homosexuality of Sodom and Gibeah give us conclusive biblical evidence that when homosexuality goes public, when it becomes bold, forceful, and even boastful, God won't tolerate it much longer. It indicates that sin is "full," that the cup of rebellious human misdeeds is filled to the brim. And that means that a swift, sure, and terminal visitation of divine judgment is soon to come.

Indeed, our generation is witnessing nothing less than "Sodom revisited," that is, an appalling revival of increasingly bold homosexuality. It is Sodom and Gibeah all over again. *Never before in the history of the world and the church has sodomy reached its current level of public acceptance.* In prominent cities across this and other nations, gay and lesbian groups march openly in our streets with the same deluded confidence their ancient predecessors displayed in the promenades of Sodom and Gibeah. No longer are they ashamed to be known. To the contrary, they are vocal, proud, and defiant. Their political action groups are well funded, articulate, and influential. They have so effectively advocated their abnormality that it is now considered a normal thing…an innocent, innate inclination rather than an acquired, pernicious perversion…a result of biological makeup, not immoral choices. It is now considered abnormal to object to this abnormality and dare suggest that traditional morality is still valid. In an attempt to force the public to accept their twisted self-view, pro-homosexual advocates are trying to redefine the oldest, most universally accepted and basic human social institution: marriage. Could any Christian a decade ago have imagined that today we would be striving to reassert publicly that marriage is between one man and one woman? Not only the manner but the madness of Sodom pervades our society! And it is becoming increasingly difficult and dangerous for anyone to speak out against homosexuality without taking considerable abuse from the insistent, immoral minority.

When asked his opinion of the United States military's "Don't ask, don't tell," policy concerning homosexuals in the military, Marine General Peter Pace, then the chairman of the Joint Chiefs of Staff, said, "I believe homosexual acts between two individuals are immoral and that we should not condone immoral acts….I do not believe the United States is well served by a policy that says it is OK to be immoral in any way."[1]

For even this very measured and impassionate criticism of the homosexual lifestyle, Pace was immediately roundly condemned, not only by the predictable gay and lesbian advocates but also by leading public figures. Senate Armed Forces Committee Chairman, Republican Senator John Warner of Virginia said, "I respectfully but strongly disagree with the chairman's (general's) view that homosexuality is immoral."[2] The Democratic Speaker of the House of Representatives, Nancy Pelosi, added that she was "disappointed in the moral judgment" of the general.[3] And I am disappointed in hers! What has caused this nation to virtually reverse its moral standards over the last sixty years?

The postmodernism ideology, which rejects any standard of truth as being fixed, universal, and absolute, and has pervaded American culture in recent decades, has greatly influenced our perception of traditional morality in general and homosexuality in particular. Christian commentator Albert Mohler Jr. writes:

> The God allowed by postmodernism is not the God of the Bible, but a vague idea of spirituality. There are no tablets of stone, no Ten Commandments...no rules. Morality is, along with other foundations of culture, discarded as oppressive and totalitarian. A pervasive moral relativism marks postmodern culture.... Homosexuality, for example, is openly advocated and accepted. The rise of gay and lesbian studies in universities, the emergence of homosexual political power, and the homoerotic images now common to popular culture mark this dramatic moral reversal. Homosexuality is no longer considered a sin. Homophobia is now targeted as sin, and demands for tolerance of "alternative lifestyles" have now turned into demand for public celebration of all lifestyles as morally equal.[4]

With incidents and philosophies like these becoming increasingly commonplace, the warning Jesus spoke originally to gospel-rejecting Israel comes to mind:

> I say unto you, that it shall be more tolerable in that day [of ultimate divine judgment] for Sodom, than for that city.
> —LUKE 10:12

Jesus here prophesied that God's judgment would be more severe upon cities that heard His gospel but rejected it than it would be on those, like Sodom, that never heard it and yet lived wickedly. This points up the biblical principle that God judges those who have the light of His Word more, not less, severely than those who don't. If the present trend continues in American culture, our generation will have a far harsher judgment than even the ancient Sodomites, who never had the light of God's salvation and the understanding of His Word taught them as we have. And they perished in a sudden, fiery flash of judgment! But the general public's adoption of homosexuality is not this generation's greatest scandal.

By far the greater outrage is the growing embrace of homosexuality by professing *Christian* people and organizations. Remember, while our first biblical example cites unrestrained homosexuality among the unredeemed (Sodom), the second describes it being embraced and defended by the redeemed (the Jews in the city of Gibeah and tribe of Benjamin)! The Jews had the full light of God's Law, which clearly forbade such practices: "Thou shalt not lie with mankind, as with womankind: it is abomination" (Lev. 18:22). "If a man also lie with mankind, as he lieth with a woman, both of them have committed an abomination [before God]" (20:13). Yet they too surrendered to the spirit of homosexuality, just as the heathen did.

Similarly, a growing number of churches today across the theological and denominational spectrum are openly known as homosexual churches. These congregations campaign to draw in practicing homosexuals and assert vociferously that their activities are normal and fully approved by God. Other more traditional churches comprised of sexually "straight" worshippers have now made it their policy to not exclude practicing homosexuals from their fellowship and communion—this despite clear New Testament condemnation of homosexuality in all its forms. (All congregations should receive *penitent* homosexuals just as they do other converted sinners, or they fail to exhibit Christ's love for all who turn from sin to Him.)

One such inspired indictment is found in the Book of Romans:

> They exchanged the truth of God for a *lie....* Because of this, God *gave them over* to *shameful lusts.* Even *their women* exchanged natural relations for *unnatural* ones. In the same way the men also abandoned natural relations with women and were inflamed with lust for one another. Men committed *indecent* acts with one another, and received in themselves the *due penalty* for their perversion.
>
> —ROMANS 1:25–27, NIV

This inspired text clearly states the following truths:

- The notion that homosexual conduct is normal is a "lie."
- Homosexual conduct is "unnatural" and "indecent."
- God has at least temporarily "given over," or abandoned to the forces of sin, those who practice homosexuality.
- God considers homosexual desires "shameful lusts."
- Lesbianism is as equally unacceptable as male homosexuality.
- Homosexuals may suffer a self-inflicted, "due" (deserved), physical "penalty" if they continue their sinful practice.

Concerning this last point, while the deadly AIDS (acquired immune deficiency syndrome) virus that emerged in the 1980s and has since spread throughout the world has unquestionably killed millions of innocently infected persons, many of its victims are not innocent. AIDS was initially, and remains today, primarily a plague that spreads through homosexual or other immoral acts (or illicit drug use). How much better this troubled world would be if all people, especially Christians, would humbly believe this lucid New Testament warning and avoid all homosexual activity!

Additionally, the New Testament includes those who impenitently "practice homosexuality" (1 Cor. 6:9–10, NLT) in a long list of people who will be excluded from residence and rewards in God's eternal kingdom.

Despite these sober warnings, the spirit of Gibeah has revisited many churches today. Homosexual activity is being justified, pacified, and defended, as it was in ancient Gibeah. Impenitent homosexuals are being welcomed, not warned; commended, not corrected; and brought into the church, not asked, if still impenitent, to leave. The holiness of God's love is ignored and unholy love is embraced. And Christ's desire for a thoroughly changed, purified church is rejected so that we may accept people who want neither change nor purity. This inexcusable affair with the spirit of this world has grieved the Holy Spirit and switched many Christians and churches from being God's friends to being His enemies: "Ye adulterers and adulteresses, know ye not that the friendship of the world is enmity with God? Whosoever, therefore, will be a friend of the world is the enemy of God" (James 4:4). But the Lord hasn't given up on His people.

The heavenly Bridegroom has recently sent us, His sleeping virgins, several stunning wake-up calls. Multiple cases of sexual abuse by Catholic priests filled the news media during the first years of this twenty-first century. And in 2003, an openly gay cleric was appointed as bishop of the New Hampshire diocese of a mainline protestant church.[5] In 2006, *the* top evangelical minister in the nation was first exposed as, and later confessed to, being a long-time secret bisexual.[6] If homosexuality has infiltrated the highest level of leadership in both high- and low-church bodies, we may assume it has permeated not only our culture but also our churches. But have these alarming incidents awakened us?

If so, what is the proper response? How should we "awake to righteousness" (1 Cor. 15:34)?

We should begin by recognizing what not to do. We must not be truly homophobic, though this misnomer will be applied to us. The Spirit in us is greater than the spirit in this world, and His power and protection remain with the righteous even when we are surrounded by great unrighteousness. (See 2 Kings 6:15–17.) Nor is hateful mockery justified. God's blessing is reserved for those who refuse to sit "in the seat of the scornful" (Ps. 1:1). Nor does it help to blow this sin out of proportion. Though abominable, homosexuality is not the worst sin. Pride, lying, murder, injustice, plotting evil—the Word identifies these sins as the worst in God's sight. (See Proverbs 6:16–19.) Furthermore, social prejudice and injustice will not make homosexuality disappear. Though darkened by sin and twisted in their moral judgment, homosexuals do have a legal right to live and work in our pluralistic society and democratic republic. (But their sin will not be tolerated during the thousand-year reign of Christ!) None of these forms of righteous indignation are the right response, for "the wrath of man worketh not the righteousness of God" (James 1:20).

Only one method of redress is proper: the compassionate, Spirit-filled intercessions of grace-redeemed, now-enlightened former sinners like you and me! If we abide in Christ and let His Word abide in us, we can pray for the conversion of any homosexual, and the supernatural delivering power of the Holy Spirit will lead him (or her) from the darkness of moral rebellion into the light of God's forgiving love, unchanging truth, and uncompromising holiness. "If ye abide in me, and my words abide in you, ye shall ask what ye will, and it shall be done unto you" (John 15:7).

Paul reminded the Christians of his day that converted homosexuals were in their churches: "And *such [homosexuals] were some of you*; but ye are washed, but ye are sanctified, but ye are justified in the name of the Lord Jesus, and by [receiving and obeying] the [Holy] Spirit of our God" (1 Cor. 6:11, see vv. 9–10). And there are upright, godly, spiritual, and fruitful Christians today that are former homosexuals.

As we pursue this path of action, we should earnestly remember the words of Jesus, who promised He would come for His bride church in a time when conditions were again "as in the days of Lot." And, believing this, we must neither fret at the current revisitation of Sodom nor compromise with its twisted values but rather quietly and diligently prepare ourselves, our churches, and our families for the Lord's appearing. And quickly. Why?

The time is short. It's "high time" that we get ready for Jesus' appearing:

> Knowing the time, that now it is *high time* to awake out of sleep; for now is our salvation nearer than when we believed. The night is far spent, the day is at hand; let us, therefore, cast off the works of darkness, and let us put on the armor of light. Let us walk honestly, as in the day; not in reveling and drunkenness, not in immorality and wantonness, not in strife and envying. But put ye on the Lord Jesus Christ, and make not provision for the flesh, to fulfill its lusts.
>
> —ROMANS 13:11–14

"High time" may be defined as "beyond the proper time but before it is too late."[7] And it is now "high time" that we wake up and face the full significance of Jesus' words, "as it was in the days of Lot." Yes, we *are* truly witnessing an important fulfillment of Bible prophecy. Yes, our generation *is* truly like Lot's. Yes, the time *is* truly very late. But it's *not* too late. We can still get ourselves ready, if we will. Surprisingly, Lot's experience gives us this hope.

God delivered even Lot, spiritually tardy though he was, out of Sodom, "the LORD being merciful unto him" (Gen. 19:16). That's encouraging news to this lukewarm generation. If we have at times lived more like Lot—self-centered, worldly, indifferent to God's will, in subtle com-promise with the prevailing immorality of our day—than we care to admit, let us take heart and believe this great sign Jesus has given us. *Because our times are clearly "as in the days of Lot," we may be certain we are now in the church's final season of preparation before Jesus appears. Soon the Bride-groom will appear and the bride will ascend to meet Him. Then, "as it was in the days of Lot," the "brimstone"—the tribulation period and its termi-nal divine judgments—will descend.* So let us forsake all that we would be ashamed of in the presence of the Lord and "give ourselves wholly" to the great duty of fully knowing and fully serving God (1 Tim. 4:15). Then we will be "accounted worthy to escape all these things that shall come to pass [the tribulation period], and to stand [delivered] before the Son of Man [in heaven]" (Luke 21:36).

As surprising as it may sound, the revival of Sodom is a sign permit-ted by God to revive the church. While we grieve over our society's descent into the dark abyss of homosexuality, and bear witness against it, let us be absolutely confident that Jesus is coming soon and, in that purifying hope, begin rising from our dark valley of non-expectation and despair. It's time to redouble our efforts at abiding very close to the Lord.

> And now, little children, abide in him, that, when he shall appear, we may have confidence and not be ashamed before him at his coming.
>
> —1 JOHN 2:28

And if any preacher, prophet, or politician tries to prove to you that Jesus is not coming soon, don't buy it. That's fool's gold—a big lie!

Chapter Ten

THE LIE STOPPER

The mouth of those who speak lies shall be stopped.

—PSALM 63:11

*H*arassed day and night by King Saul in the Judean wilderness, David closed Psalm 63 with these memorable words: "The mouth of those who speak lies shall be stopped." No passing sentiment, this was a vital part of the future king of Israel's personal faith.

At the time, David's reputation was being systematically destroyed throughout Israel by King Saul's vicious, unrelenting, and surprisingly successful slander campaign. We find a small but illuminating sampling of Saul's works of iniquity in 1 Samuel 22:6–8, where in Gibeah Saul maliciously described himself as a generous, nonauthoritarian, betrayed, terrorized victim of conspiracy and David as an unfaithful, ungenerous, power-hungry, villainous conspirator and terrorist:

> Then Saul said unto his servants who stood about him, Hear now, ye Benjamites; will the son of Jesse give every one of you fields and vineyards, and make you all captains of thousands, and captains of hundreds, that all of you have conspired against me, and there is none that discloseth to me that my son hath made a league with the son of Jesse, and there is none of you that is sorry for me, or showeth unto me that my son hath stirred up my servant against me, to lie in wait, as at this day?
>
> —1 SAMUEL 22:7–8

If Academy Awards could have been given in the eleventh century B.C., Saul would have won the Oscar for "Best Actor" by unanimous vote, because everything he said was an act—and precisely the opposite of the truth. He was churlish and David generous. He was dictatorial and David magnanimous. He was the betrayer and David the loyalist. He was power-hungry and David the content subordinate. He was the terrorist and David the peacemaker. He was the conspirator and David the object of his plotting. He was the villain and David the victim.

Nevertheless, because Saul told such lies anywhere, anytime, and to anyone who would listen, everywhere David turned, former friends were turning against him. The Lord revealed to David that the people of Keilah were fully ready to betray David to Saul for arrest, even though David's men had recently delivered the Keilahites from Philistine invaders! And Nabal, whose shepherds and flocks had prospered because of the protection of David's men, responded with bitter accusations and disdain when David, in great need, asked Nabal for food supplies for his hungry men: "Who is David?... There are many servants nowadays who break away, every man from his master. Shall I, then, take my bread, and my water, and my flesh that I have killed for my shearers, and give it unto men, whom I know not from where they are" (1 Sam. 25:10–11).

Besides these estrangements, even people David had never met were manifesting distrust and hostility without cause. When David and his men took refuge in their territory, the men of Ziph reported their presence to Saul and agreed to lead his soldiers in an ambush on David's hideout, only to discover that David had already moved on to the wilderness of Maon.

In such extreme adversity, the anointed, formerly successful, and beloved son of Jesse took comfort in realizing that his long nightmare of misjudgment would not last forever. On some divinely appointed day, though he knew not when, where, or how, God would stop the lies of Saul and every other liar: "The mouth of those who speak lies shall be stopped!" This was not wishful thinking. It was God's promise: "Thine enemies shall be found liars unto thee [lit. 'cringe,' ashamed and broken, when their false-hoods are exposed]" (Deut. 33:29). This was the basis for David's faith. And his hope. And his confession. And our lesson—a golden truth tried and proven in the fires of David's wilderness trials, and those of countless others, and ready to be proven again in our tests! But do we understand fully what lies are?

Webster's defines a *lie* as, "a false statement…an intentional untruth; a falsehood."[1] But lies are not only blatant total untruths and outlandish fabrications. More frequently they are partial truths deliberately twisted to create false impressions. *Webster's* continues, "something intended or serving to convey a false impression…an inaccurate…statement."[2] Lies are willful disseminations of damaging misinformation and malicious distortions of reality. They are biased or imbalanced presentations, inaccurate or incomplete descriptions of events, actions, words, or characters.

There are several reasons why deceivers lie. Through their mean-spirited misrepresentations, liars always seek to deceive, destroy, or divide.

They hope to deceive their listeners in order to further their own selfish purposes or malicious agendas—usually to use people for gain or to put down rivals in order to lift themselves up (in their own minds, if nothing else). Their listeners won't respond as they wish if they tell them the truth. So they use lies to manipulate them. Once their listeners buy into the lie, they then act as they wish.

Also, liars' words always harm or destroy something. For instance:

- The reputations, favor, careers, projects, businesses, or ministries of the people about whom they lie
- The souls of the people about whom they lie (if such victims become offended and embittered)
- The souls of the people to whom they lie, which are poisoned whenever they believe false reports and misjudge innocent people: "The wicked…speaking lies. Their [liars'] poison is like the poison of a serpent" (Ps. 58:3–4).
- Third parties, whose souls are damaged when they believe the lies passed on by those who initially hear and believe them: "The words of a gossip are like choice morsels; they go down to a man's inmost parts" (Prov. 26:22, NIV). This says that gossip seems like "choice morsels," or tasty morsels of good food, but it's really rotten food that "wounds"

(KJV) our souls, deeply sickening our thoughts and feelings toward, and spoiling our relationship with, innocent people.

Additionally, lies are highly divisive. Once sown and given time to grow, liars' devilish distortions invariably spring up and separate people from their fellow Christians, associates, and friends. Because He realizes all too well the needless, poignant pain this causes, God hates the sowing of discord: "These six things doth the LORD hate...*he that soweth discord among brethren*" (Prov. 6:16–19). Sowing disharmony causes enormous spiritual, psychological, and emotional damage, splitting marriages, families, and churches that God has brought together for His purposes: "One sinner destroyeth much good [union, work]" (Eccles. 9:18). But, even more importantly, lying divides impenitent liars and those who believe them from God, who has no respect for "such as turn aside to [speak or believe] lies" (Ps. 40:4). Liars may deceive their way into the favor of naïve ones, but not the divine One. He has banned them from His presence, pending repentance: "He that worketh deceit shall not dwell within my house [presence]; he that telleth lies shall not tarry in my sight" (Ps. 101:7).

Lying takes many different forms. In the American justice system, lying under oath is perjury. In American politics, which has recently perfected the art of deception in almost every form, the popular euphemism for lying is "negative politics." (And I cast my vote here and now to abolish it!) In religion, lying manifests in a variety of ways—as false religions, false doctrines, false movements, false prophets, false claims, false miracles, false epiphanies, and envious or competitive religious backstabbing. In journalism, lying in any form of print media is libel and, in radio and television reporting, slander. Socially, lying manifests as gossip, or passing on unconfirmed defamatory information about people we often don't know concerning matters that are often none of our business. Whatever form it takes, lying is despised by God, who has appointed a time and way to stop all liars: "Liars will be silenced" (Ps. 63:11, NLT).

Why was David so sure God would stop liars?

FOUR REASONS WHY GOD WILL STOP ALL LIARS

Here are four reasons why God will one day stop the mouths of all liars. David surely understood these truths at the time of his writing.

God's holy hatred

Well versed in God's Word, David understood that God positively hates willful reputation assassination. (One cannot assassinate another's character, only their reputation.) As stated earlier, two of the seven sins God despises most involve willfully misrepresenting people's characters, words, or deeds (Prov. 6:16–19). And the term the Holy Spirit selected to describe God's feelings about this practice is "abomination," which conveys the strongest possible antipathy—absolute detestation and thorough loathing. Also as we have already seen, one of the Ten Commandments is dedicated to the forbiddance of the sin of lying: "Thou shalt not bear false witness against thy neighbor" (Exod. 20:16). Furthermore, God repeatedly vows that unrepentant liars cannot presently draw near him, "He that telleth lies shall not tarry in my sight" (Ps. 101:7)—and that (if never saved) they will spend eternity far from Him, in the tormenting lake of fire, "All liars shall have their part in the lake of fire" (Rev. 21:8).

Other scriptures confirm just how strongly God detests lying. Consider these inspired, infallible declarations:

> Rescue me, O LORD, from liars and from all deceitful people. O deceptive tongue, what will God do to you? How will he increase your punishment? You will be pierced with sharp arrows and burned with glowing coals.
>
> —PSALM 120:2–4, NLT

> Nothing evil will be allowed to enter[3] [New Jerusalem], nor anyone who practices shameful...dishonesty...
>
> —REVELATION 21:27, NLT

> Outside the city[4] [New Jerusalem] are...all who love to live a lie.
>
> —REVELATION 22:15, NLT

Why is lying so reprehensible to God? Surely, the God of truth hates falsehood because, as described above, it is deceptive, destructive, and divisive. But another, and perhaps chief reason, is that lying reminds Him of the treacherous work of Satan, the "father" of lies (John 8:44), in the Garden of Eden. There, by maliciously misrepresenting God's intentions to Eve, Satan (in the serpent) successfully created a false or distorted impression of God—that He did *not* want the best for man. It was this slander that provoked Adam and Eve to rebel against God. So in the beginning of human history on earth it was a lie that separated the loving Creator from His most-beloved creature, man. And as stated in chapter seven, before creation Satan (Lucifer) used this same method in heaven to deceive a third of the angels and move them to join his rebellion against God.

So to God every human lie is but a distant, sad echo of these two original, catastrophic, malicious misrepresentations in heaven and on earth.

God's faithful, fatherly love

David was keenly aware of God's faithful, fatherly love for His own redeemed people.

In tender fatherly compassion, God has bound Himself to defend His adopted children from every adversary and attack, whether spiritual, verbal, or physical: "As a father pitieth his children, so the LORD pitieth them that fear him" (Ps. 103:13). As stated above, God promised in the Pentateuch, "And thine enemies shall be found [exposed as] liars unto thee" (Deut. 33:29). How could God do anything less when slanderers harm those who are "the apple of his eye" (Zech. 2:8)? Any loving earthly father would defend or vindicate his children, if it was in his power to do so. How much more will the heavenly Father do so?

So David realized, as we should, that God's intense fatherly love makes Him not only willing but also determined to redress the slander directed against His adopted children. He may "bear long" with us as we endure seasons of misunderstanding and reproach divinely designed to refine us and develop Christ's character within, but ultimately He will have His day with everyone who slanders us: "And shall not God avenge his own elect, who cry day and night unto him . . . I tell you that he will avenge them speedily [suddenly]" (Luke 18:7–8). His love is too faithful to leave us without a way of escape from the cruel bonds of malignment:

> God is faithful [. . . to His compassionate nature], and He [can be trusted] not to let you be tempted and tried and assayed beyond your ability and strength of resistance and power to endure, but with the temptation He will [always] also provide the way out (the means of escape to a landing place) . . .
> —1 Corinthians 10:13, AMP

God's Abrahamic covenant

Very familiar also with the details of the Abrahamic covenant (Gen. 12:1–3), David remembered that God swore to curse those who cursed Abraham or, by extension, His believing seed: "I will . . . curse him that curseth thee" (v. 3). Lying is but another form of cursing, since by spreading malicious distortions liars hope to bring a "curse"—disfavor, misfortune, and ruin—on the people they lie about.

Haman's lie, for example, claimed that the Jews were disobedient to Persian law and therefore an intolerable liability to King Xerxes: "Then Haman said to King Xerxes, 'There is a certain people . . . in all the provinces of your kingdom whose customs are different from those of all other people and who do not obey the king's laws; it is not in the king's best interest to tolerate them'" (Esther 3:8, NIV). Haman used this deviously crafted half-truth (the Jews *were* different from other people but were *not* generally insubordinate to Persian law) as a hateful tool to authorize the extermination of all the Jews in Persia. Thus his lie brought a "curse" upon them when the royal decree was issued "to destroy, kill and annihilate all the Jews—young and old, women and little children—on a single day" (v. 13, NIV).

But as the reader of Scripture will note, God caused Haman's "curse" to return upon his own head and household . . . and swiftly! He was publicly humiliated when the king ordered him to lead the citywide parade honoring Mordecai, whose honorable Jewish faith and heritage he had maliciously misrepresented. Later Haman was hung—on the very gallows his lying heart had conceived and built to execute Mordecai! "So they hanged

Haman on the gallows that he had prepared for Mordecai" (Esther 7:10). And finally, Haman's sons were all executed by royal decree (Esther 9:10). Thus the children of Haman suffered the very "curse" Haman had hoped to bring on the children of Israel by his lies!

In this instance God also, "turned the curse into a blessing" for his maligned Persian exiles, as He had done centuries earlier in Balaam's case (Deut. 23:5). Note all the good He created from Haman's bad intentions.

First, He stopped their lying enemy, Haman, from killing them. This nixed the "curse" and returned them to their former position. Second, God removed their most powerful enemy, Haman. This put them in a better position. Third, He removed Haman's sons, thus preventing otherwise sure retaliation from them. This strengthened the Jews' position. Fourth, God removed all their other enemies throughout the entire Persian Empire: "Thus the Jews smote all their enemies with the stroke of the sword...and did what they would unto those who hated them" (Esther 9:5). This strengthened their position even more. Fifth, God gave the Jews a new respect throughout the land. Rather than being despised, they and their godly leaders, Mordecai and Esther, were now held in awe throughout Persia: "For the fear of the Jews fell upon them...the fear of Mordecai fell upon them...Mordecai grew greater and greater" (Esther 8:17; 9:3–4). This raised them, however briefly, to favor and prominence in Persia. Sixth, God caused many people to convert to the Jewish faith: "Many of the people of the land became Jews" (Esther 8:17). So the Jews' living conditions in Persia were *much better* at trial's end than they were before Haman released his vicious slander. Why? God transformed Haman's curse into a blessing.

And why did He do so? He remembered His solemn covenant with their forefather in the life of faith, Abraham.

Abraham is our forefather in faith also: "They who are of faith [in Christ], the same are the sons of Abraham [by faith]" (Gal. 3:7). And Abraham's covenant blessings are ours just as much as they were the Jews': "They who are of faith are blessed with faithful Abraham" (v. 9). Do we believe God will "curse him that curseth thee"? If so, we will never again fret at or fear those who lie about us. Why? They're going the way of Haman.

God's just nature

Finally, David understood that God's divine nature is perfectly and unchangeably just. As surely as He is love and truth and faithfulness, God is justice.

Therefore, using many different expressions and examples, God's Word promises that every unrepentant sinner will eventually reap precisely what he has sown. The apostle Paul encapsulated this universal principle:

> For *whatsoever* a man soweth, *that* shall he also reap.
> —GALATIANS 6:7

In the Pentateuch, Moses required that a false witness suffer the very penalty he hoped to inflict upon his accused: "If a false witness rise up against any man…then shall ye do unto him, as he had thought to have done unto his brother" (Deut. 19:16–19). God did this to Haman, not judicially but providentially; not in a court of law, but in the circumstances of life.

In the Psalms, David wrote of liars who by their words had digged "pits" of ruin for good men, yet fell in them themselves: "He [the 'persecutor' who 'conceived…and brought forth falsehood'] made a pit, and digged it, and is fallen into the ditch which he made" (Ps. 7:15). He also prophesied that liars who shot "arrows" of sudden, bitter false accusations at others would receive the same—God would use honest, just, and honorable men to "shoot" arrows of just indictment at them: "The workers of iniquity…bend their bows to shoot their arrows, even bitter words…at the perfect. Suddenly do they shoot at him, and fear not.…*But God shall shoot at them with an arrow; suddenly…*" (Ps. 64:2–4, 7). He added that this judgment would be caused entirely by their own lying words: "He will turn their own tongues against them and bring them to ruin" (v. 8, NIV). The apostle John asserted that all those who lead others into spiritual captivity through their lies will be led into captivity by God: "He that leadeth into captivity shall go into captivity" (Rev. 13:10).

Because willful slanderers will reap what they've sown, they must not only be silenced, but they must also be slandered. Because they have misrepresented others, they must be misrepresented themselves. Again, Haman is our example.

Before Haman was hanged, God, in a surprising turn of events, permitted him to look like a sex offender. When King Xerxes returned from his garden, Haman "was fallen upon the couch where Esther was" to plead desperately for his life (Esther 7:8). To the king, it looked as if Haman was trying to force his affections upon her: "Then said the king, Will he force the queen also before me in the house?" and he promptly ordered Haman's execution (v. 8). While Haman was guilty of crimes against God, and probably the Persian state also, he was *not* guilty of rape! But God let him look guilty. Why? God's divine nature is permanently and perfectly fair: Haman the misrepresenter had to be misrepresented. So it was.

It was with unchanging biblical principles such as these in mind that David wrote confidently, "The mouth of those who speak lies shall be stopped." And in other writings he promised vindication for all who have been wrongfully vilified: "And he shall bring forth thy righteousness as [surely as] the light [or dawn comes], and thy justice as [clear as] the noonday [sun]" (Ps. 37:6).

The apostle Paul went one step further, putting this issue in the imperative: "Whose mouths *must* be stopped" (Titus 1:11). Why must God stop liars? If He didn't, His maligned servants would never be trusted by His people and therefore free to serve Him fruitfully among them. If permanently slandered and misjudged, they would be forever defeated—prevented from advancing God's will, kingdom, and glory on earth—and their enemies victorious.

HOW GOD LIBERATES HIS SERVANTS FROM LIARS

God liberates His servants from liars in one of three ways:

1. By confounding and dispiriting liars
2. By exposing liars
3. By terminating liars

Confounding and dispiriting liars

By helping Nehemiah rebuild Jerusalem's walls in a remarkably short time, God showed His support for him—and His opposition to the Samaritans who had slandered and resisted Nehemiah every step of the way (Neh. 6:15–16). By restoring David to power after Absalom's rebellion, God showed His continuing favor for David—and His displeasure with Shimei who had bitterly denounced David when Absalom had taken power and seemed invincible (2 Sam. 19:18–20). By making Aaron's rod miraculously revive and bear fruit overnight, God showed that Aaron was His sovereign choice as Israel's high priest—and that He strongly disapproved of those who had falsely accused Aaron of appointing himself to the post (Num. 17:5).

In each of these cases, God intervened to show His overwhelming favor for His maligned servants. And suddenly their detractors were confused, discouraged, and without anything further to say.

Exposing liars

In the Book of Proverbs, God vows to expose malicious liars as the crafty deceivers they are: "He whose hatred is covered by deceit, his wickedness shall be revealed before the whole congregation" (Prov. 26:26); "His malice may be concealed by deception, but his wickedness will be *exposed* in the assembly" (NIV).

The envy-driven Jewish religious leaders tried to discredit Jesus' increasingly popular ministry by claiming that the source of His supernatural powers of healing and deliverance was not divine but demonic: "And the scribes who came down from Jerusalem said, He hath Beelzebub, and by the prince of the demons casteth he out demons" (Mark 3:22). The heavenly Father exposed—brought into the daylight of open recognition—this lie over time as the people witnessed more and more of Jesus' acts of divine compassion and words of profound spiritual truth. Soon many people realized that *their* religious leaders' official assessment, not Jesus' ministry and message, was a lie: "These are *not* the words of him that hath a demon. Can a demon open the eyes of the blind?" (John 10:21). Other observers, even Gentiles, discerned the real reason for their animosity toward the popular Nazarene preacher: crass religious rivalry! Even Pilate, a thorough pagan, could see this: "He knew that for envy they had delivered him" (Matt. 27:18).

So the Pharisees, Sadducees, and Herodians' wide, powerful river of damaging falsehoods slowed, shrank, and narrowed until it became a meaningless, weak streamlet of hollow accusations. Why? As He promised in Proverbs, God had "exposed" their "wickedness" in the "assembly" of clear-seeing Jews and Gentiles. The falseness of their statements was evident and their hidden, true motive for opposing Jesus was brought out into the light of full public recognition.

Terminating liars

By confounding, discouraging, or exposing them, God stops many liars from continuing to slander His servants. But not all. Some are beyond repentance. Incorrigible liars, such as King Saul and Absalom, force God to deal with them more severely.

The only way God could get King Saul and Absalom to stop misrepresenting His servant David was to take them home. Tragically, they were fixated on their falsehoods, so consumed with their hatred for David and so driven to ruin him that they would rather die than give up their evil desire: "Fools detest turning from evil" (Prov. 13:19, NIV). So they persisted in their deceit until their tragic premature deaths.

Sadly, their folly is occasionally repeated in our time. There are still incorrigible liars who, because they refuse to respond to warnings and lesser forms of divine discipline, force God to terminate them. To facilitate the release of His true servants to further His gospel and plan in the earth, God has no choice but to bring the judgment of early death on their unrelenting accusers in His appointed time and way. When a soul reaches this point of no return, further intercession is futile: "There is a sin unto death: I do not say [recommend] that he [the Christian] shall pray for it" (1 John 5:16). Although this church age is primarily a season of divine grace, the apostle Paul warned us not to assume that therefore God will not bring terminal judgments on impenitent sinners: "For this cause [unconfessed, unforsaken sins, including lying] … many sleep [die early]" (1 Cor. 11:30).

Why did Paul assert this? Like David, he knew God as the Lie Stopper: "whose mouths *must* be stopped."

Do you recognize and believe in your heavenly Father in this, His vital role as the Lie Stopper? You will need to, if you continue walking faithfully with Jesus. Why?

"All that will live godly in Christ Jesus shall suffer persecution," declared Paul by the Spirit's inspiration, and one form of persecution all true disciples are sure to meet is slander. "Blessed are ye," Jesus forewarned us, "when men shall...reproach you, and cast out your name as evil, for the Son of man's sake" (Luke 6:22).

When for the first time your adversaries willfully misrepresent your motives, inaccurately describe your actions, twist your words, and demonize your character, you will get a sinking feeling in the pit of your stomach, as you ponder losing the best thing you have: your good name. You'll be furious and strongly tempted to fight back, word for word, accusation for accusation—or fearful and ready to give up. In that low and lonely hour, only faith in God will save you. Specifically, you must share David's confidence that God eventually discredits all lies and liars and honors those whom they dishonor—if they continue trusting and obeying Him!

So hold steady and refuse panic by remembering that God is still in complete control: "Be still, and know that I am God" (Ps. 46:10). Your enemies couldn't have spoken against you unless *He* let them: "Thou couldest have no power at all against me, except it were given thee from above" (John 19:11). Determine not to rebel against and forsake the Lord, but rather to abide even more closely to Him. Choose not to resist evil, as Jesus commanded—"But I say unto you that ye resist not evil" (Matt. 5:39)—but rather to persist in your God-given duties. Refuse to fear your accusers' lies, even when some, perhaps many, people believe them and reject you for a season. Choose instead to believe that God will do for you what He did for David.

David lost his reputation for the Lord's sake during his years in the Judean wilderness, but he later recovered it when the Lord removed King Saul and raised David to the kingship. If you too honor God by willingly giving up the best thing you have—your good name—for His sake, He will honor you by restoring it: "Because he hath set his love upon me, therefore will I...honor him" (Ps. 91:14–15). In His time and way, the Lie Stopper will turn your bitter vilification into sweet vindication!

That is, unless you quench the Holy Spirit.

Chapter Eleven

QUENCHING THE HOLY SPIRIT

Quench not the Spirit.

—1 THESSALONIANS 5:19

hether lied about or lauded, every Christian is called to be a channel of life and hope to this hopeless, dying world. God wants us to be spiritual riverbeds through which He can pour out the saving reality of Jesus to every life we touch. Jesus revealed this gracious divine plan in John's Gospel:

> He that believeth on me…out of his heart shall flow *rivers of living water.*
>
> —JOHN 7:38 (SEE VV. 37–39)

Indeed, every born-again, Spirit-baptized, abiding believer fulfills this destiny to some degree daily. As long as we trust and obey, "rivers of living water"—fresh streams of the life and power of the Holy Spirit—constantly flow into us and through us to bless others.

But the continuation of this invisible flow of blessing is not automatic. We may stop it at any time. For this reason the apostle warns us, "Quench not the [Holy] Spirit" (1 Thess. 5:19). The Greek word *sbennumi* (spen´-noo-mee), here translated "quench," means literally "to extinguish"[1] or "quenching."[2] Its usual New Testament usage refers to "quenching fire or things on fire,"[3] such as the true believer's fervent or burning devotion to Jesus (Matt. 25:8). To "quench" the Holy Spirit, then,

113

is to "extinguish" His burning, passionate love, devotion, and enthusiasm in our soul and our living.

But when considered in the context of John 7:37–39, quenching the Spirit refers to "extinguishing," or slowing, reducing, or terminating, the flowing of the river of the Holy Spirit in our lives. Various definitions of the English word *quench* reveal further that to quench the Holy Spirit is to "subdue, suppress, curb, decrease, or stop" His life, graces, and gifts in our lives, assemblies, or ministries. This ruinous spiritual blockage, which is exactly the opposite of God's plan, completely shuts down God's reviving and powerful life in our souls. It renders us dry, dull, weak, and of no practical value to God. The believer who quenches the Spirit ceases to be a channel of salvation to the world and revival to the church.

To prevent this, let's identify some of the things that quench the Holy Spirit in our lives.

Things That Quench the Holy Spirit in Our Lives

Not receiving the fullness of the Holy Spirit

After we are born again by the work of the Holy Spirit, we may receive a full, rich, and empowering infilling of the Holy Spirit. As already stated, Jesus called this experience the "baptism with the Holy Spirit." "Ye shall be *baptized with the Holy Spirit* not many days from now" (Acts 1:5).

To refuse or neglect to be filled with the fullness of the Spirit is to stop His work in our lives before He can start it. If the Spirit's full inflow never begins, His outflow will never occur. To give out large supplies of "living water," we must first take in all of it that is available to us. Before rivers can flow, rains must fall and fill their watersheds and tributaries. Mighty rivers of "living water," therefore, *cannot* come forth from souls who have never asked for and received the baptism with the Holy Spirit.

Jesus taught as much when, as John describes it, He announced and described the baptism with the Holy Spirit:

Jesus stood and cried out, saying, If any man *thirst*, let him *come* unto me, and *drink*. He that believeth on me, as the scripture hath said, out of his heart shall *flow* rivers of living water. (But this spoke he of the Spirit, whom they that believe on him should receive...).

—JOHN 7:37–39

Jesus used four highly significant terms here: "thirst," "come," "drink," and "flow."

To "thirst" is to *desire* spiritual life in general and Christ and the Holy Spirit in particular. (See John 4:15.) To "come" is to *respond* to Jesus' call to come to Him, the Savior, in repentance and faith, and be saved and enter into personal relationship with Him (note, "come *unto me*"). To "drink" is to *receive* the full measure of the living water, or Holy Spirit, Jesus openly promises throughout the Gospels and freely and repeatedly bestows in the Book of Acts (Acts 2:1–4, 32–33; 8:14–18; 9:17–18; 10:44–47 [11:15–17]; 19:1–6). (After this first infilling, we should continue "drinking" in the Spirit daily through Bible meditation, prayer, worship, and biblical instruction.) To "flow" is to *be a channel or outlet* of the Holy Spirit's life and power in this spiritually dry, dead world. Jesus' statements here are carefully, not carelessly, chosen. Their order is inspired, not random; inerrant, not flawed. One must "thirst," "come," and "drink in" the baptism with the Holy Spirit before the Spirit can fully and freely "flow" from one's life.

So the unbaptized Christian quenches the Holy Spirit. At best, their spiritual outreach will be a narrow or trickling streamlet. At worst, they'll be a tragically dry riverbed—and a disappointment to God.

Disregarding warnings

Warnings are an important part of everyday life. Traffic signals, highway markers, weather bulletins, sirens, labels on consumer goods, bodily pains—all these and other warnings urge us to take protective action to avoid loss, injury, or possible death in this natural world.

It is the same in the spiritual realm. Warnings keep us in the way of life. The Holy Spirit warns us about many dangers and potential pitfalls—disloyal friends, distracting pastimes, risky activities, wrong thoughts, alluring temptations, false teachings, neglecting our spiritual needs, unattended duties, broken vows, and so forth. If we ignore these, His quiet warnings, we quench His "still, small" voice.

By doing so, we suppress God's loving correction—and rush headlong into spiritual traps, confusion, emotional turmoil, and needless loss of precious time, energy, and resources. Said Paul to those who had rejected God's warning through him, "Sirs, ye should have hearkened unto me, and not have loosed from Crete, and to have gained this harm and loss" (Acts 27:21).

Denying the Lord

Jesus Christ is the only name and person through whom we may receive right relationship with God: "Neither is there salvation in any other; for there is no other name under heaven given among men, whereby we must be saved" (Acts 4:12). There is no other hope or way of salvation but through Him, world without end. With this all true Christians agree.

It's wonderful, peaceful, and preferable to agree with people whenever possible. But to agree with the advocates of religions that deny Jesus' deity and saviorship is to deny Jesus. (To doubt, obscure, deny, or contradict Jesus' emphatic claims is to "deny" the One who made them.) To allow that there are other avenues to salvation is to deny the One who lovingly but plainly declared Himself the only road to redemption: "I am *the* [only] way, the [only] truth, and the [only] life; *no man* cometh unto the Father *but by me*" (John 14:6). Desiring to gain favor with the sons and spirit of this world, overly broadminded Christians, wishing to be "positive" and avoid the culturally obsolete "negative" truths of the New Testament, sometimes fail to stand firmly on this monumental Christian fact. When pressed by unenlightened journalists, errant theologians, compromised clerics, or spiritually hostile postmodernists, they either state or tacitly imply that, yes, there are other ways people can find salvation, truth, or abundant life.

Thus they deny their Lord to delight His enemies. Instead of giving a bold confession to which the Spirit can bear witness, spineless Christians chime in with politically and religiously correct euphemisms. And the Holy Spirit—the Spirit of *truth*—is left grieving. And quenched.

Denying the Word

The Bible plainly and repeatedly declares its eternal truthfulness and preeminence over all other philosophies, ideologies, and religious writings:

I esteem all thy precepts concerning all things to be right, and I hate every false way.

—PSALM 119:128

Forever, O LORD, thy word is settled in heaven.

—PSALM 119:89

For the word of the LORD is right.

—PSALM 33:4

The scripture cannot be broken.

—JOHN 10:35

As if to sum up the Bible's declaration of supremacy, Jesus said:

Heaven and earth shall pass away, but my words shall not pass away.

—MATTHEW 24:35

Indeed, the Scriptures are an infallible revelation concerning God and mankind and their vital relationship, past, present, and future. A. W. Tozer wrote, "Whatever is stated clearly but once in the Holy Scriptures may be accepted as sufficiently well established to invite the faith of all believers."[4]

Besides its veracity and primacy, God's Word contains and conveys to us His very life and Spirit. More than a message about God, it is a medium through which we access God. Its every word, phrase, and sentence is filled with emissions of His Spirit, or very life and "breath": "Every Scripture is God-breathed (given by His inspiration)" (2 Tim. 3:16, AMP). Merely to believe and confess faith in any Bible truth, therefore, is to receive a measure of the Spirit's life-giving breath and permit it to flow into and through one's soul. To disbelieve or deny such truth is to quench or stifle the breath of the Spirit contained in and emerging from the Word.

So to the degree we reject, dismiss, or deny Bible truths we diminish the flow of the Spirit into and through our lives.

Unbelief

Jesus taught that our belief in Him causes the river of the Spirit to flow through us: "*He that believeth on me* ... out of his heart shall flow rivers of living water" (John 7:38). So if faith releases the river of life, unbelief represses it. If the Spirit is to continue flowing, we must continue believing on its heavenly source, Jesus.

Troubles, offenses, and tests of faith challenge our belief in Jesus and threaten the river of the Spirit flowing in us. If when hard pressed by seemingly impossible people and perplexities we conclude there is no way of escape or victory, our faith, and the river of life in us, run dry. We must learn, therefore, never to succumb to disbelief. At our lowest, shakiest "panic points" we must remember the words of Jesus, "All things are possible to him that believeth" (Mark 9:23), and quietly choose to continue believing in Him—His unchanging loving, faithful character and utterly reliable Word. No matter how troubled someone's emotions, twisted their thinking, or confused their circumstances, no soul or situation is beyond the redeeming reach of Jesus—if only we will keep believing in Him and interceding: "If *ye* abide in me, and my words abide in *you, ye* shall ask what *ye* will, and it shall be done unto *you*" (John 15:7). Why?

As we continue believing in Jesus, the river of His *omnipotent* Spirit continues flowing through us, making the impossible possible.

Neglect of duty

God gives us sufficient grace—divine ability, strength, and wisdom imparted to the believer—for every duty to which He calls us: "My grace is sufficient for thee" (2 Cor. 12:9). As long as we discharge our duties steadily, His grace and Spirit flow—and our joy! And rather than despise our duties, we delight in them: "I *delight* to do thy will, O my God" (Ps. 40:8). But all this changes whenever we refuse to discharge any God-given duty.

The father who does not provide for his children, the wife who refuses to submit to her husband's leadership, the pastor who neglects feeding his flock, the employee who will not fulfill his assigned tasks, these unfaithful ones disappoint Jesus. Why? He loved His duties—the will of His Father—and discharged them daily with gladness and vigor. They were as satisfying to His soul as delicious food was to His palate: "My food is to do the will of him that sent me, and to finish his work" (John 4:34). Christians who despise their duties prevent His love of duty from being reexpressed in their lives. Instead of releasing His Spirit's river of joy, they obstruct it.

Denying the Convicter

The Holy Spirit is the Convicter. Said Jesus, "When he comes, he will convict the world of guilt in regard to sin..." (John 16:8, NIV). Whenever we walk in the light of Christ's righteousness, the Holy Spirit gives us inner peace that flows like a river. This is a "fruit of the Spirit" (Gal. 5:22–23), or evidence that He is having His way. But if we disobey the Lord in thought, emotion, word, or deed, the Holy Spirit, ever the gracious-but-persistent perfectionist, calls our attention to our departure from the light by gradually withdrawing our tranquility. Holy, He refuses to give us full peace in sin.

During this time, He quietly but persistently works in our consciences. As the river of His peace within us decreases, He urges us to confess our sin to the heavenly Father and receive forgiveness and cleansing by the blood of Jesus: "If we confess our sins, he is faithful and just to forgive us our sins, and to cleanse us from all unrighteousness" (1 John 1:9). He also urges us to take whatever action is necessary to correct our disobedience to God's Word or will: apologizing to people, making restitution for losses, changing our course of action, embracing new attitudes, replacing bad habits with good ones, and so forth. Our response to His conviction is crucial.

If we confess and correct our sin, it is quenched and our peaceful fellowship with the Lord and other believers is immediately restored. And our peace continues flowing as long as we walk in the light of complete honesty and obedience before God. But if we deny the Convicter's voice, the river of His peace is further quenched, until it stops flowing altogether.

Failing to give

Financial support is necessary to Christian ministry. Without the gifts of God's people, sowers of the Word, however devoted, gifted, and anointed, cannot do their work. Even Jesus needed financial supporters for His ministry to thrive: "And certain women [were with Him]...and many others, who ministered unto him of their substance" (Luke 8:2–3).

When Christian donors give freely, the Word flows freely. When they limit their giving, the Word is limited. When they withhold their gifts, the Word is withheld. Practically speaking, this means that the works of evangelists, pastors, teachers, and prophets are hindered—and the lost are not evangelized, the saved are not taught, the erring are not corrected, and the discouraged are not exhorted. Why? Edifying publications, broadcasts, campaigns, missions, and conferences are withheld for lack of funds. And there's more.

Believers who fail to give suppress the flow of God's blessings not only to the world and the church but also to themselves. Jesus taught that God gives faithfully to faithful givers: "Give, and it shall be given unto you; good measure, pressed down, and shaken together, and running over shall men give into your bosom" (Luke 6:38). So whenever we give to ministries, God gives to us. The obvious counterpart to this spiritual law is, "Withhold, and it shall be withheld from you." When we limit our charity, God limits His charity toward us. When we stop giving to God's work, God stops giving to us. Why? Jesus taught that the very "cup" we use to measure our gifts to God is used by God to measure His gifts to us: "For with the same measure that ye measure it shall be measured to you again" (v. 38). Thus the size of our gift to God determines the size of His gift to us. Paul taught, "He who soweth sparingly shall reap also sparingly; and he who soweth bountifully shall reap also bountifully" (2 Cor. 9:6).

The same is true of any failure to give—a listening ear to those who need to share their troubles, forgiveness to those who ask it, a helping hand to those who need it, knowledge and counsel to those seeking it, patience to those who are struggling and failing, kindness to those who are grieving, and so forth.

So whenever we limit or stop our giving in any way, we suppress or decrease God's blessings to others and to ourselves—and the Spirit's outflow from our lives is quenched.

Refusing to worship

Worship is a vital part of the true Christian walk. Jesus taught that our heavenly Father yearns for us to worship Him "in spirit and in truth" (John 4:23–24). For this reason, we should freely enter into the flow of worship at Christian gatherings and also worship the Lord privately in our homes daily.

Answering Jesus' call to worship serves four key purposes. First, it pleases God because He strongly desires and openly "seeks" our worship: "the Father *seeketh* such to worship him" (v. 23). Second, worship releases the love of God that the Holy Spirit has "shed abroad" in our hearts (Rom. 5:5). A powerful river of adoration for God is loosed and begins flowing freely within us. Third, our ongoing worship increases this river of love for God. Expressing love increases love; every time we express our love for God by worshiping, it grows stronger. Fourth, worship energizes and increases our obedience to God, because the more we love God, the more we want to obey Him. Thus another spiritual river flows out from our lives: a steady stream of inspired obedience. We enthusiastically seek God, study His Word, pray, submit, serve, and, when necessary, suffer difficulties and injustices for His sake. In all these ways, worshiping regularly keeps the various "rivers" of life flowing freely within and through us: "Out of his heart shall flow *rivers* of living water" (John 7:38).

But Christians who refuse or forget to worship abide dry and lifeless. Why? They are not releasing and increasing their love for God by expressing it. So it withers—and the flowing of the Spirit dries up.

Failure to give thanks

The very placement of the biblical command, "Quench not the Spirit," is revealing. (See 1 Thessalonians 5:19.)

The preceding verse calls upon us to give thanks to God in every circumstance: "Give thanks in all circumstances, for this is God's will for you in Christ Jesus" (v. 18, NIV). Thus, by His inspired arrangement of Bible truths, the Lord makes a subtle connection between *giving thanks* and *the flowing of the Spirit*. He hints that thanking Him throughout the day, whatever our circumstances, keeps the Spirit flowing in us throughout the day.

Truly, this "sacrifice of praise…the fruit of our lips giving thanks to his name" (Heb. 13:15), releases a powerful stream of overcoming life, a deep, wide current of spiritual strength that lifts us above all the despiritualizing vexations, problems, and offenses we meet. But like all hints, this one can easily be missed.

Have we caught God's hint? To fail to give thanks, or even worse, to complain, suppresses the river of God's Spirit in us. Also, His will—that we be thankful, and channels of life to others—is quenched.

Failure to pray

Context also gives us another intimation. Two verses before the Spirit commands, "Quench not the Spirit," He orders, "Pray without ceasing" (1 Thess. 5:17). To "pray without ceasing" is (a) to not stop praying about a specific matter until God's answer comes, and (b) to not stop praying in general. The latter interpretation implies we should pray continually. That is, we should pray at our usual times of prayer and also whenever prayer is needed through the day. So the Lord makes a subtle spiritual link between *the constant flow of the Spirit* and *constant prayer*.

Talking to God puts us in touch with God—and keeps His Spirit flowing into us. Talking frequently with the Life-giver, therefore, means that His Spirit flows into us frequently. As a result, we live in the fullness of the Spirit daily and He overflows from us daily, creating an atmosphere that draws others to Jesus: "No man can come to me, except the Father, who hath sent me, *draw him*" (John 6:44).

But all this changes if we refuse or fail to pray "always with all prayer and supplication in the Spirit" (Eph. 6:18). The Spirit's supernatural life-flow stops, the riverbed in our soul dries up, and needy ones on every side are not touched by the living waters and drawn to their Source.

Neglecting the morning watch

The Bible urgently calls believers to seek the Lord: "Seek ye the Lord while he may be found; call ye upon him while he is near" (Isa. 55:6). While our attendance at Christian meetings is one way of seeking God, it isn't a true and full response to this call.

We must also go into our private chambers and seek the face of Jesus daily, meditating in God's Word and praying. While it's acceptable to seek the Lord at any time, it's best to do so in the early morning. Numerous biblical references establish this prime time for earnest seekers of God:

> And be ready in the morning, and come up in the morning unto Mount Sinai, and present thyself there to me...
>
> —Exodus 34:2

> Job...rose up early in the morning, and offered burnt offerings...
>
> —Job 1:5

> Early will I seek thee...
>
> —Psalm 63:1

> Awake, psaltery and harp; I myself will awake early.
>
> —Psalm 108:2

> Seek ye first [daily; every morning] the kingdom of God, and his righteousness...
>
> —Matthew 6:33

During His ministry, Jesus taught those who came to Him in the temple courts "early in the morning." "And *early in the morning* he came...into the temple, and all the people came unto him; and he...taught them" (John 8:2). He still does this today. Early every morning He draws near the courts of our bodily "temples" and, if we rise to meet Him, teaches us as we prayerfully read His Word and worship. Truly, whoever seeks Him "early"—in the early morning hours, before other activities, or diligently—finds Him: "I love those who love me, and those who seek me *early* shall find me" (Prov. 8:17). These early seekers drink very deeply from the living waters of the river of life. As a result, the deepest rivers of living water flow out of their lives.

The morning watch was a vital part of Jesus' earthly lifestyle. Often He rose early to acquire private time with His Father: "And in the morning, rising up a great while before day, he went out, and departed into a solitary place, and there prayed" (Mark 1:35). This early appointment with His heavenly Father refilled Jesus with the Spirit daily and powered the phenomenal flow of truth, healing, deliverance, and saving grace seen in His ministry. Without keeping the morning watch, Jesus would have quenched the Spirit—and His ministry!

If Jesus needed the morning watch to avoid quenching the channel of life in His soul, how can we get by without it?

Disobedience to Scripture

"All scripture is given by *inspiration* of God," writes the apostle (2 Tim. 3:16). Literally, this states that all scripture is *God-breathed*—the Holy Spirit has breathed the very life of God into every word of the Bible.

Just hearing the Word, therefore, gives us fresh life. Doing the Word, putting biblical commands into practice in our personal living, brings an even stronger infusion of life from above. Truly, obedience to the inspired Word inspires the one who obeys. And every time we submissively comply with the Word in our decisions, thoughts, words, and actions, we receive a new "dose" of life more abundant. Steady compliance with biblical precepts and principles keeps divine energy flowing into us steadily.

But if we stop living the Word, this heavenly life-flow stops...until we turn back to God by repentance, confession, and the resumption of obedience. (See 1 John 1:9.) That moment, by the grace of God and blood of Jesus, the living waters rush back in—and we no longer quench the Spirit.

Misapplying Bible truths

Whenever we hear sermons or messages expounding Bible truths, the Teacher—the Holy Spirit—is present and trying to say something to us that we need to hear. In the Revelation, Jesus urged us repeatedly to "hear what the Spirit saith unto the churches" (Rev. 2:7). The Spirit wants us to apply every sermon or message first to ourselves. For wise Christians, the prime issue is not what He is saying to others but what He's saying to us: "Lord, what wilt thou have *me* to do?" (Acts 9:6).

We must bring the Word straight home to the shores of our personal lives: "Where does this truth apply to my life? In what ways do I need to change my thinking, values, habits? Is this sin or fault presently in my heart or daily living? How may I further obey this principle?" These are the thoughts of the wise as they receive the ministry of the Word. They habitually judge themselves first, not their fellow believers, spouses, or acquaintances. As they remain focused on their personal responsibility to obey the Spirit, they abide in His river of life. Why? They're doing what He wants and thus allowing Him to flow freely in and through them without hindrance.

But Christians who ignore their personal spiritual condition and eagerly judge others with every Bible teaching they hear misapply the truth. By refusing to focus on what the Spirit is saying to them, they redirect His voice to others. Thus they quench His purpose in speaking to them…and the flow of His reviving river in their lives.

To prevent the prophet Ezekiel from doing this, God taught him to *eat before you speak.* "Son of man, [you] *eat* what thou findest; [you] *eat* this scroll, and [then, having first eaten] go *speak* unto the house of Israel" (Ezek. 3:1; see vv. 3–4). Ezekiel was never to "speak" (direct and apply) a message to others that he had not first "eaten" (received and applied to) himself. Like Ezekiel, we should be eager to "eat" (receive and apply to ourselves) the bread of life, not to put it on someone else's plate. The truths we hear may apply to millions of other Christians, including those by our side at home, work, or church, but what is that to us? The Teacher is speaking to *us* at the moment, not them, and we must be careful to heed Him, not redirect His voice to others. That would quench His desire to speak to us—and His life-flow.

Worldly entanglements

Through Scripture the Holy Spirit warns us to avoid *loving* the values, activities, and methods of the present Christ-rejecting social order and commands us to neither be *conformed* to nor *entangled* with it:

> Love not the world, neither the things that are in the world…
>
> —1 JOHN 2:15

> Be not *conformed* to this world…
>
> —ROMANS 12:2

No man that warreth *entangleth* himself with the affairs of this life...

—2 TIMOTHY 2:4

Therefore, as long as we maintain a healthy separation from worldliness, the Spirit is pleased and flows freely in our lives. But too much interest, involvement, or investment in purely worldly activities or goals grieves the Spirit and hinders His flow in our souls.

Jesus warned of this in His parable of the sower and the four soils. He taught that just as thorns choke the life of plants, so the cares, riches, lusts, and interests of this present fallen world may "choke" His Word in our lives, or render it unfruitful: "And the cares of this age, and the deceitfulness of riches, and the lusts of other things entering in, *choke* the word, and it becometh unfruitful" (Mark 4:19). And to choke the Word is to choke the Spirit who inspires it.

The dangers of spiritual "thorny ground" are subtle. At issue is not whether something is overtly evil, but whether it is *in God's plan* for us. If it is, God will supply plenty of grace and strength for it. If it isn't, every bit of desire, thought, time, and energy we give it quenches the Spirit. And the more we persist in such interests or activities, the more we suppress and curb the Spirit. We must remember that not only the evil but also the good is ever the enemy of the best. Any worldly interest or activity, however admirable, that hinders your fellowship with Jesus threatens the river of the Spirit in your life—and your spiritual destiny.

So for your spiritual destiny's sake, cut it off. (See Matthew 5:29–30; 18:7–9.) Quench the entanglement, not the Spirit; your distraction, not your destiny.

Submitting to erroneous instruction

Proverbs exhorts us, "Cease, my son, to hear the instruction that causeth thee to err" (Prov. 19:27). The apostle Paul further warns, "Shun profane and vain babblings" (2 Tim. 2:16). In these and similar references, the Holy Spirit urges us not to submit to pastoral instruction or counseling that we recognize to be biblically incorrect. If we do, we quench the Spirit—and pay a high price for our failure to insist on *truth*.

Paul claims that false teaching is a cancer of the soul that erodes faith: "Their [the proponents of error] word will eat as doth a gangrene [cancer]...and overthrow the faith of some" (2 Tim. 2:17–18). When pastors reject fundamental Christian doctrines (the Trinity; the deity, incarnation, and resurrection of Christ; authority of Scripture; salvation by grace alone, through faith alone, and so forth), deny experiences plainly authorized in Scripture, advance doctrines that contradict Jesus' teachings, condone sin, or claim unscriptural revelations, we continue to submit to their instruction at our peril. You cannot digest poison without suffering for it. Nor can you continue feeding on error, legalism, license, or fanaticism and expect to grow steadily in God's grace.

If your spiritual diet contains teaching that is spiritually toxic or cancerous, the Spirit says "cease...to hear" it. If you don't, it will metastasize in your soul, erode your faith, and cause the Spirit to cease flowing in your life.

Continuing in elementary instruction

Teaching that is correct but persistently shallow is also insufficient. Jesus wants committed, growing disciples to eventually launch out into the deep things of His Word.

Therefore, the writer to the Hebrews charges us, "Therefore, leaving the principles of the doctrine of Christ, let us go on unto perfection [full growth; spiritual maturity or adulthood]" (Heb. 6:1). One cannot grow strong and wise in the faith without feeding regularly on the deeper, more challenging truths of Christianity. Biblical "milk" (elementary Christian instruction) is nourishing and necessary, but a believer cannot become fully grown, much less a strong overcomer, on a diet of spiritual milk alone. Biblical "solid food" (spiritual meat, bread, and potatoes; or more difficult or demanding Bible truths) is also needed: "Someone who lives on milk is still an infant...*Solid food* is for those who are mature" (Heb. 5:13–14, NLT). The apostle Paul rebuked the Corinthians because their persistently carnal attitudes were not permitting him to feed them with deeper, stronger spiritual nourishment: "I have fed you with milk, and not with *solid food*; for to this time ye were not able to bear it" (1 Cor. 3:2).

Growing disciple of Christ, it is your church's duty to provide you with "solid food," or increasingly deep and challenging spiritual nourishment that will mature your faith and knowledge of God. If its spiritual table continually offers only milk and baby cereal (introductory Bible truths), pray and seek another. If you don't, you will limit your spiritual growth—and quench the Spirit.

Failing to exhort disobedient fellow Christians

The Bible strongly asserts that we are our brother's keeper. The Book of Hebrews urges us, "Exhort one another daily, while it is called Today..." (Heb. 3:13). Why is this?

"...lest any of you be hardened through the deceitfulness of sin" (v. 13). Unchecked sin quickly begins hardening our hearts, resulting in an ever-increasing indifference toward God, our spiritual condition, our God-given work, and other people. To prevent this subtle hardening, the Holy Spirit instructs us to talk to each other daily and, if necessary, "exhort" each other, dissuading from unrighteousness and urging to righteous action. Exhorting involves kindly calling a fellow Christian's attention to any symptoms of spiritual trouble we notice, such as irritability, sadness, anxiety, apathy, or other uncharacteristic speech or behavior, and then asking, "What's wrong?" This releases the flow of the Holy Spirit—the Convicter—to bring them to confession and repentance, preventing their hardening and restoring them to faith, righteousness, fellowship, and fruitful service.

Both Jesus and Joseph were faithful exhorters. Even in Potiphar's dark prison, Joseph lovingly exhorted his fellow prisoners: "And he asked Pharaoh's officers who were with him in the prison... Wherefore look ye so sad today?" (Gen. 40:7). This led to the butler's deliverance from depression and to Joseph's long-awaited release from prison. Jesus exhorted His apostles daily. When He noticed them arguing secretly over their own greatness, He probed them with questions, elicited truthful answers from them, and then used the occasion to teach them the imperative of humility and the superiority of servantship (Matt. 18:1–6; Mark 9:33–37). This released them (for the time) from the hardening of pride and enabled them to continue their spiritual training. After His resurrection, Jesus also famously exhorted two discouraged disciples on the Emmaus Road (Luke 24:13–32); this released them from the hardening of unbelief and inspired them to exhort their discouraged brethren to do the same (Mark 16:12–13). By so exhorting their fellows, Joseph and Jesus released the all-powerful yet tender Convicter to skillfully restore them to their former walk and work with God.

To follow their example we must first examine ourselves daily, and then exhort others. We can help others walk in the Spirit only if we first do the same. If as we abide close to Jesus we alert our troubled brethren to their substandard condition, gently prodding them to self-examination and spiritual recovery, we love them and loose the Convicter to restore them. If we refuse to do so, we don't love our brethren. And we disobey Hebrews 3:13, ignore Jesus' example, and quench the Convicter.

Being unequally yoked

Scripture warns believers against uniting with those who refuse to unite with Jesus: "Be ye not unequally yoked together with unbelievers" (2 Cor. 6:14). (See 2 Corinthians 6:14–18; 2 Timothy 2:19–21.) Yet many do just that. They enter into close relationships, contractual partnerships, or marriage covenants with unbelievers or carnal Christians. (The normal contacts, contracts, and communications necessary to live and do business in this fallen world are an exception.)

Whenever a child of light joins forces with a child of darkness, he brings upon himself needless trouble and peril. Consider the near-disastrous results of King Jehoshaphat's false and foolish union with wicked King Ahab: Jehoshaphat narrowly escaped death in a battle in which he never should have participated. (See 2 Chronicles 18:1–34, especially verses 31–32.) Besides being perilous, false unions are also corrupting. "Evil company corrupts good morals" (1 Cor. 15:33), asserts the wise apostle Paul. Rather than converting practicing sinners from corruption, being too closely associated with them always corrupts a believer's morality and weakens his or her spiritual strength. Why? It is disobedience to God's Word. It also grieves and suppresses the *Holy* Spirit whom God has given us.

Keep the Spirit who is holy flowing freely in your life. Don't forge close unions with those who despise righteousness, disrespect your faith, or deny your Savior.

Disobeying divine guidance

"As many [Christians] as are led by the Spirit of God, they are [truly living as] the sons of God" (Rom. 8:14). The rest quench the Spirit who yearns to lead them.

Disobeying divine guidance cuts off our life-flow from our divine guide, the Holy Spirit. For instance, when...

- God says, "Go ye into all the world," and we remain at home.
- God says, "Stand thou still a while, that I may show thee the word of God," and we rush ahead into ministry or good works.
- Jesus says, "Come unto Me," and we draw back from Him, preferring other things to spending time with Him.
- God says, "Arise, let us be going," and we sit and pout over our past sins, failures, or troubles.
- God says, "Trust in the Lord with all your heart," and we continue reasoning, worrying, and trying to resolve our problem in our wisdom and strength.
- God says, "The battle is not yours, but God's," yet rather than rest in our heavenly Defender we keep resisting our earthly detractors.
- God says, "Hold thy peace," and we keep talking—and lose our peace!
- God says, "Speak, and hold not thy peace," yet we remain silent—and ashamed!

When the light of divine guidance comes, there is only one way to avoid quenching the guiding Spirit. Obey Him! And at the first, not the final, opportunity! "Whatsoever he saith unto you, *do it*" (John 2:5). This will keep the Spirit's leading flowing freely in your life. "After he had seen the vision, *immediately we endeavored to go* into Macedonia, assuredly gathering that the Lord had called us to preach the gospel unto them" (Acts 16:10).

Failing to minister as commissioned

True ministry is an irreversible lifelong obligation. Once divinely commissioned, there is no release from the holy responsibility laid upon a servant of God (unless he or she receives a higher calling). Why? "For the gifts and calling of God are without repentance" (Rom. 11:29).

After we've finished God's initial ministerial training process—seeking the Lord, studying His Word, submitting to leadership, faithfully executing secular duties, and overcoming our trials in the school of the Spirit—and been ordained, our very life lies in discharging the task God has given us. If it's evangelism, we must be evangelizing. If teaching, we must be teaching. If pastoring, we must serve in the pastorate. If foreign missions, we must "go ye into all the world." If we fulfill our ministry, the Spirit who called us to it continuously refills us. If we forsake it, we grieve Him and quench His anointing on our lives and works. Turning from our heavenly commission also brings a dreadful "woe" of divine chastisement upon us. Paul testified, "Necessity is laid upon me, yea, woe [punishment, judgment] is unto me, if I preach not the gospel!" (1 Cor. 9:16). To every minister, then, the word of the Lord is one: fulfill your ministry! "Take heed to the ministry which thou hast received in the Lord, that thou fulfill it" (Col. 4:17).

Are you fulfilling or forsaking your ministry? The answer will explain why the Spirit's life-flow is being sustained or suppressed in your life and labor.

Failing to say what the Spirit wants said

Ministers are the Spirit's messengers to the church: "To the messenger of the Ephesian assembly write..." (Rev. 2:1, YLT). Messengers don't author messages; they just relay them. They speak others' words, not their own. Accordingly, ministers must faithfully deliver the messages the Spirit lays on their hearts for God's people. As they do so, He continues flowing and speaking to them.

The master Minister, Jesus, was careful to teach and preach what the Father laid upon His heart: "I have many things to say...but...I speak to the world [only] those things which I have heard of him [the Father]" (John 8:26). If Jesus was obligated to say what the Spirit wanted Him to say to God's people, so are His ministers. Not what we want to say, nor what the people want to hear, but what the *Holy Spirit* wants said to each audience is the word we must bring. This issue will test our courage and loyalty to Christ aplenty.

As long as we faithfully say what the Spirit wants, He continues flowing and speaking to our hearts timely, nourishing, inspiring messages for God's people. But if we begin diluting, twisting, or withholding "what the Spirit saith unto the churches" (Rev. 2:7) to please people or to profit or protect ourselves, we quench the messenger-Spirit in our hearts and ministries—and the spiritual life of our listeners and readers. And we all dry up together.

~

Christians who quench the Holy Spirit begin not only to dry but also to die. When the Christians at Sardis quenched the Spirit, Jesus told them, "I know all the things you do, and that you have a reputation for being alive—but you are dead" (Rev. 3:1, NLT). Those who detect and correct their spiritual blockages reverse this lethal process. Released, they immediately begin to live, thrive, and bear fruit again.

God urges us to turn from everything that quenches the Spirit: "Turn you at my reproof" (Prov. 1:23). If we will, He promises us two wonderful blessings. First, we will receive an immediate, powerful refilling with the Spirit: "Behold, I will pour out my spirit unto you" (v. 23). Rivers of living water will rush back into our parched souls. Second, the Spirit will give us fresh insight into God's Word: "I will make known my words unto you" (v. 23). The dry, dead letter of the Bible will suddenly become the live, flowing words of the living God speaking life and hope to us from chapters and verses previously silent.

Now that you've identified some of the things that extinguish the Spirit in your life, you've but one thing left to do: eliminate them! So whatever is quenching the Spirit in your life, *quench it!*

Your personal supply of spiritual gold will immediately increase—and your meekness.

Chapter Twelve

SEEK MEEKNESS!

Seek the LORD ... seek meekness.

—ZEPHANIAH 2:3

For many years the Jews quenched the Holy Spirit by persistently worshiping idols. With the awesome, unprecedented judgment of the Babylonian captivity looming on Judah's horizon, the prophet Zephaniah called on its idolatrous people to repent and "seek the LORD" (Zeph. 2:3). Then he added, "Seek meekness." Why this additional call?

The man of God realized that, despite the almost certain impending national judgment, God could yet spare meek Judeans in the day His wrath visited their proud and impenitent peers: "It may be ye shall be hidden in the day of the LORD's anger" (v. 3).

But how did they, and how should we, "seek meekness"?

HOW TO SEEK MEEKNESS

The verb *seek* implies a search or hunt demanding a sustained, conscious effort to find and obtain a particular object. To "seek meekness" requires several things of us.

First, we must study meekness. How will we seek something unless we discover its existence, purpose, and worth through study? Second, we must idealize meekness, or esteem it highly as an ideal. How will we sustain a search for something unless we admire and desire it strongly? Third, we must pursue meekness not just intellectually but practically, choosing

133

to act, speak, and think meekly, and, yes, to actually *become* meek. How can we fully understand meekness unless we take the steps necessary to possess it in our experience? Fourth, we must then practice meekness, walking in it daily for the duration of our lives. Like every other grace or talent, meekness is perfected by practice; its beautiful blossom develops, not overnight, but over years.

Let's begin our search by defining meekness.

DEFINING MEEKNESS

Succinctly, and obviously, meekness is the condition of being meek. The Hebrew word most often translated "meek" in the Old Testament is *anayv* (aw-nawv´) and means, "depressed in mind or circumstances."[1] This speaks of both a general outlook on life and a specific condition of and attitude toward adversity.

Considering the naturally proud, or uplifted, state of mind present in sinful human nature, to be "depressed in mind" means, not necessarily to be psychologically depressed, oppressed, or troubled as we think of these terms today, but to be "pressed down" in one's natural self-view—or *not* lifted up with pride. Meek souls, then, are simply humble souls. For their righteousness, faithfulness, and work's sake, they sometimes also find themselves "depressed [pressed down, persecuted, or troubled] in circumstances."

Another Hebrew word with practically the same meaning as *anayv* is *aniy* (aw-nee´), meaning "poor, humble, or meek."[2] W. E. Vine observes, "Especially in later Israelite history, just before the Exile and following, this noun came to have a special connection with those faithful ones who were being abused, [or] taken advantage of, by the rich."[3] Again, this speaks not of their mental depression but of their quiet repose and full acceptance of the adverse circumstances God permits to test their faith, loyalty, and endurance. Rather than rebel (in pride) against God's arrangement of their lives and thus fail to please Him, the meek choose to fully accept their unpleasant conditions for the time being. Picking up their crosses and following Jesus, they endure injustice and rejection until God, in His time and way, releases them. Because God's grace is sufficient for every trial He sends (2 Cor. 12:9), the meek abide strong in the spirit, not weak or depressed, despite their adverse circumstances. Therefore, meek souls react trustingly and submissively toward God when He permits difficult trials to come their way. When proud souls rebel and turn back because the way is hard, the meek stay true, trusting, and faithful in their God-ordained duties.

Other Hebrew words closely associated with *anayv* convey the meaning of "mildness, modesty, [being] saintly."[4] Indeed, to be consistently humble in attitude and nonresistant to God when He lets us suffer is to be "saintly."

Consider the meekness of these consensus saints.

Except on two occasions, Moses meekly endured all the false accusations, bitter insults, and deadly rebellions of the Israelites—whom he was called of God to love, lecture, and lead.

When the apostle Paul learned that his "thorn in the flesh," or demonic enemy, was part of God's wise plan to keep him humble, Paul meekly accepted it. And gladly: "*Most gladly*, therefore, will I rather glory in my infirmities" (2 Cor. 12:9).

When God let the Romans banish the apostle John to the island of Patmos, John humbly accepted his trial of persecution and made the best of a bitter situation. He walked so closely with Jesus that he was "in the Spirit" (Rev. 1:10) when others would have been "in rebellion."

The Philadelphian Christians humbly accepted the Lord's command to wait for His help while they were opposed and maligned daily by their proud, cruel Jewish critics: "*Since you have kept my command to endure patiently*, I will also keep you from the hour of trial that is going to come upon the whole world to test those who live on the earth" (Rev. 3:10, NIV).

After being commissioned, the prophet Ezekiel meekly submitted to God's plan that he remain in his house, not speak or travel in public ministry, be mute (physically unable to speak, except when given special messages), prophesy primarily through symbolic actions, and bear bodily burdens daily for the sins of the Jews until the fall of Jerusalem—over seven years later!

How meek, how saintly, these were! Nevertheless, let's seek a broader description of meekness.

FURTHER DESCRIBING MEEKNESS

Meek ones are sober-minded, not high-minded. They are quietly thankful to God, not loud and boastful, about their gifts, graces, blessings, and accomplishments. Yet they see and speak of themselves accurately, not with false humility. They will frankly acknowledge not only their shortcomings but also their strengths, as Moses did when he meekly wrote this self-assessment: "Now the man Moses was very meek, above all the men who were upon the face of the earth" (Num. 12:3). And they'll calmly take it when abusive epithets like "conceited" or "arrogant" are hurled at them for doing so!

So biblical meekness must not be mistaken for mousiness or mere human introversion, timidity, or lack of resolve. Such terms describe not meekness but weakness—and heaven neither needs nor wants any Walter Mittys! To the contrary, biblical meekness involves being *meek toward God*, or docile toward Him, pliable in His hands, easily conformed and never resistant to His will; even when, as stated earlier, this involves inescapable and sometimes prolonged sufferings.

Meek ones are not self-willed, self-interested, self-serving, or self-preserving, but are rather dominated by an overriding desire to please God. Jesus of Nazareth, the meekest man ever to live, said, "I do always those things that please him [God the Father]" (John 8:29).

Paradoxically, meek ones are strong, yet not in themselves but in God. Spiritually mature, they don't depend on their own strength, ideas, or methods, but instead they rely entirely on God's power, wisdom, and ways of working. When in difficulty, trouble, or danger, they consistently choose to trust God to save them rather than try to save themselves: "They who know thy name [unchangeably faithful character] will put their trust in thee; for thou...hast not forsaken those who seek thee" (Ps. 9:10). Because they firmly believe Christ's testimony that the Judge of all the earth will ultimately rule in their favor (Luke 18:7–8), they need not and do not seek revenge. Lamblike, they are nonresistant toward their oppressors, not strongly self-defensive or bitterly vengeful: "Ye have condemned and killed the just, and *he doth not resist you*" (James 5:6; see vv. 7–9.)

Though strong, meek ones are soft-hearted. Forgiving, they are ready to reconcile with even their worst offenders, if they will only repent. And if they won't, the meek will never utter a word or move a finger to harm them, even when given repeated opportunities to do so. (See 1 Samuel 24, 26.) This is the stuff of true saintliness.

As growing Christian disciples idealize, pursue, and practice these qualities of meekness, the Holy Spirit transforms them from contentious, reactionary, injurious, raptor-like, immature Christians to peace-loving, dovelike, meek, saintly followers of Jesus Christ.

MEEKNESS: A BIBLICAL IDEAL AND INCARNATION

Meekness is one of the Bible's prime ideals and is incarnated in the life and teachings of its most central character, Jesus.

In the Beatitudes, Jesus openly praised, not the proud and self-assertive, but the meek: "Blessed are the meek; for they shall inherit the earth" (Matt. 5:5). He also demonstrated meekness by quickly and fully accepting His cruel betrayal—because it was His Father's will: "The cup which my Father hath given me, shall I not drink it?" (John 18:11). He furthermore checked raptorial (attacking, retaliatory, injurious) behavior among His students: once, when John prayed for fire to consume the Samaritans (Luke 9:51–56), and again, when Peter resorted to violence to try to stop Jesus' arrest (John 18:10–11). The apostle Paul cited Jesus' meekness (humility) as the chief reason God "highly exalted" Jesus and gave Him "a name...above every name" (Phil. 2:9; see vv. 5–11). After describing Himself as "meek and lowly in heart," Jesus called us to take on His meekness and find soul-rest by cultivating it in our lives: "Learn of me; for I am meek and lowly in heart, and ye shall find rest unto your souls" (Matt. 11:29). Others have answered or anticipated the call of meekness incarnate.

Paul demonstrated Jesus' amazing meekness in Philippi in three different ways: (1) by accepting his unjust conviction and cruel beating (surely the work of his "thorn"); (2) by continuing to pray and worship despite his pain; and (3) by refusing to accept a personal deliverance that would harm an innocent person (Acts 16:16–28). Isaac exhibited the Master's meekness by repeatedly refusing to resist the mistreatment the Philistines so spitefully and persistently visited upon him (Gen. 26:15–22). Moses, *the* meekest man alive in his day, showed Jesus' marvelous meekness by not defending himself against Miriam and Aaron's groundless criticism: "Now the man Moses was *very meek, above all the men* who were upon the face of the earth" (Num. 12:3).

So we see that, not only in the Nazarene but also in His devoted disciples of the present and past ages, the most marvelous meekness was incarnated.

THE MANY BENEFITS OF MEEKNESS

Biblical idealism is not the only reason to pursue meekness. Its practical benefits are many and enviable. God delights in lowly souls so much that He lavishes upon them His highest blessings.

For instance, He gives them deep contentment with their present earthly provisions: "The meek shall eat and be satisfied" (Ps. 22:26). He grants them growing inner joy: "The meek also shall increase their joy in the LORD" (Isa. 29:19). He provides them heavenly guidance throughout their earthly walk: "The meek will he guide in judgment; and the meek will he teach his way" (Ps. 25:9). He will ultimately give them *everything*—"the earth"—permitting them to access at will every part of His splendid creation for their delight: "But the meek shall inherit *the [entire] earth*, and shall delight themselves in the abundance of peace" (Ps. 37:11). And He rises to rescue them from their enemies' ruinous plots: "when God arose to judgment, to save all the meek of the earth" (Ps. 76:9). And that's not all.

He turns even their ugliest trials into beautiful victories: "He will beautify the meek with salvation" (Ps. 149:4). He promotes them, never the proud or self-promoting, to higher service: "The LORD lifteth up the meek" (Ps. 147:6). He overturns unfair judgments made against them and recompenses their losses for His name's sake: "But with righteousness shall he judge the poor, and reprove with equity for the meek of the earth" (Isa. 11:4). He revives them through the inspired words of His anointed messengers, especially the greatest Messenger, Jesus: "The Spirit of the Lord GOD is upon me...to preach good tidings unto the meek" (Isa. 61:1). And, lastly, as the prophet Zephaniah anticipated, He protects the meek from harm when He visits the earth in judgment: "All ye meek of the earth...it may be ye shall be hidden in the day of the LORD's anger" (Zeph. 2:3).

These are the many benefits of the Lord's meek ones.

My friend, our times are similar to Zephaniah's. Because of this world's, and our nation's, persisting sinfulness, a day of divine reckoning and unprecedented judgments looms before us. We know this because the Bible prophesies, "The time is come that judgment [the End-Time divinely enforced worldwide restoration of divine order] must begin at the house of God [the church and those nations in which it is concentrated]" (1 Pet. 4:17). Shouldn't we obey Zephaniah's inspired advice to "seek meekness"—studying, idealizing, experiencing, and practicing it—so we will receive benefits rather than chastisements in the day the Lord visits?

For that, we must know how to humble ourselves.

Chapter Thirteen

HOW TO HUMBLE YOURSELF

Humble yourselves in the sight of the Lord, and he shall lift you up.
—JAMES 4:10

ointedly, persistently, and passionately, in both Old and New Testaments, the Bible calls its readers to humility.

In Deuteronomy 8, Moses told the Israelites three times that God tested them in the wilderness for the express purpose of humbling them: "The LORD thy God led thee these forty years in the wilderness, to *humble* thee…and he *humbled* thee…that he might *humble* thee" (Deut. 8:2–3, 16). By inspiration the apostle Paul added that their trials were recorded as examples to us in this Christian era: "Now all these things happened unto them for examples, and they are written for our admonition" (1 Cor. 10:11). In his epistle, therefore, James exhorts Christians everywhere, "Humble yourselves in the sight of the Lord" (James 4:10). Peter orders the same in his general epistle, "Humble yourselves…under the mighty hand of God" (1 Pet. 5:6).

In these and many similar biblical references God implies a fact too clear to deny or ignore: *In our natural (fallen) state we are all proud creatures—thinking too highly of ourselves, not highly enough of God, and too lowly of other people. Therefore, even after we're redeemed by God's grace, we need to be humbled.*

Consequently, the Redeemer seeks to deliver His redeemed ones from our overinflated sense of self-esteem and bring us into humility—a sober perception of ourselves, an appreciative view of others, and an awestruck and worshipful outlook on God. This mental transformation is essential if we hope to live and work close to God throughout eternity, because He has repeatedly declared His holy hatred of all pride. In Proverbs, pride ranks *first* on God's definitive list of most-hated sins: "These six things doth the LORD hate; yea, seven are an abomination unto him: *A proud look…*" (Prov. 6:16–17). The writings of Isaiah and Ezekiel reveal that pride was Satan's (Lucifer's) primary sin and caused his permanent ouster from paradise before the creation of man. (See Isaiah 14:12–15; Ezekiel 28:1–19.) And if God rejected Lucifer from His presence due to his pride, He won't receive people into His presence who are still proud.

James says that instead of receiving the proud, God resists them: "God resisteth the proud" (James 4:6). The apostle Peter agrees verbatim: "God resisteth the proud" (1 Pet. 5:5). And as if to dash even the feeblest hopes of impenitently proud ones somehow spending perpetuity close to God, David declares that not only he but more importantly God will not tolerate them: "Him that hath an high look and a proud heart will not I tolerate" (Ps. 101:5). (In Psalm 101, David's standards for choosing his companions and co-workers mirror God's.)

What is God's underlying message here? If we are ever to know and abide near the God who hates pride, we must be humbled.

Obviously, if we were already humble in our natural state, or even as born-again Christians, God's Word would not repeatedly call us to "humble yourselves…" Nor would Jesus have warned even His closest disciples to humble themselves: "Except *ye* [My very own twelve handpicked disciples!] be converted, and become as [humble as] little children, *ye* shall not enter into the kingdom of heaven" (Matt. 18:3). Nor would two of the highest-ranking leaders of the early church, Peter and James, have written general epistles to Christians everywhere summoning them to humility. So we conclude that God's call to humility is addressed to everyone, redeemed and unredeemed, regardless of their station and status in this world or in the church.

While becoming humble is easier said than done, it is not mission impossible. If it were, we could justly charge God with unfairness, because through His inspired writers He plainly orders us (imbued with and assisted by His grace) to accomplish this task, using imperative language: "[You must] humble yourselves in the sight of the Lord" (James 4:10). In

His mind, therefore, this is something that we, not He alone, must do. The only question remaining, then, is *how?* How do we humble ourselves? Pride is like a stubborn inner beast with seven lives. How do we mortify our hubris and replace it with Jesus' humility?

As with every other spiritual problem, the Bible provides us with clear and available solutions. Here are some biblical ways by which we may humble ourselves.

Biblical Ways to Humble Ourselves

Obedience to God's will

The ultimate example of righteous living, Jesus has shown us the chief way by which we may rid ourselves of the curse of pride. As a man, Jesus humbled Himself by obedience to His Father's will.

The Holy Spirit captures the essence of Christ's humility in these words: "As a man, he humbled himself and became obedient" (Phil. 2:8). By use of the conjunction "and," an inspired link is made between Jesus' humility and His obedience to His Father's will: "He humbled himself *and* became obedient." We could paraphrase this, "He humbled Himself *as* He became obedient." Or we could say, "He humbled Himself *by* becoming obedient." All of these expressions convey the same thought: it was obedience that humbled Jesus as a man. If as a man Jesus could not humble Himself without obeying His Father's will, neither can we.

Our obedience to God's will and our humility are inseparable. Every time we obey the Father's will (revealed generally by the Bible and specifically by the Spirit's guidance), we exalt God above ourselves. A.W. Tozer taught that this puts our sovereign heavenly Father in the right position—above us. And it also puts us in the right position—beneath Him. Disobedience to His will, however, does just the opposite. It places our selfish will above our Father-God's sovereign will. Thus we put ourselves above God, dishonor Him, and walk in pride. Every act of obedience helps correct this overinflated self-esteem and bring us into a right view of ourselves and of God. The more we obey, the more humble in spirit we become...and the more like Jesus. This is the humbling process the apostle Paul had in mind when he wrote, "*Let this mind be in you*, which was also in Christ Jesus, who…humbled himself" (Phil. 2:5–8).

All the other biblical methods by which we humble ourselves are linked to this primary way, because they each constitute some form of obedience to God's Word or will.

Sober thinking

Physically, we are what we consistently eat. Mentally, we are what we consistently think. Proverbs teaches, "As he [any person] thinketh in his heart [mind], so is he" (Prov. 23:7), meaning, our usual thought stuff and thought patterns determine our character. While sinful behavior may arise spontaneously, sin usually exists first in our minds.

In His famous catalog of human sins, Jesus cited "evil thoughts" first before listing various kinds of wrong behavior:

> For out of the heart [mind] proceed evil thoughts, [and then] murders, adulteries, fornications, thefts, false witness, blasphemies.
> —MATTHEW 15:19

To eliminate pride, then, from our life actions, we must first root it out of our thought life. Why? Proud thoughts produce proud words and acts, but if we cease thinking proudly, our proud words and actions will cease. If we determine to think humbly, our conversation and behavior will naturally follow the new viewpoint we embrace.

With this in mind, the apostle Paul calls us to sober thinking: "For I say…to every man…not to think of himself more highly than he ought to think, but to *think soberly*, according as God hath dealt to every man the measure of faith" (Rom. 12:3). We must not think we are special because we have faith, wisdom, or spiritual gifts, for God has given every Christian similar graces with which to serve and glorify Him. And if every Christian is so endowed by God, obviously we are not special and therefore have no reason to boast in thought or word: "For who maketh thee to differ from another? And what hast thou that thou didst not receive [as a free gift from God]? Now if thou didst receive it [as a gift from God, as others have], why dost thou glory [delight, boast], as if thou hadst not received it?" (1 Cor. 4:7).

144

Sober-thinking Christians practice honest mental self-examination continually. They quickly and firmly dismiss "every high thing that exalteth itself against the knowledge of God [in one's life]" (2 Cor. 10:5), such as thoughts of self-importance, self-promotion, arrogance, or vanity. They refuse to yield to their ego's cravings to seek self-praise or indulge in memories of past achievements or victories. Thus their excessive self-esteem dies a slow but sure death. If practiced, sober thinking produces a properly *dis*-illusioned mind—one in which every illusion has been *dislodged* and removed. Consequently, we no longer build fantastic air castles or harbor foolish visions of grandeur but consistently estimate ourselves accurately, as Peter urges:

> Therefore *humble yourselves [demote, lower yourselves in your own estimation]* under the mighty hand of God, that in due time He may exalt you.
>
> —1 PETER 5:6, AMP

Another way to describe sober thinking is *seeing ourselves exactly as God's Word describes us*. As stated above, Paul urged us not to think "more highly" of ourselves than we should. He implies, then, that we should think "highly" (respectfully, worthily, honorably) of ourselves, though not "more" highly. This means we should realize our immense potential value in God's sight and kingdom. Why are we valuable to Him, His work, and His realm?

As His Word reveals, every Christian possesses the priceless life of Jesus; the person, gifts, and strength of the Holy Spirit; and the potential to bear much fruit for God's eternal kingdom. Through just one believer wholly yielded to God, God can reach and bless people throughout the whole earth. But we should not think "too highly" of ourselves because, as already stated, other Christians are also similarly endowed by God and equally valuable to Him. Additionally, we should remember that, whatever our potential or actual kingdom value, we still possess a sin nature and can stumble through sin or folly at any moment if we don't stay close to Jesus and watch ourselves. It's hard for us to inflate with pride when freshly deflated by a memory or recurrence of the "plague of our own heart" (1 Kings 8:38).

Full acceptance of the "lowest place"

Wherever there is pride there is ambition. And the worst kind of ambition is religious ambition. Ever disruptive to sin, Jesus' teachings rudely uproot the tree of religious ambition growing in our heart.

While attending a chief Pharisee's Sabbath-day luncheon, Jesus discerned the Pharisees coolly but carefully choosing the most honorable seats for themselves: "Jesus noticed that all who had come to the dinner were trying to sit in the seats of honor near the head of the table" (Luke 14:7, NLT). This prompted Him to tell a story about an ambitious guest at a wedding feast (vv. 8–11). Every Christian has been invited to attend the wedding feast of the Marriage Supper of the Lamb (Rev. 19:7–9). So what was His advice to them, and to us?

He illuminated this simple but sure path to freedom from religious ambition: when God puts you in life's lowest places, fully accept them! "But when thou art bidden, go and *sit down in the lowest place...*" (Luke 14:10), or "take the lowest place at the foot of the table" (NLT). Make no mistake, His doctrine here is radical, anti-everything the world holds dear (and most churches and Christians too, I lament). Rather than eagerly climb the various "ladders" of life—social, financial, commercial, political, or religious—Jesus here teaches Christians to humbly accept the positions they currently occupy, however low, and work faithfully there until His Father providentially lifts them higher.

He closes His powerful vignette with a rock-solid spiritual law. If we refuse to accept our low places, but work instead to exalt ourselves, our future humiliation is assured: "Whosoever exalteth himself *shall be abased*" (v. 11). But if we accept our humble stations, our future promotion is equally sure: "And he that humbleth himself *shall be exalted.*" This is no idle remark. Jesus made this same statement on at least three different occasions recorded in the Gospels. (See Matthew 23:12; Luke 14:11; 18:14.) Thus, as a recurring theme, it was one of the central pillars of His teaching.

Note that in this instructive parable everything hinges on our *reaction* to being placed in the "lowest" places of life. The circumstances of life are many, but Christ calls every disciple sooner or later to live and labor in the humble places of this world. These overlooked training grounds for Christ's future honorees are on three levels—low, lower, and lowest—and

Christ calls His student-followers to the "lowest" places: "Go and sit down in the *lowest* place..." (Luke 14:10). He wants us to be fully, restfully content in very humble circumstances, realizing that He, not chance, enemies, or the devil, has led us there: "In all thy ways acknowledge *him*" (Prov. 3:6). This contentment is symbolized by the posture of sitting: "*Sit down in the lowest place.*"

When waiting, our physical postures and actions often betray our disposition.

When we *pace back and forth*, we are in full rebellion against whatever or whoever is delaying us. We are waiting, but we hate every minute of it. We're tolerating our delay but not embracing it. So we're waiting, but impatiently.

When we *stand still*, we demonstrate at least partial acceptance of our delay. We're waiting, and with patience, but not with perfect patience.

When we *sit down*, however, we have fully accepted our required wait. We rest and occupy ourselves with thinking, reading, conversation, or other useful activities without a trace of impatience or discontent. Thus by waiting patiently, we wait perfectly: "Let patience have her perfect work, that ye may be perfect and entire, lacking nothing" (James 1:4). This is the attitude Christ calls us to embrace in the lowest places of life: "*Sit down* [neither pace nor stand but *sit*, fully accepting your circumstances as from God]." This releases the Holy Spirit to work in us mightily, uprooting our ambitious pride of life and planting instead the very humility of the Son of God. We know His humility is taking root when we no longer feel we must have a more honorable station in life to be happy. It is enough that we know we are where our heavenly Father has placed us and we are growing daily in knowledge of Him and readiness to do His will.

The psalmist says amen to this parable, testifying that he would rather have a very low position in the will of God than a more desirable one outside of it: "I had rather be a [humble, ignored] doorkeeper in the house [and will] of my God, than to dwell [freely and self-satisfied] in the tents of wickedness [outside God's will]" (Ps. 84:10).

Try as we may, none of us can choose when, where, how, or how long God humbles us. Only He has the right to do that. He did so for His

Son, selecting Nazareth, its carpentry shop, its synagogue, and Mary and Joseph's home as the "lowest" place for Jesus' *thirty-year* training in humility. But we can choose to "sit down" in our "lowest places," as Jesus did in His. "Let this mind be in you, which was also in Christ Jesus…"

Are we pacing, standing, or sitting just now, amid our present mortifications?

Receiving the chastening of God

To American Christians today chastening (training and corrective discipline meant to perfect moral character) is a distant concept, long lost in the annals of yesteryear. Decadent decades after the advent of baby boomers and proliferation of (Dr. Benjamin) Spockism, most of us now believe that if we love our children we should never displease them. But the Bible teaches otherwise, namely, that if we love our little ones, we not only nourish, protect, and educate them, but also, when necessary, we reprove and discipline them. This helps them know right from wrong and guides them into a lifestyle that God can bless.

It also does something else that God considers very important: it humbles them. Early in life children learn that parents have authority over them and expectations of them and that they, their children, have obligations—and limitations. Just as God limits the uprisings of the ocean tides and storms, "Thus far shalt thou come, but no farther" (Job. 38:11), so parents limit the rebellion of their children. This quenches their innately arrogant "I'll do whatever I want, whenever I want, however I want, with whomever I want, and you can't stop me" attitude and gives them a sober, realistic self-view.

Whether we choose to chasten or coddle our children, the fact remains that the heavenly Father chastens His—and not just a select few: "He chasteneth…*every* son whom he receiveth" (Heb. 12:6). He considers chastening so important that He devoted nearly an entire chapter of the New Testament to the topic. (See Hebrews 12:5–17, 25–29.) Also, key Bible characters testified of its benefit in their lives. David expressed deep appreciation for the Good Shepherd's rod: "Thy rod and thy staff they comfort me" (Ps. 23:4). The Palestinian shepherd's wooden "rod" was used not only to drive away predators but also to discipline disobedient sheep.

When we disobey God, we force Him to visit us with His rod. Our reaction then is vital. If we rebel, we remain proud and unfit to know the Lord deeply or be used by Him widely. And the more we resist His correction, the more we unfit ourselves and forfeit the rich blessings of sonship. But if we "endure" His chastening—submissively confessing our faults and correcting them—we are on the road to full-fledged sonship: "If ye endure chastening, God dealeth with you as with sons" (Heb. 12:7). And every time we yield to our heavenly Father's correction, which sometimes comes through troublesome circumstances or difficult people, we become more humble. It is a fixed spiritual law: chastening rejected is pride enthroned; chastening received is pride destroyed.

So don't despise the Lord's chastening because it's humbling. It's supposed to be. You need to know your heavenly Father's expectations, which are, in a word, obedience. And you also need to know your limitations, what God will and will not tolerate. Wise children learn quickly to stop wherever their Father draws the line: "Thus far shalt thou come, and no farther."

Submitting to spiritual leaders

Constructive criticism is an important part of success in any endeavor. Accordingly, the Bible urges Christians to always hear and obey the instruction that comes through loving, wise spiritual leaders: "Obey your spiritual leaders, and do what they say. Their work is to watch over your souls, and they are accountable to God" (Heb. 13:17, NLT).

Divinely approved Christian leaders (pastors, elders, teachers, counselors) are ministers of constructive criticism, sent into our lives by God to help us see our faults that our present level of spirituality may not permit us to see (or current level of pride admit). The experiences of life eventually open even the blindest inner eyes of understanding. So those who have gone before us in the way of discipleship usually possess keener spiritual vision than we do. These who "are of full age [spiritually mature], even those who by reason of use have their senses exercised to discern both good and evil" (Heb. 5:14), are quicker to perceive spiritual signs and conditions than we are. When such leaders graciously point out our faults and advise corrections in our attitudes or actions, we are foolish and proud to reject their counsel. We do well to remember that they gain nothing by our obedience and we gain everything by it. God rewards them for *telling* us the truth, not for trying to make us obey it. Their wisdom is offered entirely for our help and growth, "for they watch [solely] *for [the benefit of] your souls*" (Heb. 13:17). Why should we object to that? The only thing in us that squeals or squirms is pride. The more we obey our spiritual leaders, the more pride dies, and we emerge more refined and humble. Why, even the unredeemed humble themselves and receive constructive criticism from their leaders. Let's look to the world and learn.

Athletes receive the instruction of seasoned coaches or trainers. Interns use the information they glean from the experienced physicians training them. Green troops heed tips from battle-hardened soldiers. Young business students seek and retain the practical advice of successful entrepreneurs. Novice politicians are glad to use any proven advertising strategies taught them by often-elected officeholders. Why? They realize that receiving constructive criticism from their superiors pays enormous dividends, and they'll gladly humble themselves to get them! Christian, the sons of this world are trying to teach us. Their advice? *Listen to your leaders!*

Let's not reject their wisdom, or God's! When the Lord prompts a caring bishop, pastor, or elder to counsel you—"Simon, I have somewhat to say unto thee" (Lk. 7:40)—hear him. You'll be humbler and wiser for obeying your minister of constructive criticism.

Being subject one to another

In Peter's inspired call, "Humble yourselves, therefore, under the mighty hand of God" (1 Pet. 5:6), note the word *therefore*. This directs our attention to the previous statement in verse 5, where we find two ways of humility presented.

First, as discussed above, we humble ourselves by submitting to the advice of our elders and leaders: "In like manner, ye younger, submit yourselves unto the elder" (v. 5). Second, Peter urges us to "be subject one to another." That is, we should listen to each other's wisdom and consider and serve one another's needs: "All of you, serve each other in humility" (v. 5, NLT). As we do these two things we put on the beautiful garment of humility: "and [so] be clothed with humility."

Humble believers are pliable, willing to receive wisdom from any source, whether an elder or peer. And they're ready to change their plans, when necessary, to serve their fellow Christians' needs. Are we clothing ourselves with these two beautifully humble "garments"?

Casting all our worries on the Lord

The verse in which Peter calls us to humility closes with a colon, not a period (1 Pet. 5:6, KJV). Several excellent translations also close the verse with either a semicolon or comma.[1] Rather than terminating its line of thought, therefore, verse 6 flows on to the next verse: "Casting all your care upon him; for he careth for you" (v. 7).

Thus Peter, and his heavenly Inspirer, the Holy Spirit, link the thoughts in these verses, which speak of:

- Humbling ourselves under God's hand
- Casting all our cares on the Lord

This inspired order and linkage of thought implies that we humble ourselves under the mighty hand of God by casting all our cares on Him. As long as we insist on worrying our way through problems, depending not on God's wisdom, ways, and strength, but on ours or other people's, human pride still rules in our hearts. But when we decide to "[cast] all our care on him," we begin growing in the humility of faith. That *utter dependency on God* is essential if we are to not only be saved but also "live" by faith: "The just shall *live* by his faith" (Hab. 2:4).

The apostle Paul, who lived daily in this humble reliance on the Lord, taught us precisely how to "cast all our cares on him." He says we should refuse to worry and choose instead to pray for, believe we receive, give thanks for, and patiently expect God's help: "Be anxious for nothing, but in everything, by prayer and supplication with thanksgiving, let your requests be made known unto God" (Phil. 4:6). All who humbly comply will receive the wondrous reward of the peace of God: "The peace of God, which passeth all understanding, shall keep your hearts and minds" (v. 7). This special tranquility is the special reward of the humble.

Receiving help freely

In Matthew 10:8, Jesus ordered His original disciples to "freely give" the gracious message and benefits of salvation to everyone. His introductory phrase reveals that the Twelve had already learned to freely receive help from others: "*Freely ye have received*, freely give." This tells us Jesus had already begun to humble them. How do we know this?

Human pride resists accepting any help from anyone at anytime, because it doesn't want to look weak. Accepting help is a silent admission of need and acquiescence in dependency. Though we all need some kind of help daily from God and people, we don't like admitting it.

While that irresponsible and sinful indolence that freely lives off other people's labors is no better than pride, Jesus nevertheless aims to train His disciples to, like simple sheep, humbly live off *His faithfulness* however He chooses to send it (Ps. 23:1). We work hard at education, jobs, sales, and friendships, but ultimately He alone withholds or gives us success. As we learned in chapter four, "A man can receive nothing, except it be given him from heaven" (John 3:27). Christians who are growing in humility learn to receive God's help, whatever form it takes, but proud Christians refuse it. Why? They must maintain their superior sense of independence. While lauded by this world, this fiercely independent spirit isn't Christlike.

When the heavenly Father sent Jesus on His earthly mission, He deliberately put His Son in a position of need. For years Jesus earned His income by laboring humbly in Nazareth's carpentry shop. But when He entered ministry, all this changed. Throughout His three-year campaign, Jesus' ministry team was financed, not by His personal savings or ongoing labors (though by all accounts His labor in ministry was *more* exhausting than that in any carpentry shop! See Mark 6:31), but by donations from mainly female disciples:

> And…he went throughout every city and village, preaching…. And certain women…Joanna, the wife of Chuzas, Herod's steward; and Susanna; and many others, who ministered unto him of their substance.
>
> —LUKE 8:1–3

Some of these supporters referenced above were wealthy. Joanna's husband was Herod's steward. His was a most lucrative employment, so we may assume Joanna was wealthy. But whether wealthy or not, these women were all Christ's divinely appointed helpers, sent by the heavenly Father to assist Him in some phase of His work. And, humbly, Jesus freely received what they freely gave.

If we are to partake of His humility, God will deliberately put us in some position of need for a season. There, in some way, we will be dependent on others for some kind of support or assistance. It may have nothing to do with money, but in some way they will help us with the difficulties and trials we face. Because this divine assistance will come through human agency—ordinary people like you, me, or "Joanna"—we may be tempted to refuse it, lest we look weak and dependent on others. If we do so, we fail the Lord. But if we receive God's help, we delight Him—and grow humbler.

So when the Lord sends you help in any area of your life, work, or ministry, receive it. And freely! "*Freely* ye have received." And don't consider your helpers burdened. They will be blessed, not burdened, for helping you: "I will bless them that bless thee" (Gen. 12:3).

Confessing faults and errors

It is amazing how far some of us will go to avoid saying these words: "I'm sorry, I was wrong." Why do we dread this admission so badly? Our pride. Jesus' teaching reveals that this must go if we hope to follow Him.

In the Sermon on the Mount, Jesus taught that if we have given someone cause for offense, we should take the initiative and be reconciled: "If thou bring thy gift to the altar, and there rememberest that thy brother hath anything against thee, leave there thy gift before the altar, and go thy way; *first be reconciled* to thy brother..." (Matt. 5:23–24).

The first step in reconciliation is to say we were wrong. The second is to resume normal friendly relations, if possible. The third is to draw near and resume worshiping the God of humility: "...and then come and offer thy gift." In his epistle James echoes Christ's teaching, exhorting us to confess our sins and failures "one to another" (James 5:16) when we seek release from the chastisements they have brought upon us.

This confession of our faults and failures need not be a teeth-pulling affair. It can be quick, easy, and minimally painful. When pressed by the prophet Nathan, David said simply, "I have sinned against the LORD" (2 Sam. 12:13). And that was it. In a moment he was a forgiven, free man (though discipline lay ahead). And a humbler one.

Are we following the pattern of David's humility?

Returning thanks sufficiently for every blessing

One day normally humble King Hezekiah grew proud—and his normally adoring Father-God became angry! "There was [divine] wrath upon him [Hezekiah], and upon Judah" (2 Chron. 32:25). Why did Hezekiah swell with pride? He neglected to return thanks for a great blessing.

After being healed of a deadly illness, Hezekiah "rendered not again [thanksgiving] according to the benefit done unto him" (2 Chron. 32:25). Apparently, Hezekiah didn't thank the Lord at all for his healing, or not enough, not "according to the [exceptional] benefit done unto him." Considering the great kindness God had shown him by delivering him from certain death, Hezekiah's thanksgiving, if any, was inadequate. By failing to thank the Lord sufficiently, he failed to exercise humility. As a result, his formerly dormant pride arose and filled his heart: "his heart was lifted up" (v. 25). We must watch lest we repeat his error.

As commanded, we should form the habit of thanking God every day in every situation, whether wonderful, woeful, or mundane: "Give thanks in all circumstances" (1 Thess. 5:18, NIV). And when He gives us special blessings, favors, or deliverances, we should take time to return special thanks to Him, "according to the [special] benefit done" to us. If we don't, we repeat Hezekiah's folly. By failing to duly credit God, we tacitly credit ourselves. And swell with pride. And grieve God. And stop walking humbly before Him.

Waiting patiently

While humility is patient—willing to wait calmly for its needs or wants—pride is a very impatient spirit. Without apology it demands gratification instantly. When uplifted, we imagine that others should "hop to" our every request. Then we enter God's school of humility.

When God wants to let the air out of us, He arranges for us to deal with folks who have the twin gifts of stubbornness and slowness. These dear souls, fearing neither God nor man, are decidedly unimpressed with our swollen sense of self-importance. They care neither to please nor appease us and are quite at peace with making us wait. And wait. And wait! When at their mercy, our willingness to wait is the key to our becoming humble. If we will "let patience have her perfect work, that ye [we] may be perfect and entire, lacking nothing" (James 1:4), our humility will be perfected along with our patience. We will emerge from our wait genuinely meeker souls.

Nothing is said of Moses's meekness at age forty, when, still possessing his Egyptian pride, he tried to initiate a premature fulfillment of God's vision. But later, after forty years of waiting on God in Midian, his meekness had grown significantly and so was cited by the Spirit in the biblical record: "Now the man Moses was very meek [humble] . . ." (Num. 12:3). What is the Spirit saying to us?

Pride is reduced, and meekness produced, as we wait patiently for God—forty years, if necessary! Are you keeping the word of His patience *patiently*?

Accepting humiliations

There is no such thing as life without occasional humiliations. In fact, Christian growth demands that embarrassments, demotions, and indignities come our way. Jesus declared, "It is impossible but that *offenses will come*" (Luke 17:1). So the question is not, will humiliations come, but rather, how will we react when they come?

When intentionally misunderstood, unfairly criticized, slandered, or ignored for Jesus' sake, or when rebuked and punished for our sins or errors, will we respond with a spiritual or carnal attitude? Will we react as Christ's students or as people who don't know Him? Jesus taught us to acknowledge our heavenly Father's hand in everything and by His grace practice the rare art of nonresistance: "Ye have heard that it hath been said [retaliation is permissible], An eye for an eye, and a tooth for a tooth; but I say unto you . . . *resist not evil* [unfairness, insult, injury, or any adversity]" (Matt. 5:38–39).

If we inwardly resist humiliations, harboring anger at our mortifying circumstances, we move and grow in pride. If we acquiesce, yielding to Jesus' words, "Resist not evil," and then quietly follow His guidance, we grow in grace and humility, despite the humiliation.

These ways to humble ourselves are neither antiquated nor theoretical. They are proven, golden biblical methods. We may safely trust that, as we practice them, they will release us from the stressful yoke of pride and bring us under the restful yoke of Jesus' humility:

> Take my yoke upon you, and learn of me; for I am meek and
> lowly in heart, and ye shall find rest unto your souls.
> —MATTHEW 11:29

If we continue in this, His yoke, Jesus will establish us in healthy, biblical humility. Finally, and forever, our perspective will be right. We will think worshipfully of God, highly of others, and soberly of ourselves.

And that will enable God to put His glory on our tabernacles.

Chapter Fourteen

GLORY ON YOUR TABERNACLE

By him, therefore, let us offer the sacrifice of praise to God continually, that is, the fruit of our lips giving thanks to his name.
—HEBREWS 13:15

Written in part to compare things Jewish with things Christian, the Book of Hebrews contains many golden jewels of spiritual knowledge. One is the "sacrifice of praise" we are to offer to God "continually."

The writer to the Hebrews commands us:

By him, therefore, let us offer the *sacrifice of praise* to God *continually*, that is, the fruit of *our lips giving thanks to his [Jesus'] name.*
—HEBREWS 13:15

Self-interpreting, this verse describes the "sacrifice of praise." It is "the fruit of our lips giving thanks to his [Jesus'] name." This mandate of thanksgiving is neither novel nor mystical to the experienced Bible student. Throughout its pages, the Word repeatedly commands us to bless, praise, and thank the Lord incessantly.

Consider these references:

In *every thing* [*circumstance*] give thanks; for this is the will of God in Christ Jesus concerning you.
—1 THESSALONIANS 5:18

I will bless the LORD *at all times*; his praise shall *continually* be in my mouth.

—PSALM 34:1

Every day will I bless thee, and I will praise thy name *forever and ever*.

—PSALM 145:2

Let such as love thy salvation *say continually*, Let God be magnified.

—PSALM 70:4

Let my mouth be filled with thy praise and with thy honor *all the day*.

—PSALM 71:8

Even so, the inspired language used by the writer to the Hebrews hints at something more. He says we are to offer God a "sacrifice," or offering, of praise, and that it is to be rendered "continually." These words call to mind the *continual burnt offering* God commanded the Israelites to offer during the Old Testament period. It too was a "sacrifice." And it too was offered "continually." It is described in Exodus 29:38–46.

There God ordered the Jews to offer two lambs to Him every day: "Thou shalt offer upon the altar: two lambs…day by day continually" (Exod. 29:38). They were to begin offering one lamb at 9:00 a.m. and the other at 3:00 p.m.: "The one lamb shalt thou offer in the morning; and the other…at evening" (v. 39). Since the morning offering would continue slowly burning until the evening sacrifice was offered, a sacrificial lamb would be burning on Israel's altar continually. So God concluded, "This shall be a *continual* burnt offering" (v. 42). He further described it as "an offering made by fire" (v. 41) to be "before the LORD" (v. 42) always. As with other Old Testament types, all these details speak of New Testament realities: "Now all these things happened unto them for examples…for our admonition [warning or instruction]" (1 Cor. 10:11). So let's bring forth the meaning of the symbolism hidden in this passage.

Obviously, the two lambs speak of Jesus, "the Lamb of God, who taketh away the sin of the world" (John 1:29, 36). All the other details speak of His cross. The times at which the two lambs were offered correspond with the times at which Jesus was offered on the cross for the forgiveness of our sins. His crucifixion began at 9:00 a.m. and He expired at 3:00 p.m. Jesus' entire life, but especially His suffering, was "before the LORD ['s or the Father's loving, watchful eyes]." And His offering of Himself was "an offering made by fire," or fiery passion to His heavenly Father. So by obeying Jehovah's instructions for the continual burnt offering, the Israelites were worshiping Him for what He would yet do through Jesus on the cross. If verbalized, their actions would have said: "Jehovah, we praise and worship You for saving us by the blood of the Lamb. We are thankful to You always. Continually we adore You. At all times we bless You. You are worthy of our worship every hour, every day, every generation."

While the Israelites faithfully worshiped, God faithfully worked. While lamb was ascending from the people to God, life was descending from God to the people. While the glorifying of God went up, the glory of God came down: "my glory" (Exod. 29:43). As long as the people offered the continual burnt offering, God poured out His glory, not sporadically but "continually." Every hour of every day of every year of every generation, the marvelous awe-inspiring Shekinah glory—the visibly manifest presence of God as a glowing fire by night and pillar of cloud by day—rested on the tabernacle of God's people.

<h2 style="text-align:center">THE BENEFITS OF ISRAEL'S CONTINUAL BURNT OFFERING</h2>

The benefits of Israel's continual burnt offering were nothing less than a wonder. Let's ponder them.

Manifestation: God drew near His people.

God's first promise was, "I will *meet* you" (Exod. 29:42–43).

Never far away, the faithful but invisible Husband of Israel promised to show His betrothed people the reality of His perpetual nearness in a distinctly detectible way. He wanted them not just to believe He was there, but also to sense, see, and feel He was there. So He swore to rendezvous with His beloved "at the door of the tabernacle" (v. 42).

And the holy One kept this holy tryst faithfully.

Communication: God spoke to His people.

God's second promise was to "*speak* there unto thee" (v. 42).

Communication is essential to any healthy, growing relationship. So the Redeemer wanted His redeemed ones to know and meditate upon His sacred written Word, the Law recently given through Moses. But He also wanted them to detect His spontaneous *voice*: calling them to specific duties and ministries, guiding them at crossroads, exhorting them when they were low, and warning them when deception or danger lay ahead.

So He spoke, and so they grew to recognize the "still, small voice" of the Lord. (See 1 Samuel 3:7–10, 21; 1 Kings 19:11–13.)

Sanctification: God consecrated the priests, people, and tabernacle.

God further pledged to sanctify the people and the tabernacle for His service: "And the tabernacle shall be *sanctified* by my glory. . . . I will *sanctify* the tabernacle . . . the altar . . . [and] Aaron and his sons, to minister" (vv. 43–44).

To "sanctify" is to *make holy or pure; to consecrate or dedicate to God, or set apart exclusively for Him and His use.* So He set apart Israel and its worship center, ministers, and priests and thereafter used them to minister to Him and make known His greatness to the nations.

Visitation: God dwelt among His people continually.

Remarkably, Jehovah next promised to give Israel what no other nation has ever had, before or since—a perpetual visitation, the glory of God dwelling among them constantly: "And I will *dwell among* the children of Israel . . . *dwell among* them" (vv. 45–46).

Thus He officially "moved in" to the tabernacle they built for Him. Thereafter they could look up and see the cloud of His presence daily, confirming His nearness and shielding them from the sun's deadly heat. Nightly they could see its (His) glowing light, feel its comforting warmth (in the cold desert evenings), and hear its gentle but fervent burning. Month after month, year after year, generation after generation, this ongoing miracle was theirs, exclusively theirs.

God's uninterrupted visitation served three purposes. First, it satisfied God's heart because His express purpose for the tabernacle and its priesthood was to enable Him to live, walk, and work among His beloved people: "that I may *dwell among* them" (Exod. 25:8). He longed to be with them; now He was. Second, it fascinated the Israelites, inspiring them to want to know more about their wondrous living God. Third, it secured peace for them by intimidating their enemies. Who would dare to defy a nation when their God was so visibly alive and present to defend them?

So God and His people lived, walked, and worked together in bliss. It was a most happy marriage of the Holy One and the holy people in the holy land.

Confirmation: God caused them to firmly "know" He was their God.

Lastly, God gave the assurance, "They shall *know* that I am the LORD their God" (Exod. 29:46).

All the elements of God's ongoing visitation in the tabernacle—His nearness, voice, sanctification, and glory—combined to give the Israelites an unshakable *knowing* or impenetrable confidence that:

1. God was real.
2. He was really with them constantly.
3. They were perfectly secure in Him.

With God not only for but also among His people, who or what could be against them? There is no security on earth like the confirmed presence of Immanuel—*God with us.* All other sources of confidence pale, and fail, before this consummate confirmation.

⌒

All these amazing benefits—divine manifestation, communication, sanctification, visitation, and confirmation—belonged to the Israelites as long as the glory rested upon their tabernacle. And that lasted as long as they offered the burnt offering, "day by day continually." What does all this mean to us?

Let's review the application of Exodus 29:38–46 to our lives.

- Israel's "tabernacle" represents our *individual bodies*. 2 Corinthians 5:1 draws the same analogy between tabernacles (tent dwellings) and our bodies: "If our earthly house of *this tabernacle* were dissolved . . ."
- The "altar" of the tabernacle represents our *lips*, the primary place from which we offer our audible worship to God.
- The "continual burnt offering" is our *sacrifice of praise*, the steady worship of "our lips giving thanks to his name" (Heb. 13:15).
- An "offering made by fire" reminds us that, like Jesus' sacrifice, our sacrifice of praise should be an *expression of our inner passion, or fiery devotion*, to God.
- "Before the Lord" reminds us that *God's eyes are always watching over us*, His dear children, just as they did the Israelites, His beloved people, and Jesus, His beloved Son.
- "Day by day, continually" refers to *all our waking moments*.

THE BENEFITS OF OUR SACRIFICE OF PRAISE

The benefits of rendering God our "sacrifice of praise" continually parallel those Israel enjoyed for offering the continual burnt offering. They are most enviable—yet, by grace, fully within our reach. Let's consider them.

Manifestation

God will draw near us, or manifest His abiding nearness, in a way our human senses can detect. This is exactly what Jesus promised Christians who love Him with their whole hearts: "He that hath my commandments, and keepeth them, he it is that [truly, fully] loveth me . . . and I will love him, and will *manifest [reveal; disclose; cause to sense, feel, hear, or see] myself to him*" (John 14:21).

While believing God's presence is with us—based solely on His promises, "I will never leave thee, nor forsake thee," or "Lo, I am with thee always"—is more important than feeling it, the manifest presence of God is nevertheless a very sweet redemptive benefit Jesus plainly wants us to savor. Sensing that our ancient, loving Redeemer is truly near and blessing us in the middle of this callous modern world and our swirling personal troubles is the purest and highest ecstasy redeemed creatures can enjoy on earth: "In thy [realized] presence is fullness of joy" (Ps. 16:11).

Communication

With growing frequency, clarity, and confidence, we will detect God speaking to our hearts.

The still, small voice of God may come to us in many different ways. It may come while we read or study God's Word or while we worship privately. It may come in public worship or prayer meetings. It may come while we're walking or resting. It may come in the night or as we awake in the morning. Or it may come in the heat, noise, and activity of the day. But come it will, if we will only do three things consistently: (1) ask the Lord to speak, (2) listen for His voice, and (3) obey it. When the child prophet Samuel followed this simple method (1 Sam. 3:4–18), God established very clear communication with him and later through him to His people (3:19–4:1).

As we follow this "Samuel pattern," we too will develop an "ear to hear" what the Spirit is saying to us and to the churches: "He that hath an ear, let him hear what the Spirit saith unto the churches" (Rev. 3:22). Once established, this open, unerring communication with heaven makes us *prophetic*, or able to hear God's voice accurately, as the prophets did, and, having obeyed it, pass it on to God's people. This sure discernment of God's voice makes us very valuable, like faith-saving spiritual refuges for confused, shaken Christians who aren't yet able to clearly hear God's voice for themselves.

Sanctification

Offering thanks regularly releases a methodic deep-cleaning work of the Holy Spirit in our lives: "In everything give thanks...and the very God of peace sanctify you wholly...your whole spirit and soul and body...preserved blameless unto the coming of our Lord Jesus Christ" (1 Thess. 5:18, 23).

As we persist in offering thanks, the Spirit persists in cleansing our inner and outer life. Increasingly, He will show us how to, and graciously help us, change our thinking, speech, actions, and reactions to please Him. Thus we will grow in true holiness—the loving pureness of Jesus. And as we become more "sanctified, and fit for the master's use, and prepared unto every good work" (2 Tim. 2:21), He will use us more. "Separate me Barnabas and Saul for the work unto which I have called them" (Acts 13:2).

Visitation

In the fullest sense possible in this life, the glory of God will rest on our bodily tabernacle.

No, our bodily presence will not be shadowed by a cloud, fire, or even halo visible to others. But in some way, we will be very much aware that God is with us wherever we go. God's precious promise to Joshua will become our precious possession: "The LORD thy God is with thee wherever thou goest" (Josh. 1:9). Such a rare, sustained presence cannot go forever unnoticed.

Consequently, like the rising of the sun, the light of Christ's truth, grace, strength, and beauty will shine ever brighter through us in ways unnoticed by us but unmistakable to others. The result? They will be drawn to the light.

Life-changing inquiries will arise: "Sir, we would see Jesus" (John 12:21). "Sirs, what must I do to be saved?" (Acts 16:30). Then life-changing instructions: "Believe on the Lord Jesus Christ..." (v. 31). Then life-changing experiences: "And they spoke unto him the word of the Lord, and to all that were in his house...and [he] was baptized, he and all his" (vv. 32–33). Why?

The glory resting on our tabernacle is now visiting others through our tabernacle.

Confirmation

As time passes, this ongoing visitation in our bodily tabernacles will confirm to us as never before that the Almighty is not only with us but has also established us to do His will: "And David perceived that the LORD had established him..." (2 Sam. 5:12).

This growing verification gives us an undefeatable knowing, a rock-solid confidence that can't be broken by life's worst adversities: "Because [I know] he is at my right hand, I shall not be moved" (Ps. 16:8). Though spiritual winds, rains of discouragement, and floods of trouble beat vehemently against our souls, we will stand firmly in our faith and places of service with thanksgiving on our lips, glory on our tabernacles, and hope in our hearts—until the Lamb appears to take us to His heavenly tabernacle.

So rejoice in this fact: *if the continual burnt offering brought God down upon the Israelites, the sacrifice of praise will do the same for us today!* And if enough of us practice it, it will bring down God's glory upon our homes, churches, and ministries. Then, as a mighty river of supernatural life, the glory will overflow into our cities and nations and to the ends of the earth. And people everywhere will respond to its (His) reviving touch: "And every thing shall live where the river cometh" (Ezek. 47:9). So let me ask you a question.

Do you want glory on *your* tabernacle? It's yours for the taking, if you will just pay this small price: "the fruit of our lips giving thanks to His name." Begin paying it today!

I will offer to thee the sacrifice of thanksgiving…
—PSALM 116:17

Would you like a book specially designed to help you form the habit of thanking God at all times? I know just the one you need.

Chapter Fifteen

MAY I RECOMMEND THE PSALMS?

For it is written in the book of Psalms...

—ACTS 1:20

*M*ost Christians have heard that the Bible is the all-time, best-selling book in print.

Not all, however, are aware that within its sixty-six-book library of inspired literature, one book stands out as *the* most comforting, prayer-ready, and praise- and worship-inspiring of all. That sacred scroll is the Book of Psalms—a multi-authored, five-part collection of plaints, prayers, and praises used for over twenty-five hundred years as the highest hymnal, widest prayer book, and deepest solacer of innumerable Jews and Christians alike.

THE PURPOSE AND PLACE OF THE PSALMS

It is evident that the psalms are written to inspire the faithful to praise and worship. They are tailor-made, or more accurately divinely designed, for sacred music. All we have to do is add the key, melody, and chords to the psalmists' lyrics and we're off and flowing in worship: "Sing unto him, *sing psalms* unto him" (Ps. 105:2). The entire Book of Psalms seems to build to a grand crescendo of glorious praise to God. The last five psalms each begin with the urgent prompt, "Praise *ye* the Lord," as if urging the reader to rise and praise Jehovah along with the psalmists. The last, Psalm 150, urges all creation to rise and form one stupendously large orchestra and chorus worshiping God in His temple courts—every creature, every person, and every instrument spontaneously erupting in soaring sacred song:

> Praise ye the LORD. Praise God in his sanctuary; praise him in the firmament of his power. Praise him for his mighty acts; praise him according to his excellent greatness. Praise him with the sound of the trumpet; praise him with the psaltery and harp. Praise him with the timbrel and dance; praise him with stringed instruments and flutes. Praise him upon the loud cymbals; praise him upon the high sounding cymbals. *Let everything that hath breath praise the Lord.* Praise ye the LORD.
>
> —PSALM 150:1–6

One popular study Bible cites the last verse—"Let everything that breathes sing praises to the LORD!" (NLT)—as the keynote to the entire Book of Psalms.[1]

Taking these scriptural prompts literally, the Scottish reformers threw off the intricate music of the Medieval high mass and took up the singing of psalms in their greatly simplified reformed worship services.[2] Many other reformers also sang psalms, as they reveled in their newly liberated congregational worship. While for centuries Protestant sacred music has been dominated largely by hymnals and hymnists—Charles Wesley alone penned the lyrics to over six thousand hymns—in the latter years of the twentieth century, many worship leaders and Christian musicians turned afresh to using psalms in their congregational worship or recordings. Some refer to themselves as "psalmists." Psalms are still sung in many churches and fellowships today. Surely such praise and worship is one chief reason God breathed the Psalter into existence through David and other inspired writers.

Another is prayer. A strong case could be made that the psalms were written as much for prayer as for praise and worship. Realizing this, about A.D. 540 Benedict of Nursia made the praying of the psalms an integral part of the "divine office" (or "God's work") he ordered his monks to observe daily during the Middle Ages. According to Benedict's "rule," or plan for orderly, fully dedicated Christian living, the "divine office" required his monks to gather for group devotional exercises at eight different hours during the twenty-four-hour day. Once gathered, they, among other acts of devotion or worship (singing, readings, homilies), prayed psalms to the Lord. Benedict assigned different psalms for different days' "office" so that by the end of every week all one hundred fifty psalms were prayed.[3] Thus solemnly charged, his monks had to memorize all one hundred fifty psalms! What a lesson and challenge to us today!

We do well to follow the spirit of the monks' commitment by uttering to God as our own those psalmic prayers that express our present problems, needs, fears, griefs, or joys.

This brings us to the third great purpose for the Psalms, which we want to expound more fully in this chapter—to comfort tried souls.

When those who would live righteously are forced to live temporarily in a world that is stubbornly, impenitently, and sometimes demonically unrighteous, they invariably experience troublemakers, trials, and tribulations—and in these last days, terrorists! The Scriptures repeatedly affirm this: "Yea, and all that will live godly in Christ Jesus shall suffer persecution" (2 Tim. 3:12). And again, "Though now, for a season...ye are in heaviness through manifold trials" (1 Pet. 1:6). To endure the unsettling and sometimes deconstructive adversities of life, we need steady doses of the calming, reconstructive consolations of God. The Psalms provide us with this powerful "soul medicine." In the next world, the leaves of the tree of life will heal injured bodies; in this one, the words of the psalms mend wounded, hurting souls.

Specifically, the Psalter affords us *comfort through inspired identification and expression.* As we prayerfully and meditatively read the Psalms, the Holy Spirit, the divine Comforter, causes us to notice similarities between the situations the psalmists describe and those we face. Their troubles are different and distant from our confusing circumstantial crucibles, but the parallels are clear, many, and meaningful. As a result, we identify with the psalmists and feel they speak to us and, in a sense, for us.

With amazing sensitivity they accurately and fully express our innermost feelings, such as perplexity, need, fear, frustration, despair, trust, hope, relief, jubilation, and thankful adoration of God. When we confess their words, speaking them slowly and thoughtfully to ourselves before God (again, as Medieval Benedictine monks practiced *lectio divinia*, or "godly reading," by slowly pondering and pronouncing every verse[4]), our souls, whether weary or jubilant, find perfect expression and powerful release. Instantly, emotional relief and spiritual refreshment visit and liberate us. Our spiritual shackles of fear and anger drop off, and we are refilled and reinvigorated by the Holy Spirit. The apostle Paul urges us, "Be filled with the Spirit, [by] *speaking to yourselves in psalms...*" (Eph. 5:18–19). This resurgence of the "sap" of the heavenly Vine promptly restores the key fruits of faith and hope on our personal "branches." Then we go forth to a peaceful, loving, fruitful day's walk and work, thanks to the Spirit's ministry through the psalms.

Furthermore, the psalms strengthen us with a reassuring sense of companionship. Going through difficult experiences with sympathetic companions is always easier than going it alone. As few as six, and perhaps as many as fifty-five, sacred writers penned the one hundred fifty songs and prayers in the Book of Psalms. (There are six known authors—David, Asaph, Solomon, Moses, Ethan, and the sons of Korah—plus forty-nine anonymously authored "orphan" psalms, each potentially with its own separate writer.) As we read the record of their struggles and ultimate victories, two realizations grip us: (1) these godly believers have "been there, done that" before us; and (2) the God who helped them through their trials will help us through ours. So no matter how lonely we feel, we realize that, actually, we're not alone at all. God's victorious Spirit is with and within us on earth, and a band of overcoming brothers, the troop of biblical psalmists, are cheering us on from heaven: "Seeing we also are compassed about with so great a cloud of witnesses" (Heb. 12:1). Just as athletes draw energy from their roaring fans, so overcomers draw strength from the empathetic psalmists who have gone before them. When about to drop the ball or faint in the final stages of our grueling contests of endurance, we hear them roaring to us from heaven's grandstands:

I [too] had [almost] fainted, unless I had believed to see the goodness of the LORD in the land of the living. Wait on the LORD; be of good courage, and he shall strengthen your heart.

Wait, I say, on the LORD.

—PSALM 27:13–14

Have you listened to the messages from your "fan base" today?

Why is this ministry of comfort through inspired identification and expression necessary? Why aren't our personal, spontaneously generated expressions to God in prayer enough to fully relieve our burdened souls?

Two reasons stand out.

First, we don't always face our true feelings. We tend to ignore our unpleasant feelings and soul burdens. As a result, many of us are not fully conscious of our true core feelings and thoughts. Then, when others ask us of them, we deny them—and remain bound in the darkness of falsehood. Why? Only "the truth," and nothing less, "shall make you free" (John 8:32).

Second, we lack fully developed communication skills. Most of us are unable to translate all the emotional and mental impulses that throb within us into clear descriptions and accurate messages. We mumble and stumble and bumble, and the words just don't seem to come out right. What we say or write falls short of what we really think or feel.

Enter the ready writers of the psalms—and now even the simplest, most stoical, or most rhetorically ungifted believer can find the words— beautiful, inspired, perfectly accurate words—that fully express the pathos of his soul and motivate him to rise above his adversities, however difficult, painful, or perplexing.

One Bible commentator states:

> In the course of dealing with the adversities of life, people are often frustrated by not being able to express adequately their emotional pain or mental anguish. The Psalms release us from that frustration. With emotionally drenched complaints, humble confessions, desperate pleas, penitent prayers, or screams of pain, the writers of the Psalms skillfully expose and express the yearnings of our deepest thoughts. This use of the Psalms is often the first step toward our own deliverance…they [the Psalms] comfort the lonely, strengthen the weary, bind the brokenhearted,

and turn the eyes of the downcast up toward their Creator. Hope returns, faith is renewed, and life again becomes bearable.[5]

Another observes:

This is the book to which the soul naturally turns for its devotional needs.... In the Psalms we find ourselves mirrored, because we recognize in the words of the inspired writers our own deepest desires, our own searching after God, and our own spiritual longings that only God can satisfy...[6]

So perhaps the most practical purpose of the Book of Psalms is to comfort us, and thus see us through all of life's many trials. The Psalms' proper place, therefore, is *near us*. That is, we should keep this book close at hand day and night.

A REVELATION OF ADVERSITY—AND ADVERSARIES

Besides being an extraordinary hymnbook, prayer book, and personal comforter, the Book of Psalms is also an educative revelation. It informs spiritually naïve Christians that adversaries and adversities are part and parcel of the true Christian walk. Or, in the words later penned by Paul, "For you have been given not only the privilege of trusting in Christ but also the privilege of suffering for him" (Phil. 1:29, NLT).

By my own humble count, the psalmists refer directly to their "enemy" or "enemies" approximately eighty-five times in one hundred fifty psalms and refer to them indirectly even more frequently. Thus they testify that certain individuals were committed to making life miserable for them. They also clearly and repeatedly refer to the many conflicts these troublemakers made. Though to a person the psalmists were Jews, and not Christians, the troubles they describe parallel our Christian trials. Why? Jews of the Old Testament era and church-age Christians share a common calling: both are redeemed people struggling to know God and do His will in an unredeemed and spiritually hostile world. By inspiring David and his fellow psalmists to write so frequently of their "enemies," God is trying to send us a message. It reads something like this:

If you walk with Me faithfully, as David and the other psalmists did, you too will have enemies one day. When that day comes, this book will help you survive and overcome your conflicts, and soar to new heights in your walk and work with Me.

I remember well when this first hit me. After turning to the Lord in my college days, I began searching and devouring the Word of God. When meditating in the Book of Psalms, I wondered, Why did David and the other inspired poets write so frequently of their enemies? Who were these "evildoers," "wicked" ones, and "workers of iniquity"? I was happily saved and filled with the Spirit, but I didn't have any personal enemies. The burden of my sin was gone, and the blessing of the Lord made my formerly confused and uncertain life simple, productive, and full of flowing joy and sure hope. I knew nothing of perplexing trials, offensive injustices, oppressive burdens, and relentless, mean-spirited slanderers. Looking back, I now know the reason for that early trouble-free time: I was a babe in Christ enjoying my blissful, protected spiritual infancy. Mercifully, and fittingly, the good Lord was temporarily withholding strong trials until the words and ways of God I was learning had time to take root in my soul.

Sometime during this period, however, based largely on the testimony of the Psalms, my wondering heart concluded that if I went the way David went, one day I would face my own devilish detractors. So I went on perusing God's Word, growing in His grace, and studying music education at Appalachian State University in Boone, North Carolina.

A few years later, in God's time, the reality of David's words visited my personal life and I began experiencing the difficulties he so eloquently expounded. Then a new dependency on, and affection for, the Psalms was born in my soul. I've lived and loved them ever since.

A REMEDY FOR ALL ILLS

In late nineteenth- and early twentieth-century America, it was not uncommon for traveling merchants to peddle "miracle tonics." These bottled wonder fluids, sold to legions of gullible sufferers, were sure to heal everything from aching feet to serious internal illnesses. Or so their audacious labels and salesmen loudly claimed. Over time these cure-alls proved to be cure-nothings. So, having been tried and found false, these peddlers and their dubious panaceas gradually went the way of all the earth.

Unlike these bogus medics and medicines, the Psalms perform precisely as advertised. No matter what kind of adversity you may be in, from minor irritations to major offenses, they deliver! And when taken in steady doses, they never fail to stop every pain, heal every wound, calm every upset, and reinvigorate every exhausted soul with spiritual pep. This is no academic estimate; I know this to be true experientially.

For years now, when ailing from the distresses of my Christian trials, I have drunk deep from the psalmists' bottle of miracle tonic. And time and again I have found it to contain much more than sugar water and water coloring. To the contrary, I've found every drink full of pure supernatural life, inexhaustible strength, and abounding grace. Evidence of my secret dependency on this Psalm-tonic surfaced a few years ago.

When the leather binding on my primary study Bible began falling apart due to age and use, desperate measures were needed. I loved that Bible and didn't want to part with the innumerable annotations I had inscribed in its margins over the years. So off to the book rebinder I went, worn Bible in hand. At the bindery, an expert examined my Bible and gave me some tips for further preservation. It was then I noticed that by far the most heavily worn pages in my Holy Writ were the Psalms. In the other books the pages still retained their white color, but there the pages were incriminatingly yellow. Here was solid evidence, admissible in any court, that, more than on any others, these were the pages upon which my hands had rested during many a prayerful morning reading or workday study session.

Convicted without a jury of my peers, I made my confession to the Judge of the quick and the dead: "Lord, I'm guilty as charged: I *love* the Psalms!" And I still do. Never do I begin a day without reading in the Psalms, and I've often done the same in the evening. (But I don't rest my hands on the pages any more!)

AN ABBREVIATED DIRECTORY OF PSALMS

Before the advent of Internet Web sites, search engines, and e-mails, the telephone directory yellow pages were the best device for getting in touch with the right person in the least time. They are still very useful. When in need of specific supplies, skills, or services, we may simply reach for the telephone directory, search the yellow pages, and dial. Soon we're in touch with our desired source and our need or problem is no more. We should employ this same simple method in times of spiritual need.

When hard pressed by troubles and troublemakers, we should get before the Lord and ask Him to do two things: (1) to lead us to the psalm that best fits our present spiritual needs; and (2) to help us understand what He is saying to us in that psalm or through its biblical chain references.

To assist you in this search of your biblical "yellow pages," here is an abbreviated directory of selected psalms that fit specific needs, conditions, or topics:

- Anger at evildoers—Psalm 37
- About fools—Psalms 14, 53
- About promotion—Psalms 75, 113
- Blessings on faithful givers—Psalm 41
- Blessings on the God-fearing—Psalms 112, 128
- Convicted of sin—Psalms 51, 32
- Deliverance from fear—Psalm 34
- Discouraged—Psalm 138
- Don't harden your heart! —Psalm 95
- Envious of sinners—Psalm 73
- God's omniscience—Psalm 139
- God's personalized help—Psalm 146
- God's worldwide sovereignty—Psalms 24, 47
- Hope for family and future—Psalm 115
- Hope for more Spirit and growth—Psalm 92
- Hope for restoration—Psalms 80, 147
- Injustice—Psalm 9

- Intimidated—Psalm 27
- In calamity—Psalm 46
- In danger—Psalm 91
- In doubt—Psalms 42, 43
- In reproach—Psalms 69, 79, 109
- In triumph—Psalms 124, 126
- Justice assured—Psalms 7, 50, 64, 96
- Longing for God—Psalm 63
- Low and lonely—Psalm 88
- Needing strength and a sign—Psalm 86
- On God's ways and works—Psalms 104–107
- On God's Word—Psalms 1, 19, 119
- On the morning watch—Psalm 5
- Overwhelmed—Psalms 56, 57, 61, 142, 143
- Praise for answered prayer—Psalms 21, 116
- Praise for deliverance—Psalms 18, 30
- Praying for guidance—Psalm 25
- Resting amid distress—Psalm 4
- Surrounded by enemies—Psalm 3
- The power of praise—Psalms 8, 29, 149
- Thankful to draw near—Psalm 65
- Thankful for humble duty—Psalm 84
- Thankful for mercy—Psalm 136
- Vows for holy living—Psalms 26, 101
- Waiting for God—Psalms 27, 40, 62
- Weak and weary—Psalms 6, 71, 77
- Worshipful—Psalms 100, 148, 150

For decades, twentieth-century American consumers heeded the slogan, "Let your fingers do the walking" (through the yellow pages), and they usually found help quicker by phone than by foot. Why shouldn't twenty-first-century Christians, Internet-wise though we are, practice this same proven principle? Every day, and in every dilemma, let's open the Book of Psalms, pray, and search for timely, golden truths as the Spirit leads—and let God do the talking!

One Bible expositor's summation of the importance of the Book of Psalms serves as a fitting postscript to this chapter. He says simply:

There is no other book like it in all literature.[7]

Need I, need anyone, say more? Have you read a psalm today? Besides blessing you, it will also prepare you to meet and master injustice.

Chapter Sixteen

THE LORD WILL PAY YOU BACK

And the man of God answered, The LORD is able to give thee much more than this [you have lost].

—2 CHRONICLES 25:9

Very small situations sometimes teach us very large truths about our Lord. Let me share one such experience that caused me to more fully know Him. It happened many years ago.

A TEST OF TIRES

"Do you know when you'll be finished with my minivan, sir?" I asked the manager of a local tire store where my Dodge Caravan was being fitted with new tires. "We'll have you ready in just a few minutes," he responded, adding, "As soon as I finish the paper work, you'll be on your way." I turned and went to the front of the store to wait, walking slowly through the tire display area, quietly pondering what I had just witnessed and inwardly praising God for His help. Let me explain.

Two years earlier, almost to the very day, I had also needed a set of tires for the same minivan. Scheduled to leave that day for a retreat, I had visited another tire store, one where I had purchased and serviced my tires for the previous seventeen years. They had always offered excellent products and services for acceptable prices. But this time, things would be different.

After my new tires were installed and the wheels aligned, I paid the manager and drove off. The minute I left the parking lot, I felt a distinct

179

vibration on the steering wheel at both low and high rates of speed. (I later learned that this vibration, which was not present while my old tires were in use, indicated that I now had either a bent rim on one of my wheels, a bad tire, or a tire that was sufficiently "out-of-round" to need replacing.) When I returned to my office, I called the store, reported the problem, and set an appointment to have the matter corrected after the retreat.

After the retreat, I returned to the tire dealer. After examining, rebalancing, and test-driving my new tires, the manager said everything was now fine. So, again, I drove off, thinking all was well. But all was not well. Not five minutes off the lot, I noticed that the vibration was virtually unchanged, and at highway speeds it was very pronounced. So back to the dealer I went, explaining that the problem was still there. The manager, a young man obviously new to the business and the public, responded that there was nothing more he could do, unless, of course, I wanted to buy yet another set of tires. I then realized that this was a golden opportunity to practice the biblical truth I preach.

Specifically, this would be a "count it all joy" day:

My brethren, *count it all joy* when ye fall into various trials, knowing this, that the testing of your faith worketh patience. But let patience have her perfect work, that ye may be perfect and entire, lacking nothing.

—JAMES 1:2–4

So, by grace, I did just that. As I left the tire store, I first gave thanks to the Lord while still "in" this test: "*In* everything give thanks; for this is the will of God in Christ Jesus concerning you" (1 Thess. 5:18). I then asked the Lord for wisdom and help, thanked Him for answering, and decided for the time to "let patience have her perfect work." The next day I asked a second opinion from another tire dealer. Maybe their professional opinion would diffuse the problem. Perhaps my trust in or love of the almighty dollar (or partial Scottish heritage) was for the moment getting the best of me, but I just didn't want to pay good money for bad tires!

After examining the new tires and rims, the second tire dealer confirmed that two of the tires were "out-of-round" and kindly put this in writing. So, with renewed hope and hard facts in hand, I returned to the dealer who sold me the tires. Surely this would terminate my trial of tires. But my heavenly Examiner had another surprise.

The manager wouldn't budge. I was patient and gracious, but he simply was *not* going to replace those tires, second opinion or no second opinion, satisfied customer or no satisfied customer. I will admit, in this day when the customer can do no wrong, I was taken aback by this young man's attitude. And the raw unfairness of the situation—having paid for a defective product—angered me. But very quickly the Spirit made me sense that this was a test, not merely of patience, as I previously thought, but of injustice. So I dutifully reported the day's events to my heavenly Father in prayer and prayerfully considered my options.

Like the years of Jacob, they seemed "few and evil":

- Take the (non-Christian) tire dealer to small claims court, make a fuss, and dishonor the Lord for a few measly dollars
- Pay to replace the two new but defective tires
- Choose to "resist not evil [injustice, adversity]" (Matt. 5:39), but simply use the tires—and vibration—as they were

Here was a small but sure dilemma. The first option was out of the question. I'm a poor debater. The second was the most reasonable, but still unfair. Why should I have to pay more when I had already paid for a set of tires? The third option, though scriptural, went against my natural desire to *do* something to rectify the obvious injustice of the situation. So I prayerfully pondered what to do next.

Then the divine Teacher (Holy Spirit) gave this diminutive instructor a word of pure gold.

THE TEACHER SPEAKS

Quietly but distinctly, the Spirit reminded me that just a few weeks earlier a brother in our fellowship, whom we shall call "James," had a trial of financial injustice.

James is a gifted draftsman with years of experience in drawing both commercial and residential structures. After completing a set of plans for a woman's proposed new home, he presented her with her blueprints and his bill (several hundred dollars). But instead of receiving a prompt payment, he received a puzzling telephone call from her a few days later, informing him that because she had decided not to build at this time she wouldn't be paying for her plans. Well, not building was her option, but not paying for her construction plans wasn't her option. It was her obligation. She had ordered the plans, reviewed and requested changes in the preliminary drawings, and approved the final draft. James had in good faith invested labor, time, and expense in the project. For services rendered, therefore, he was due his pay, and he politely told her so. But this lady, bless her heart, thought otherwise. So James' bill went unpaid. Her brazenness surprised him. He had never had a client flatly refuse to pay a bill.

Within hours James telephoned to tell me of his offensive encounter. After reflection, we both realized this was no accident. If Christians walk in faith and obedience, the enemy can have "no power at all against [us]," unless it is "given…from above [God]" (John 19:11). Nor was it a chastisement for disobedience. Having pastored him for years, I knew James was a man of faith, obedience, and integrity, besides being a committed tither and extraordinary donor. No, this was neither an accident nor a punishment but a test. So privately I asked the Lord to give me wisdom and counsel for James. What could I say to comfort and strengthen my puzzled brother?

Sometime later the Lord brought this scripture clearly to mind:

> The Lord is able to give thee much more than this.
> —2 Chronicles 25:9

After examining the biblical context, I realized that this word was perfect for James' trial.

In 2 Chronicles 25:5–10, the children of Judah were preparing for battle with the Edomites when a man of God advised King Amaziah to cancel his plans to hire Israelite mercenaries. Unlike the more righteous Judeans (southern kingdom), the Israelites (northern tribes) were practicing idolaters. This was very offensive to the Lord. If these unholy soldiers fought beside the Judeans, the Holy One would withdraw His supernatural aid from Judah and they would lose the battle. To please the Lord, therefore, and assure victory, the Israelite warriors had to be sent away (vv. 7–8). This would almost certainly mean offending them and also losing the mercenary fee Amaziah had already paid them (v. 6). Pained by this thought, Amaziah blurted out, "But what shall we do for the hundred talents which I have given to the army of Israel?" (v. 9). The prophet then assured him that the Lord—who owns all the earth's resources (Ps. 24:1) and can make all grace abound toward us at any time (2 Cor. 9:8) and can do "exceedingly abundantly above all that we ask or think" (Eph. 3:20)—would more than make it up to him: "The LORD can give you *much more* than that" (2 Chron. 25:9, NIV). But obedience was required. Amaziah had to send the Israelite mercenaries home.

Grateful for precise guidance, I passed this word on to James, advising him to just let the matter drop and trust the Lord to restore his financial loss. Submissively and wisely, he obeyed this biblical counsel. The Lord's response was quick and clear.

That same week three individuals called James requesting new building plans. Their business alone far exceeded the income he had lost! Elated, he telephoned me with the good news, and we gave thanks and rejoiced. He later shared this testimony with our fellowship. We all thought, "What a faithful God!" Suddenly we didn't fear financial injustice any more; our Provider was greater than any thief! What a wonderful conclusion to James' unexpected foray into the land of unfairness! But we were wrong. The Lord wasn't finished yet.

A few months later, James received a telephone call from a local building contractor, who is also a Christian, informing him that the lady who had refused to pay James had now hired him to build her new home. At his insistence, she agreed to pay James for her house plans! Again, he shared the good news with our fellowship, and again, we rejoiced! Truly almighty, our God not only repays all our losses but also bends our enemies' wills! He put this stubborn woman in a position in which, to be on good terms with her Christian contractor, she had to pay James for his services. Praise Him! God can overreach any injustice and overrule any offender—if we, His children, will just trust and obey His voice: "When a man's ways please the LORD, he maketh even his enemies be at peace with him" (Prov. 16:7).

So the Teacher reminded me, and so I pondered.

INSPIRED BY THE TEACHER'S WISDOM

Inspired by the Teacher's wisdom and faithfulness in action, I chose simply to follow James' example in my test of tires. Why argue with confirmed success in God?

Taking 2 Chronicles 25:9 as *my* word, I committed the entire matter to God, trusting that, in His own time and way, He would give me "much more" than what I had lost. I also took consolation in knowing that my somewhat bumpy tires would at least serve the basic purpose of transportation for the time being. God's grace was sufficient, and I soon completely forgot about the whole matter. For the next two years I learned to enjoy driving with a vibrating steering wheel. Then the time came for another set of tires.

Ironically, but not accidentally, I was again preparing for a trip when I realized I needed new tires. So I called a newly opened tire store to decide which tires and prices best fit my needs. The tires the manager offered me were durable and affordable—and on sale! So I advised him I would come in later that morning to get the work done.

Meanwhile I returned to my work, calling a woman in our fellowship, whom we'll call "Lynn," who needed pastoral counsel that morning. Like James, Lynn is a committed disciple with a long record of exceptional stewardship. During the conversation she asked when I would be leaving for my trip. "As soon as my tires are installed," I said. Promptly, and unaware of my tire troubles two years earlier, she offered to pay for my tires. Just as promptly, I "freely received" her generosity and, after the conversation, fully thanked the Lord for kindly "[making] all grace abound" to me (2 Cor. 9:8). And I asked Him to bless and recompense Lynn, which He faithfully did.

When I arrived at the tire store, I noticed the manager was very eager to help me. He told me there was a rebate on the tires I had chosen. I wouldn't have thought to ask for this on a sale-priced item. When asked, he agreed to buy two of my old tires, which had resale value for their remaining tread. Together, these price breaks reduced my total price (and

Lynn's gift) considerably. Besides this, the service I received was outstanding. Aware that I hoped to leave for my trip as soon as possible, and that his technicians had stopped to lunch before finishing my installation, the manager finished the job himself on their (and his) lunch hour, just so I wouldn't be late. Not done yet, he also filled out my rebate application, addressed it, and affixed postage. All I had to do was drop it in the mail as I left town! I was really impressed, and humbled, by this royal treatment.

Then it hit me: how different it was two years ago! Then my "cup" was not the royal but the rude treatment—the bad tires, the vexing vibration, the manager's stubborn attitude, my unsuccessful appeal for fairness, James' example, the voice of God's Word, and my simple trust in and obedience to His voice. Everything happening now—the sale-priced tires, the rebate, the credit for my used tires, Lynn's generosity, the manager's super attitude, the extraordinary service—was no coincidence. It was providence—God's gracious and faithful response to my obedience through seemingly ordinary events. There was a direct, divine link between this triumph and my earlier trouble. I being in the way, *the Lord led me* to this exact time and place to show me the "much more" He had promised.

These were my thoughts as I stood in the front of the tire store, waiting for the manager to finish my paper work. Quietly, I offered a sacrifice of praise on the altar of my lips: "Thank You, Lord. Bless You. Praise You." And soon the peace of God settled down heavily on the tabernacle of my soul. I didn't know it, but one more blessing awaited me.

As I drove away, it came to me: I didn't feel any more vibration. Unlike their imperfect predecessors, these tires were perfect.

~

You may wonder why I share these testimonies when the financial losses and recompenses were so small—hundreds of dollars, not thousands or millions. Here are three reasons.

First, small trials are most often those that stumble us. Wise King Solomon noted the power of little frustrations to spoil large fruitfulness: "...the foxes, the little foxes, that spoil the vines" (Song of Sol. 2:15). Second, small victories can make Jesus very real, very near, and very precious to us. There is something about seeing His hand in mundane moments that awakens the thought, "Surely the LORD is in this place; and I knew it not" (Gen. 28:16). Third, small triumphs convince us that the principles of God's Word are true under any conditions and will therefore deliver us in the larger trials of life. (The Lord has since fulfilled the principle of 2 Chronicles 25:9 for me in *much larger* financial trials involving *thousands* of dollars!) When confronted by the dreadful giant Goliath and his fearsome well-armed Philistine warriors, David simply obeyed the same biblical principles he learned in his earlier, smaller confrontations with a lion and a bear. The result was a huge victory. What will you do in your day of injustice?

Don't make the mistake of thinking *you* will never be treated unfairly in this unfair world. It's not a matter of if, but of when, where, and how much injustice will come your way. Jesus hinted that, at the very least, we would have our shirt stolen someday: "If you are sued in court and your shirt is taken from you, give your coat, too" (Matt. 5:40, NLT). Paul testified that he had suffered thievery: "…in perils of robbers" (2 Cor. 11:26). Who are we to think ourselves exempt from trials of injustice?

Have you been cheated out of anything lately? After reasonable inquiry and follow-up, and sufficient prayer for God's guidance, has it become clear to you that you are dealing with either an unreasonable or dishonest person? If you cannot recover your loss without ruining your peace, why not take the high road? Why not trust God—your immensely wealthy heavenly Father—to faithfully perform this Word in your life?

The LORD is able to give thee much more than this.
—2 CHRONICLES 25:9

Indeed, He is *able,* for His heavenly and earthly resources are inexhaustible: "My God shall supply all your need according to His riches in glory" (Phil. 4:19). "The earth is the LORD's and the fullness thereof; the world, and they that dwell therein" (Ps. 24:1).

Indeed, He will *give* to you, meaning easily bring to you, quietly arrange for you, or unexpectedly drop into your life-basket all you need as you need it, without stress, strain, or strife. "The blessing of the LORD brings wealth, and he adds no trouble to it" (Prov. 10:22, NIV).

Indeed, His recompense will be *much more than this*. He will restore not merely what you lost, but considerably more in quantity and quality.

And best of all, as you continue trusting God and seeing His unfailing provision, you will grow spiritually rich, rich in faith and truth. You will become an overcomer exceptionally blessed, not with abundant stores of metallic gold but with tons of spiritual gold—priceless confidence in and proven knowledge of God—not temporally but eternally wealthy! Jesus is calling you to become spiritually rich in these last days: "I counsel thee to buy of me gold tried in the fire, that thou mayest be [truly, spiritually, eternally] rich [in confidence in God]" (Rev. 3:18)! Answer His call!

And remember, as with King Amaziah, your obedience is the key to this rich blessing. So don't fall into the trap of resisting injustice.

Neither design nor desire revenge. That solemn duty is God's: "Recompense to no man evil for evil…avenge not yourselves, but, rather, give place unto [leave room for God's] wrath; for it is written; Vengeance is mine; I will repay, saith the Lord" (Rom. 12:17, 19). So don't threaten or harry those who wrong you. Don't waste your time, peace, or health recovering mere rights and dollars.

Instead be spiritually minded. Meditate on Jesus' teaching: "I say unto you that ye *resist not evil [injustice]*" (Matt. 5:39). See your unfair treatment from God's viewpoint. It's not Satan's destructive plot, it's God's developmental plan: "In every thing [situation] give thanks; for *this [situation] is the will of God in Christ Jesus concerning you*" (1 Thess. 5:18). "For *this thing is from me*" (1 Kings 12:24). Your opposition is really your opportunity, a chance to prove your submission to God and trust in His Word. So don't blindly fight your circumstances. Follow God through them, day by day, step by step, until you reach the good end He has planned, and the spiritual gold He has reserved, for you.

Have faith: the Lord will pay you back! That's good news—and cause for worship!

Chapter Seventeen

ON LEADING WORSHIP

And Ezra blessed the Lord . . . and all the people
answered . . . and . . . worshiped the Lord.
—Nehemiah 8:6

idway through the twentieth century, A. W. Tozer concluded, "Our religious mood is social instead of spiritual. We have lost the art of worship"[1] He was correct then and he is correct today. With all our renewed emphasis on worship over the last decades, surprisingly, mere religious entertainment or staid rituals still pass for real worship in too many churches. We still need, as Tozer urged us, to regain the "lost art of worship." Why?

The reason is simple: God the Father greatly desires our worship! Jesus taught, "The Father *seeketh* such [true worshipers] to worship him" (John 4:23). Jesus' use of the word *seeketh* reveals that the heavenly Father is actively, eagerly, and constantly searching for, as He put it, "true worshipers." True worshipers worship God not as they please but as He pleases, and Jesus specified that the Father seeks us to worship Him "in spirit and in truth" (v. 23). If our congregations are to please Him who seeks to be worshiped "in spirit and in truth" and who indwells the praises of His people, we must offer Him much more than religious entertainment. Nothing less than real worship will satisfy Him.

How, then, should we worship? And how should we lead others in worship? Here are some helpful thoughts for worship leaders, praise teams, and any Christian who wants to worship God acceptably, privately or publicly.

HELPFUL THOUGHTS ON WORSHIP

The purpose of worship

We must understand the purpose of worship. Worship has one great primary goal: to please God! The blessing worshipers receive is a by-product of worship, never its central objective. While God delights to bless those who worship Him, true worshipers focus on filling His nostrils with the gratifyingly "sweet smell" of worship, blessing His heart, and permeating His being with joy. Worship leaders must frequently remember this basic truth—and never turn aside to seek their own pleasure or praise in worship.

If a worship leader, or any worshiper, craves pleasant feelings during worship, he (or she) stops giving unto the Lord and becomes a self-centered spiritual sponge. Designed to turn us from this "give me" to a "give to God" mind-set, Psalm 29 urges worshipers *four* times in its first two verses to focus on giving loving adoration to God:

> *Give unto the* LORD, O ye mighty, *give unto the* LORD glory and strength. *Give unto the* LORD the glory due unto His name; *worship the* LORD in the beauty of holiness.
> —PSALM 29:1–2

This inspired insistence to "give … give … give … worship the Lord" is the theme of true worshipers. They fix on it every time they draw near to bless God's heart. Ironically, this giving attitude causes them to receive. Why?

Honoring Jesus' principle of giving ("Give, and it shall be given unto you," Luke 6:38), the heavenly Father commits Himself to give sensations of His loving approval to those who commit themselves to give Him expressions of their loving adoration. (Though we should worship as we live—*by faith*, Jesus also kindly promised to "manifest" His presence and love to those who truly love Him, John 14:21.) Specifically, Psalm 29 promises that He will give true worshipers "strength" and "peace" either during or after their offering:

> The Lord will give *strength* unto his [giving, worshiping] peo-
> ple; the Lord will bless his people with *peace.*
>
> —Psalm 29:11

Thus, paradoxically, those who are set on *giving* to God get His blessing, while those who are set on *getting* from Him get nothing.

Also, when a worship leader turns and begins thinking as an enter-
tainer, he attracts attention unto himself—and away from the Lord! The
worshipers' adoration is diverted and the Lord is left deserted, robbed of
His due offering of praise, and unsatisfied. Thus the self-centered, religiously proud worship leader is really a thief. He or she steals the admira-
tion that belongs rightfully to God. Not only that, but he's also a promoter
of idolatry, one who knowingly puts false objects of adoration—himself!—
before God's people. And if he doesn't repent of this, he will eventually
bring God's punishment, not His praise, on himself.

Preparation for worship

Before we can pursue the purpose of worship, we must first prepare
for worship. And if we are to lead worship, we must also lead in preparation for worship.

A worship leader can't force others to prepare for worship, but he can,
and must, prepare himself. For that, he must ask honestly, "Am I walking
in sin or sanctification? Faith or fear? Truthfulness or hypocrisy? The flesh
or the Spirit?" Always, a worship leader's first responsibility is thorough
self-examination and self-preparation. The apostle John illustrates this.

An exemplary Christian leader and experienced worshiper, John practiced rigorous self-examination, not only in advantageous circumstances
but also in adverse. Very adverse! Despite being exiled and lonely on the
isle of Patmos, John prepared himself for worship every Sunday morning: "I was in the Spirit on the Lord's day" (Rev. 1:10). His words imply
he examined himself, confessed his sins, forsook wrong attitudes, and forgave his offenders. How do we know this? He could not have been "in the
Spirit" without doing so. Also, John repeatedly urged others to examine
themselves and warned of the dangers of not doing so: "If we walk in the
light as he is in the light...If we confess our sins, he is faithful and just to

forgive us…If we say we have not sinned…" (1 John 1:7, 9–10). "Watch yourselves, so that you may not lose what we have worked for, but may win a full reward" (2 John 8, ESV). Such consistent ministerial counsel implies that John himself was deeply rooted in self-examination—and a spiritually prepared church and worship leader.

Are we "in the Spirit on the Lord's day"? If not, we're worthless as a worshiper, and especially as a worship leader. Unconfessed sins of any kind (attitudes, words, actions, omissions) render us "out of the Spirit," or momentarily not under the Holy Spirit's influence. As such we are in an unspiritual (carnal) frame of mind, mood, and manner, thinking and acting as if we were not spiritually reborn, Spirit-baptized, and biblically taught. The apostle Paul rebuked the Corinthians for being out of the Spirit, or, as he put it, "carnal." "Ye are yet *carnal…and walk [think and live] as [unredeemed] men*" (1 Cor. 3:3). This "carnally minded" (Rom. 8:6) condition renders our worship unacceptable to God. We know this because Jesus insisted that His Father only receives worship offered "in spirit and in truth." Note His use of the imperative: "They that worship him [acceptably] *must* worship him in spirit and in truth" (John 4:24).

Worshiping God "in spirit and in truth" implies the following:

"In spirit"

- In the right attitude (adoring, reverential awe)
- From the heart, with sincere motives, with the right purpose
- In the presence, and by the prompting and help, of the Holy Spirit (without which no worship is acceptable to God)

"In truth"

- In honesty (truthfulness) before God and man
- In a state of knowing and obeying God's Word (truth)

Pondering these, Jesus' conditions for acceptable worship, leads us to another conclusion: to lead in worship, we must lead in obedience. Why? We can't walk simultaneously in our fleshly and spiritual natures, our "old man" and "new man." To worship "in spirit and in truth" as Jesus mandates, and to be "in the [Holy] Spirit" on Sunday as John illustrates, we must obey the Spirit and Word (truth) of God every day. And, as already stated, this includes regularly examining ourselves and humbly confessing and forsaking anything that displeases God.

So don't be spiritually lazy, worship leader! Don't depend on the Spirit-rich atmosphere created by self-examined worshipers to help you get right. Get yourself right! And before the worship, not during or after it! "Look closely at yourselves. Test yourselves to see if you are living in the faith" (2 Cor. 13:5, NCV); or, "Examine and test and evaluate your own selves to see whether you are holding to your faith and showing the proper fruits of it" (AMP). God's plan is for worship leaders to be more obedient than other worshipers, not less. He wants you so attuned to Him that through your praises He may fill your assembly with His powerful presence and touch and restore disobedient worshipers.

And remember this. Your public usefulness for God is determined largely by your private fellowship with Him. To be a powerful public worship leader, you must be a practicing private worshiper. Every day you must examine yourself and offer God acceptable worship in the "secret place" (Ps. 91:1); then you're ready to minister in the holy place. No mere religious entertainment, the worship you lead will be a natural extension of the life you lead. And it will be easy and uncomplicated, as Jesus promised: "My yoke is easy, and my burden is light" (Matt. 11:30). You will simply worship in your congregation as you worship in your "closet"—and God will visit His people and work powerfully to conform them to Jesus' image.

The promptings of worship

When we worship solely to please God, a Spirit-inspired flow of love is released upward toward Him. This in turn prompts Him to release the Holy Spirit to flow down and work afresh among us. As stated above, the Spirit imparts strength and peace to us. Additionally, He speaks to us, or acts for us, according to our present needs and God's will.

As the leaders of the Antioch church "ministered to the Lord," the Holy Spirit spoke, calling Paul (Saul of Tarsus) to his first apostolic mission: "The Holy Spirit said, Separate me Barnabas and Saul for the work unto which I have called them" (Acts 13:2). Apostolic ministry was God's will for Paul and He called Paul to it as he worshiped.

Similarly, the Spirit may call us to a specific work or ministry while we are worshiping. Or He may prompt us to correct ourselves by convicting us of unconfessed or unforsaken sin. He may call us to closer fellowship with Jesus: "Come unto Me" (Matt. 11:28). He may prompt us to spend more time studying God's Word: "Study to show thyself approved unto God" (2 Tim. 2:15). He may prompt us to resume praying for someone in need: "Pray without ceasing" (1 Thess. 5:17). He may warn us that danger or temptation awaits us in a particular relationship or activity. Or He may encourage us to trust God when we are afraid, hindered, or oppressed: "Fear thou not; for I am with thee...I will strengthen...help...[and] uphold thee" (Isa. 41:10).

Besides prompting the Spirit's voice, our worship also prompts His action or intervention in our lives. Though stripped of their rights, severely beaten, lacerated, bloodied, and bound in Philippi's dark, filthy "inner" prison, Paul and Silas kept focusing on the purpose of worship: "At midnight Paul and Silas prayed and sang praises *unto God*" (Acts 16:25). This extraordinarily selfless act of love prompted an extraordinarily powerful act of God to help them. "Suddenly," God caused a prison-opening earthquake, released Paul and Silas, converted the jailer, saved his family (who nursed and fed Paul and Silas), and moved the corrupt city judges to apologize for their illegal and cruel treatment of Paul and Silas (vv. 25–39).

True worship still prompts God to act for us. Often when we're worshiping Him in one place, He's acting in our behalf somewhere else, subduing critics, ending divisions, opening doors, releasing provisions, blessing our works, and answering our prayers. As long as our worship is aimed at blessing Him, He "show(s) himself strong in the behalf of them whose heart is perfect [in their worship] toward him" (2 Chron. 16:9).

This is one reason most Christian assemblies begin their meetings with praise rather than preaching. When, as Paul and Silas, we "sing praises unto God," we prompt Him to speak to us or act for us.

He may move our pastor to teach a biblical truth or principle we need at the moment. These personal "messages" may take the form of Bible quotations or insights, life stories, or other "rabbit trails" the pastor adds spontaneously to his teaching. Or the Lord may prompt him to set aside his prepared talk and speak on something altogether different but currently needed by us or other worshipers present. Or the Lord may speak to us in unusual ways—through the words of a song, testimony, prophesy, interpretation, or even a conversation following our service. When the power of the Spirit is present, the Lord may act in extraordinary ways, supernaturally healing sick bodies, troubled minds, or oppressed souls in the congregation.

Why does He speak or act in these special ways? Like Paul and Silas's, our worship has prompted Him to do so.

Leading worship by example

When after the Babylonian captivity God visited and revived the Judean Jews, Ezra the scribe led their worship by example. His actions demonstrate how God would have us lead in worship. (See Nehemiah 8:1–18.)

While standing before the congregation, Ezra audibly "blessed the LORD, the great God" (Neh. 8:6). The people, hearing his voice, sensing his attitude, and observing his gestures, then responded accordingly: "and all the people answered…and worshiped the LORD." Thus Ezra's personal worship inspired and molded the Jews' corporate worship. His lead evoked an "answer," a response of worship, from God's people. He didn't try to make them worship. He merely worshiped in their presence. The Holy Spirit did the rest, inducing the attitude and acts of true worship throughout the congregation: "All the people…[were] lifting up their hands; and they bowed their heads, and worshiped the Lord with their faces to the ground" (v. 6).

Like Ezra's worship, a good worship leader's praises are infectious. If his praise and worship are real, they spread quickly among the people. The Holy Spirit, who is the chief lover of God the Father and the Son, uses the worship leader's praise offerings as a kind of spiritual "match" to ignite the church's worship fires. His love for Jesus rekindles theirs. His fervent heart stimulates theirs. His passionate utterances of God's names—"Father, Savior, Redeemer, Healer, Lord, King, Master," and so forth—induce theirs. His words of gratitude stir theirs. His worshipful gestures prompt theirs. One such genuinely "Ezraic" worship leader can tremendously impact a church. Through him God can transform respectful reciters of hymns into passionate singers of songs and lavish lovers of God.

"Behold, how great a matter a little fire kindleth!" (James 3:5). A single spark can set an entire forest ablaze—and one true worshiper who leads by example can set a previously non-worshiping congregation aglow with New Testament worship "in spirit and in truth."

The order of worship in song

Just as the priests had their order of service in the Jewish temple, so there's an order to Spirit-led Christian worship in song: "Let all things [including worship] be done...*in order*" (1 Cor. 14:40). Here are some suggestions on how to worship in Spirit-led order.

Ideally, praise should precede worship. Louder, quicker-tempo praise songs should come first in our meetings, followed by slower, more worshipful songs. Once these slower songs begin, it's best not to reintroduce loud, upbeat tunes, because doing so breaks the sweet flow of worship that is ascending to the Lord—and the reviving, empowering flow of life, peace, and joy descending from Him to the worshipers.

Always be ready for the sovereign spontaneity of the Spirit and never fear His prompts: "As many as are led by the Spirit of God, they are the [true, worshiping] sons of God" (Rom. 8:14). God has not only general but also specific purposes in every meeting, and His spontaneous promptings always take priority over our set plans. So always prepare songs for every meeting, asking the Lord to lead your selection. But don't become inflexible after you form your song list. Remember that system and spontaneity can work together perfectly. So be in order, but don't be insensitive. Learn to detect the flow of the supernatural river of God and go with it.

Worship leader, when you sense the Spirit's special blessing on a song or stanza, repeat it, reducing the tempo slightly, and really *worshiping* God as you sing. If led, do so several times. Why? The Spirit's blessing (witness or anointing) is telling you that *that* song is very pleasing to the heavenly Father or very meaningful to one or more of the worshipers. So by following His leading and repeating *that* song, you are permitting His blessing to soak deeply into the heart of God and the worshipers He is touching. No longer mere worship music, this is *worship ministry*.

During the worship, if the Spirit impresses you to add or substitute a song, do so freely, as long as it doesn't cause confusion. Quietly redirecting the worshipers or worship team to a new song on the overhead projector screen, or PowerPoint monitor, or in the hymnal need not be disruptive. But obviously, this will occur rarely, not routinely.

Here are two further suggestions. First, after the speaker's message has been delivered and you move to close the meeting, it's good to worship the Lord again in song. In this way praise and worship prepares us for the Word and the Word prepares us for more praise and worship. Thus the beginning and ending of our gatherings are bathed in worship of the Alpha and the Omega. Second, some worship leaders choose a song from each meeting to include in the next. This links the church's gatherings—Sunday to Wednesday to Sunday—in one continuous flow of worship.

The concentration of worship

True worshipers easily and lovingly focus on the Lord, looking away from other interests and concentrating affectionately on Him. This glorifies, or honors, Jesus above all other venerated people or things. It also activates the Holy Spirit, whose prime mission is to glorify Jesus—"He shall glorify *me*" (John 16:14). Then wonderful things follow. Why? The Lord receives our concentrated stream of worship and returns it to us as a concentrated stream of blessing. This isn't novel.

Numbers 21:4–9 tells us that when even the sinful, fallen Israelites concentrated on the brazen serpent, miracles of mercy began flowing. Thousands of dying, hopeless Jews were suddenly forgiven, healed, and restored in a spontaneous release of God's compassion.

Similarly, when Christian worship leaders concentrate on Jesus, many mercies flow. The powerful, reviving river of the Spirit begins moving through the congregation, bringing conviction, conversion, and comfort wherever its "living waters" flow. Obedient worshipers are the first to be gripped and drawn into the prevailing current of worship. Soon all present, saved and unsaved, are gripped by God's grace. Disobedient Christians return to obedience. Slumbering ones awake to righteousness. Rebels submit to God's authority. Sinners' hard hearts are plowed and softened; when the gospel is "planted," they repent, believe, and enter into the worship. Then all these begin focusing on Jesus for the rest of the meeting—and their lives.

Indeed, when we concentrate our worship on Jesus, the Spirit concentrates His river of mercies on us, and "every thing shall live where the river cometh" (Ezek. 47:9).

Hindrances to worship

To remain calmly concentrated on worshiping the Lord, the worship leader must evade a host of inward and outward distractions. Here are seven common hindrances to worship.

1. A wandering mind.

Worship leader, you can't worship well with a wandering mind. Thoughts of tomorrow or yesterday, offenses or offenders, or problems or irritations break your concentration and hinder your worship flow.

These wrong thoughts and emotions don't have to be big to distract. Even the smallest psychological "foxes" may "spoil" your "vine" of worship (Song of Sol. 2:15). So heed Paul's apostolic orders: "Whatever you do," including worship, "do it heartily" (Col. 3:23). While worshiping, give yourself entirely to worship. Refuse to let your mind wander. Rein in every distracting thought or emotion. Look beyond them by thinking of Jesus or the words of the songs you're offering Him.

Persist in these corrections until your soul is quiet and your worship steady.

2. Self-consciousness

Innocent as it seems, self-consciousness blocks Christ-consciousness. So refuse to think about yourself as you worship.

Don't consider how you look, sound, or feel. And don't imagine what others think of you as you worship. Such thoughts breed fear of man and sever the ties of restful trust that unite us to God and enable us to peacefully worship Him. Conversely, don't get impressed if you sing or play an instrument exceptionally well, or pride will arise and quench the humble Spirit of true worship. God detests pride and resists proud worship leaders: "God resisteth the proud" (James 4:6).

Truly, the worship leader who lifts himself up in his heart is an amateur antichrist, a small-time "abomination of desolation" in the holy place that grieves God and moves Him to withdraw His Spirit.

3. Church pride

Church pride is as bad as individual conceit. Some congregations are worship-conscious—impressed with the way they worship.

The renown of your choir, skill of your musicians, size of your orchestra, excellence of your sound system—all these elements of music making play "second fiddle" to the higher purpose for which they exist: to worship God! Their job is to bless Him, not impress people. So don't puff up if yours is an exceptionally musical or worshipful church. Keep things in perspective. All churches worship God, and He is more impressed by our "spirit and truth" than our playing and singing (though He calls us to sing and play "skillfully" [Ps. 33:3]). By worshiping acceptably, your church is obedient, not special. It's just doing its congregational duty, not competing for a Dove award! For healthy deflation, self-impressed churches should end their worship by thinking, "We are unprofitable servants; we have done that which was our duty to do" (Luke 17:10).

Worship leader, don't worship the worship you're leading; "worship God" (Rev. 19:10).

4. The congregation's condition

Don't let the congregation's condition distract you. The Israelites' persisting carnality provoked Moses to unbelief and anger. Then he scolded his brethren and smote the rock instead of focusing on God and gently leading His people.

Don't repeat his error. Often many in your flock will *not* be "in the Spirit on the Lord's day." It's your job to get them there, to focus on the Lord so steadily that His Spirit quickens them through you. So watch for petty provocations. Disregard the discouraging or irritating "things seen"—problems with the sanctuary lighting or sound system, the looks people give you or others, their inattention, or any other audible or visual interruption. Don't fret at misplaced music, instrumental mistakes, off-key singing, crying infants, or infantile adults! If members of the worship team are showy or sullen, or forget or disobey instructions, rise above it. Refocus! Never succumb to unbelief: "Oh, they'll *never* worship in spirit and truth!" Remember, God can easily do in them what He has done, and is yet doing, in you!

And never hold anger. Anger lets the devil into your disposition: "Be ye angry, and sin not...*neither give place to the devil*" (Eph. 4:26–27). When you hold anger, the devil holds you, and he will quickly move you to speak or act foolishly in front of the congregation: "Be not hasty...to be angry; for anger *resteth* in the bosom of a *fool*" (Eccles. 7:9). Wherever anger rests, folly reigns. Anger at the congregtion's condition will cause you to repeat Moses' folly—scorning and callously scolding your brethren and smiting the heart of the Rock!

5. *Working up enthusiasm*

Worship doesn't have to be exciting and loud to please God.

When your love for Him wells up, release it in loud and enthusiastic praises: "Make a *loud noise*, and rejoice, and sing praise" (Ps. 98:4). "Praise him upon the *loud symbols*" (Ps. 150:5). But never try to generate or force enthusiasm artificially. God enjoys soft praise and worship just as much as louder, more energetic offerings. True worship doesn't have to be "worked up." It flows naturally in and from the heart of the Spirit-filled, abiding believer: "He that believeth on me...out of his heart shall flow rivers of living water" (John 7:38). Even when our feeling intensifies and volume rises, true worship is a gloriously steady stream. It is never turbulent or wild. So don't mistake perspiration for inspiration. We don't have to sweat to satisfy God's heart.

To the contrary, God doesn't want a lot of sweat in the holy place! He has ordered the priests of the kingdom age to wear garments of linen, not wool, or "anything that causeth sweat" (Ezek. 44:18). Baal's prophets had plenty of sweat but no Spirit. They "leaped upon the altar" all day in the "flesh" (raw human energy) of their religious but unspiritual natures...but no heavenly fire fell! Christ's humble disciples sat quietly praying and worshiping in the upper room...and holy fire enveloped them! Do we want fleshly fervor or holy fire in our meetings?

In sum, Spirit-stirred enthusiasm pleases God, but not mere religious excitement. It is the froth of our religious "flesh," not the wine of the Spirit.

And God has declared, "No flesh"—even energetically religious flesh!—"should glory in his presence" (1 Cor. 1:29).

6. Condemning non-worshipers

Never condemn—curtly dismiss as hopeless and helpless—non-worshipers, those who are present but don't participate in worship. You too were once uninterested in true worship. Trust the Spirit who drew you to also draw them. Or melt them.

God's presence is like a "consuming fire" (Heb. 12:29). As true worshipers praise and worship God, His presence manifests, melting the hardness and worldliness of non-worshipers and releasing them to enter into the flow of worship: "A fire goeth before him, and…the hills melted like wax at the presence of the LORD" (Ps. 97:3, 5). Thus through the praises of true worshipers, God liberates non-worshipers.

Paul and Silas' praise and worship freed non-worshipers in the Philippi jail. Rather than condemn the other prisoners for not worshiping God in adversity, they chose to do so themselves. And as they "prayed and sang praises unto God," God acted. Soon not just Paul's and Silas' bands but *every one's* bands were loosed" (Acts 16:25–26).

Why not follow their example in your worship services? Rather than write off non-worshipers, why not worship God and trust Him to melt and free them during the meeting?

7. Rejecting those who worship differently

Never reject those who worship differently than you do. As stated previously, the only New Testament requirement for worship is that it be "in spirit and in truth." Beyond that, Christ specified no "right" or "wrong" way to worship.

Worship is a personal expression, not a programmed display, of love for God. Therefore, it's an individual, not an institutional, matter. All are required to worship but not in one "correct" way. Amazingly adaptable, Jesus accepts worship offered in vastly different ways. Some worshipers sit, while others stand. Some bow low or lie prostrate, while others kneel. Some are very still, while others sway, step, or dance. Some raise their arms, while others clasp their hands as if praying. Some churches are liturgical, while others are informal. Some ministers don colorful robes, while others wear business suits or casual shirts and slacks. Some churches have choirs, while others do not. Some use instruments in their worship, while others sing acappella. Some church buildings have stained glass windows, vaulted ceilings, and elaborate altars; other buildings are small, unadorned, and unattractive. Some worship in traditional church buildings, while others worship in houses, storefronts, abandoned warehouses, grass huts—or outdoors!

If Jesus accepts all these different people, places, and procedures, who are we to object, if they worship sincerely, "decently, and in order"? (1 Cor. 14:40). "If God says something is acceptable, don't say it isn't" (Acts 10:15, NLT).*

And never judge worshipers because of their appearance. Whether they dress up or down, wear or shun jewelry, have short or long hair, or are smooth skinned or tattooed,[2] "the LORD looketh on the heart," not the "outward appearance" (1 Sam. 16:7). We should, too.

It was spiritual immaturity, not maturity, that caused the apostles to reject other sincere believers merely because they didn't follow them and their ways: "We forbade him, *because he followeth not with us*" (Luke 9:49). Let's not repeat their religious prejudice by rejecting those whose methods of worship differ from ours. Instead, let's live and let live, worship and let worship. Jesus sat and quietly sang hymns with His disciples, while David on at least one occasion danced before God with all his might. God accepted the worship of both. Let's not, as Michal, despise either.

~

Let worshipers, worship teams, and especially worship leaders take heed. These are biblical ways to worship and lead worship. They are as valuable in God's house as the finest "gold of Ophir" in antiquity and their usefulness is thoroughly proven. May God establish them in and through us for His pleasure and glory—and lead us on to the highest ministry.

---

* This verse is from the 1996 version of the New Living Translation.

Chapter Eighteen

THE HIGHEST MINISTRY

But now hath he obtained a more excellent ministry...
—HEBREWS 8:6

orship leading is truly an important ministry. But have you ever wondered which ministry is the highest? By "ministry," I mean not the highest ministry *office*, authority, or rank, but rather the noblest, loftiest, and most heavenly ministry *activity*, or spiritual labor.

It isn't, as already referenced, the work of a worship leader, musician, or music director. Nor is it the work of a deacon, elder, board member, or church administrator. Nor is it the labor of a Christian counselor or mentor. It isn't the ministry of an evangelist, foreign missionary, or charitable worker among the poor, orphans, or substance abusers. And it isn't that of a Christian educator, teacher, or pastor. It isn't the work of a Christian scholar, writer, editor, or publisher. It isn't the work of a producer, director, or technician in Christian television, radio, video, or Internet broadcasting. Nor is it the labor of those specially gifted to prophesy, heal the sick, expel demons, or work miracles. It isn't the work of a bishop, superintendent, or even an apostle, though his ministry office ranks "first" (1 Cor. 12:28). You may wonder, what ministerial activity, or spiritual labor, could possibly be higher than the work of an apostle?

The highest ministerial activity is *intercessory prayer*. On a purely human level, to "intercede" is "to attempt to reconcile differences between two people or groups; [to] mediate,"[1] but we will not address this mere earthly interpersonal interposition in this chapter. Instead we will focus on Christian intercessory prayer, which is, "a prayer to God on behalf of another."[2] From a biblical perspective, to "intercede" is to *stand between God and people to plead for reconciliation, relief, or benefit.* The interceding Christian approaches God the Father by the blood of His Son, and, with the help of His Spirit, he makes petitions for people, families, churches, cities, and nations.

This vital spiritual interposition between God and humanity is conducted "in the name" (at the command, on the authority, as an agent, in the stead) of the only Mediator between God and man, Christ Jesus, who said:

> Hitherto have ye asked nothing in my name; *ask*, and ye shall receive, that your joy may be full.
> —JOHN 16:24

> And whatsoever ye shall *ask* in my name, that will I do.... If ye shall *ask* anything in my name, I will do it.
> —JOHN 14:13–14

> I have chosen you, and ordained you, that ye should go and bring forth fruit, and that your fruit should remain; that whatever ye shall *ask* of the Father in my name, he may give it you.
> —JOHN 15:16

These and similar prayer mandates from our Master form a firm foundation of biblical authority for every Christian intercessor.

But the question still remains, why is intercession the highest ministry work?

WHY INTERCESSION IS THE HIGHEST MINISTRY ACTIVITY

The reason intercessory prayer is the highest ministry activity is simple: intercession is Jesus' current ministry in heaven. On earth He worked faithfully in many of the ministerial capacities mentioned above. He served as a missionary, pastor (shepherd), counselor, teacher, evangelist, prophet, healer, charity worker, miracle worker, bishop (chief shepherd), and "Apostle" (Heb. 3:1). Then, leaving these earthly works to His disciples, He ascended to a *higher work* at the right hand of the Father in heaven. The writer to the Hebrews reveals:

> But now hath he obtained a *more excellent [honorable or higher]* ministry.
>
> —HEBREWS 8:6

There, as the church's heavenly "High Priest" (Heb. 3:1), Christ gives Himself ceaselessly to intercessory prayer. Again, in the memorable words of the writer to the Hebrews:

> He *ever liveth* to *make intercession* for them [Christians].
>
> —HEBREWS 7:25

That He was promoted, or raised higher, from His earthly ministerial labors to this "more excellent" labor of intercession, and that He now "ever liveth" to "make intercession" for believers settles it: intercession is the highest ministry! Still, let's get further confirmation.

For that, we need only consider the present ministry of the Holy Spirit. One of the *Parakletos'* chief labors in this church age is also intercession. Every minute, every hour, every day, He pursues this mystical but vital labor in our bodily temples. Paul reveals:

> The Spirit himself maketh intercession *for us* with groanings...he maketh intercession *for the saints* according to *the will of God.*
>
> —ROMANS 8:26–27

For whom is the Holy Spirit praying? "For us...for the saints"—for you, me, and every other living believer. For what is He praying? "The will of God"—that we discover and obey God's good and perfect plan for our lives. The Spirit pursues this vital petitioning of the Father below the threshold of our consciousness.

When *the Holy Spirit* intercedes in us, we play no active part in the praying. Our bodily temple is merely His earthly base from which He intercedes for us and other believers. And He does this constantly. Note that His supplication is described in neither the past nor future but continuous tense: "The Spirit himself *maketh intercession* for us...he *maketh intercession* for the saints." This divine praying is entirely separate from our human praying, either "with...understanding" (1 Cor. 14:15) or "in the Spirit" (Eph. 6:18). (For more on this topic, please read 1 Corinthians 14:2, 14–15 and Jude 20.)

But when *we* intercede, the Holy Spirit *assists* us as *we* pray. When we pray "with understanding," or in the language we understand, the Holy Spirit provides us with inspiration (willingness to pray) and initiatives (people's names, needs, or desires, and God's Word pertaining to them) with which we formulate prayer requests in our own language. Thus we pray in the atmosphere of the Holy Spirit and in or by His assistance. When we pray "in the Spirit," or in our Spirit-given prayer language, He imparts to us the actual "utterance," or speech sounds (phonetics) and words, we speak spontaneously: "They...began to speak with other tongues, *as the Spirit gave them utterance*" (Acts 2:4). As we thus pray, the Holy Spirit is praying through our human spirit and by our words, yet apart from our intellectual faculties.

Summing up, if the holiest and highest beings ever to visit this world, the very second and third persons of the Godhead, give themselves constantly to intercessory prayer, it must be the holiest and highest labor of love. Case closed!

Why, then, do so many Christians fail to climb this summit of spiritual ministry?

WHY MANY CHRISTIANS NEVER BECOME INTERCESSORS

While there may be many reasons Christians prefer and seek other ministries more than the work of intercession, one is certain: other ministries are more noticeable.

While biblical evidence suggests that both demons (Dan. 10:12–13) and our heavenly "cloud of [redeemed] witnesses" (Heb. 12:1) may be aware of our petitions, intercession remains essentially a hidden work seen only by God. People certainly don't notice our intercession. And, like the

Pharisees, we tend to seek the highest church offices and most noticeable ministry works "to be seen of men" (Matt. 6:1–2, 5, 16). But however vain and "yet carnal" most Christians may be, God always has His remnant of spiritual Christians, faithful souls who are willing to take the more humble, less trodden paths and pursue the more vital, less recognized works in order to do God's will. It is to these humble ones that I write. They will recognize what proud Christians overlook, namely, that intercession is our most vital, powerful, and enduring kingdom work: "The humble shall hear of it, and be glad" (Ps. 34:2).

Though low in profile, intercessory prayer is high in priority. Men forget it, but God focuses on it. We covet visible ministries, but God craves vital intercessors. In a word, our obsession is recognition. In brief, His passion is reconciliation—which comes only through the persistent labors of committed intercessors.

Today God is actively recruiting intercessors, as He did in Ezekiel's generation:

> And I sought for a man among them, that should make up the hedge, and stand in the gap before me.
>
> —EZEKIEL 22:30

And He will richly reward all who respond. He certainly rewarded the leadership of the early church in Jerusalem.

A WATERSHED MOMENT IN THE EARLY CHURCH

It was a great day for the fledgling Judean Christians when their leaders, the apostles, chose to emphasize intercessory prayer. After increased membership led to new problems in their ranks—a prejudice-spawned squabble over the care of the Hebrew and Hellenist widows—they decided to reprioritize.

After seeking God they issued the following decision:

> We will *give ourselves continually to prayer,* and to the ministry of the word.
>
> —ACTS 6:4

We will *continue steadfastly in prayer . . .*

—ACTS 6:4, ASV

We will *devote ourselves to prayer . . .*

—ACTS 6:4, ESV

It was a watershed moment, dividing their previous day of small beginnings from their subsequent period of sustained, supernatural growth.

God was evidently pleased with their decision, because He began working powerfully among them. Wonders they had witnessed only sporadically began occurring steadily, and many divinely touched converts flooded into their assembly to become student-practitioners of Christ's Words and ways: "And the number of the disciples multiplied in Jerusalem greatly" (Acts 6:7). So strong was the Spirit's surge that even leaders of the Jewish priesthood—the resident, ruling, rival religion!—were converted to Christianity in large numbers: "And a great company of the priests were obedient to the faith." Indeed, God's very "glory"—the highest, most Christlike manifestation of His truth, love, and power—visited Jerusalem and its environs. Why? All evidence points to one answer: the church's leaders made a firm commitment to pursue the ministry of intercession daily.

Spiritually minded, they realized that intercession was not an incidental but rather an indispensable integral part of their church's life and ministry. Without it, they could neither generate nor sustain spiritual growth.

OTHERS WHO "GAVE THEMSELVES CONTINUALLY TO PRAYER"

Over the centuries many other churches and groups have practiced persistent intercessory prayer just as did the Jerusalem church. We'll cite two, the Moravian Brethren and the Metropolitan Tabernacle church.

After a season of spiritual self-examination and growth, the Moravians experienced a visitation of the Holy Spirit during a routine meeting in the summer of 1727 in Herrnhut, Saxony (near present-day Dresden, Germany). After this dynamic spiritual reinvigoration, the Brethren committed themselves to a round-the-clock, seven-days-a-week intercessory prayer watch. (Fittingly, Herrnhut means "the Lord's watch.") Their extraordinary labor of importunity continued for over a hundred years.[3] This exceptional "giving (of) themselves continually to prayer" produced exceptional kingdom fruit.

Moravian missionaries launched Spirit-led, spiritually prolific missions all around the world: to England, Greenland, and the West Indies; to South Africa, Guiana, and Ceylon; to Romania, Algeria, and, yes, America, where strong Christian communities were founded in towns such as Bethlehem, Pennsylvania, and (Old) Salem, North Carolina. These unprecedented Protestant outreaches prompted other missionaries to take giant leaps with and for God. Inspired by the Moravian paradigm, William Cary said, "See what these Moravians have done...Can we not follow their example?"[4] Cary's subsequent mission to India challenged and changed that great nation forever.

Additionally, powerful ministers were touched and movements spawned. It was at a Moravian meeting in London that John Wesley's heart was "strangely warmed" by the reading of Luther's introduction to his commentary on the Book of Romans. John's brother, the prolific hymnist, Charles, was also converted through Moravian influence. Chief benefactor and leader of the Moravians, Count Nicolaus Von Zinzendorf, contributed significantly to both the Pietist and Methodist movements, which were powerful positive forces for change in the eighteenth century and beyond. All this fruit, and much more, was harvested from the Moravians' humble but fertile tree of incessant intercessory prayer.

Charles H. Spurgeon, the remarkably gifted and renowned "prince of preachers," passionately believed in and practiced intercessory prayer in his Metropolitan Tabernacle in London. Formerly known as the New Park Street Church, the nineteenth-century megachurch grew from a congregation of around two hundred (eighty heard Spurgeon's first sermon) to a throng of six thousand during Spurgeon's long tenure (1854 to 1892). A dedicated intercessor, Spurgeon led by example when he taught his people to give themselves continually to prayer. When visitors toured the Tabernacle, he sometimes escorted them to the basement room where his intercessors, like the Moravians a century earlier, prayed without ceasing. Of their indispensable prayer labors Spurgeon said simply, "Here is the powerhouse of this church."[5] Indeed, there were the real cylinders, pistons, and fuel driving the phenomenal growth and spiritual influence of London's, and the world's, largest evangelical church.

Clearly, Spurgeon and the Moravians were convinced of the monumental importance of intercessory prayer.

THE MONUMENTAL IMPORTANCE OF INTERCESSION

Have we grasped the monumental importance of intercessory prayer? Are we practicing it?

Before we will make the kinds of commitment described above, we must be convinced that intercessory prayer is a worthy, not a worthless, work. We must also accept that it requires time and energy—two precious resources we must take from other nonvital interests. Yet, thankfully, it requires no money! A poor church can pray as often and effectively as a rich one! Nor does it require a large congregation! A small church can make intercession as effectively as a larger one! Nor does it demand elaborate buildings! We can pray as powerfully in small, old, ugly buildings or houses as in new, expensive, beautiful ones! Nor does it require special committees, programs, or marketing! Intercession is a simple, hidden work strictly between God and His children, requiring neither specially gifted people, innovative methods, nor public support.

Yet intercessory prayer requires the help of the Holy Spirit and invokes His fresh refillings. It exercises faith and builds it. It demands patience and increases it. It requires persistence and perfects it. Thus it transforms not only those who are prayed for but also those who pray by leading them into a fuller revelation of, and union with, God's kingdom purposes and ways. Indispensable, intercession creates, grows, and preserves God's plan on earth. Without it, God does nothing; with it, He may do anything. Soaringly supernatural, intercession redefines what is possible.

Steady intercessory prayer convicts the hardest, most hopelessly corrupt sinners and makes them advocates of holiness and ambassadors of heaven. It saves the poorest, emptiest souls and fills them with spiritual riches. It heals chronically and incurably sick bodies and gives them stable, radiant health. It releases people bound and burdened with condemnation and lifts them until rivers of joy flow from them daily. It reconciles long-estranged spouses, friends, and family members and gives them the sweetest fellowship. It restores tormented, delusional minds until they are sound, sharp, and efficient. It corrects foolish thinking and errant beliefs and instills a wise, biblical perspective and balanced faith. It transforms weak, vacillating Christians into unflappably brave, immovable overcomers.

Furthermore, incessant intercession causes hungry Bible students to discover deep truths and lasting life lessons. It enables ministers to receive strong, timely messages for tired churches. It causes God to intervene with just judgments that relieve worn and weary Christians. It causes mighty outpourings of the Spirit to rain down on dry churches, cities, and nations. It awakens sleeping Christians and stirs them to take the Word to the world. Why is intercession so all-powerful?

It engages an all-powerful God: "*All power* is given unto me in heaven and in earth," Jesus assured us (Matt. 28:18, KJV). Because of His limitless power, intercessory prayer is limitlessly powerful; it alters people and situations all over the earth. It is irresistible; no earthly or heavenly forces—even the "gates [or strongest powers] of hell" (Matt. 16:18)—can withstand sustained intercession. It is lasting; intercession prevails forever before God, who is still answering prayers faithful intercessors uttered decades, even centuries, ago. It is safe; Oswald Chambers taught that, unlike preaching, intercession has no snare of pride.[6] It is accessible; any Christian may become an effective intercessor anytime, anywhere. And who are effective intercessors?

EFFECTIVE INTERCESSORS

Why don't all Christians intercede with equal success? Why does God answer the requests of some more readily, evidently, and fully than those of others? Clearly, some believers are ineffective intercessors, praying much, yet receiving little, while others are effective intercessors. To a person, effective intercessors *abide in close fellowship with Jesus.* In John 15, Jesus taught that *abiding* causes our intercessory prayers to bear "much fruit," "glorify" God, and give us the "full" joy of effective intercessors. And there is no other way; He didn't reveal any Plan B. John recalls His teaching:

> *Abide* in me … *abide* in me … He that *abideth* in me … the same
> bringeth forth *much fruit*; for without me ye can do nothing
> [including pray effectively] … *If ye abide in me*, and my words
> *abide* in you, ye shall ask what ye will, and it shall be done unto
> you. *In this* [fruitful intercession] is my Father *glorified*, that ye
> bear *much fruit* … These things have I spoken unto you, that my
> joy might remain in you, and *that your joy might be full.*
> —JOHN 15:4–5, 7–8, 11

Believing Jesus' words with childlike faith, effective intercessors focus on abiding in Him. How do they do this?

They abide in prayer, praying regularly and spontaneously. They abide in God's Word, reading, studying, pondering, and talking it. They abide in obedience, doing Christ's commands in their circumstances. They abide in God's will, following the Spirit's leading. They abide in the light of righteousness, living by God's standards of right conduct; and the light of honesty, quickly confessing all sins to Him. They abide in God's love, rejecting unmerciful attitudes—judging, condemning, unforgiveness, stinginess, and so forth—and choosing goodwill and kindness toward all. They abide in contentment, rejecting covetousness and cultivating thanksgiving for everything they have, especially their sweet fellowship with Jesus! (See Hebrews 13:5.) While others play at prayer, these abiding Christians pray with power.

Like Abraham, they pray their "Lots" out of "Sodom." Like Moses at Rephidim, they exert their spiritual "rod" of intercession and turn the tide of earthly conflicts. Like the anonymous Hebrew slaves who prayed for deliverance from Egypt, their supplications bring deliverers and launch exoduses from sin and oppression. Like the prayers of the Jerusalem church, their unceasing pleas save "Peters"—persecuted spiritual leaders—from hindrances, detentions, and premature deaths. Like Jesus' high priestly prayer (John 17), their requests remain on God's heart and the Spirit's agenda long after they leave this world. Lord, help us become like these abiding, effective intercessors!

There is no greater spiritual work, no more heavenly ministry activity, in this life! Because effective intercessors have chosen the most valuable, or golden, ministry, their eternal home and rewards will be golden—of highest, purest, and indestructible value! "And the city [New Jerusalem] was pure gold, like clear glass...and the street of the city was pure gold" (Rev. 21:18, 21).

~

Have you entered the highest ministry? Have you prayed for anyone today?

> And Abraham drew near, and said, Wilt thou also destroy the righteous with the wicked?
>
> —GENESIS 18:23

> But prayer was made without ceasing by the church unto God for him [Peter].
>
> —ACTS 12:5

Transformative, intercessory prayer will change your viewpoint on many things, including small churches.

Chapter Nineteen

TO THE PASTORS AND PEOPLE OF SMALL CHURCHES

I... have taught you publicly, and from house to house.
—ACTS 20:20

While traveling across North Carolina one Sunday morning, I noticed how many church buildings dotted the various cities and counties. Some were large with full parking lots, but most, by far the majority, were smaller structures and had fewer cars present. Then it hit me: many Christians today admire very large congregations, yet most worship in medium to small ones. And instead of finding fulfillment, many are frustrated in their church experience because their flocks are not larger. Why?

Many Christians and church leaders put too much emphasis on, and trust in, big religion. They equate large congregations with success and seek spiritual security in numbers rather than truth. These draw more confidence from fellowship with people than from fellowship with God. (This attitude is the opposite of that held by the great reformers and revivalists, who wisely and bravely sought security in *conformity to God's Word and divine approval alone*, whether found in large or small groups.) Whatever their, and our, core misconceptions and insecurities, one thing is sure: Christianity's recent love affair with megachurches has been neither healthy nor biblical, nor has it advanced what the Spirit is trying to say or do among us. Instead it has been a distracting obsession and futile exercise in religious pride. Subconsciously, and at times consciously, churches boast of their attendance much as David gloried in the swelling numbers of Israelites—to his confusion and judgment!

My concern, and motivation for this chapter, is the detrimental psychological effect all this numbers-madness has had on us. It has left many larger churches puffed up, rejoicing over impressive but biblically unimportant talking points, such as attendance figures, income, popular programs, and buildings. Conversely, it has left many smaller churches and their pastors wondering, "What's wrong with us? Why don't we draw great crowds every Lord's Day?" It has also prompted some in larger churches to misjudge smaller churches: "What's wrong with that church, that pastor, those elders? Why aren't their numbers, building projects, and programs increasing like ours?"

These subtly competitive comparisons provoke many pastors and people in smaller churches to religious envy. Instead of rising and soaring in the peace and joy of the Lord, these eagles are grounded with chronic, crippling inferiority, disappointment, and discontent. Instead of praising and worshiping God, they pine and pray for a larger congregation, imagining that that will validate them as a bona fide and blessed New Testament church. And when other Christians or pastors prejudge or ignore them, they worry that their worship and works may also go unnoticed by God. Though His presence, voice, and opened Word tells them better daily, such thoughts still harass and discourage them. So, like Hannah, they weep and beg the Lord for more visible fruit, notwithstanding the wondrous love He shows them daily, even hourly. Jesus never intended us to be preoccupied with this numbers-consciousness.

His words fully authorize even the smallest gatherings of genuine Christians:

> Where *two or three* are gathered together in my name, there am
> I in the midst of them.
> —MATTHEW 18:20

Some preachers would scorn an invitation to speak at a small church, yet here the most prestigious Preacher in history has promised to appear and by His Spirit minister if only a handful of believers gather to sincerely study, worship, and serve Him. The more Christian messengers become like the master Messenger, the more they too will adopt His humble readiness to minister to His faithful few.

OSWALD CHAMBERS: A HUMBLE MESSENGER

Oswald Chambers was one of Christ's humble messengers. One of Chambers' hosts, William Ramsay, recalled how Chambers reacted when one of his meetings in Arbroath, Scotland, drew a surprisingly small turnout:

> At the first meeting Mr. Chambers and I were the only ones present at the appointed time. He saw that I was a bit concerned and I well remember his saying, with his fine spirit and smile, "Never mind, Brother Ramsay, I will speak to five people as readily as to five hundred." God took him at his word, for almost immediately four others came in. He led the singing, played the organ, and preached to those five, and I never heard him preach better.[1]

This was no exceptional moment but rather a true illustration of Chambers' usual attitude toward whatever work God put before him. Later he served as principal and lecturer at the Bible Training College in London, where over his brief four-and-a-half-year tenure (1911–1915) the school averaged about twenty-five students. Imagine that, twenty-five students sitting under a young Scottish Bible teacher so Spirit-filled and gifted that many Christians all over the world regard his prime literary work, the best-selling devotional *My Utmost for His Highest*, as one of the finest devotionals in print and Chambers as one of the church's greatest Bible teachers and intellects. And I cast in my humble vote with the many.

WORSHIPING AND TEACHING "FROM HOUSE TO HOUSE"

Chambers was just one of many examples of ministerial humility. Rather than undermine Jesus' words in Matthew 18:20, church history underscores them. For approximately the first two centuries, due chiefly to persisting persecution, Christians met almost exclusively in homes, usually the larger houses of wealthier believers.

Without question, the apostle Paul spent almost all of his time ministering in house churches. He wrote frequently of the various house churches in which he ministered and with whom he maintained fellowship and ministerial oversight. To the Corinthians, he wrote, "Aquila and Prisca greet you heartily in the Lord, with *the church that is in their house*" (1 Cor. 16:19, NAS). To Philemon, he penned his greeting to "the church *in thy house*" (Philem. 2). To the Ephesian elders, he testified:

I...have taught you publicly, and *from house to house.*
—ACTS 20:20

During this key, formative "house church" period of church history, individual congregations were typically limited in size. Why? You can't fit a megachurch into someone's upper room, study, or atrium! In larger cities, several, sometimes many, of these diminutive domestic churches coexisted and commingled in fellowship, ministry, worship, and communion.

Public worship buildings and services, and larger congregations, gradually replaced these smaller, private meetings. Down through the centuries, however, many Christian groups opted to again worship in homes. This "back to the Acts" trend resurfaced most notably when pre-reform and reform groups were being persecuted by the powerful Roman church; and later, after Protestantism was established, when new branches of Christianity suffered at the hands of Roman and Protestant (or national) churches. Among these latter groups were the Separatists, Pietists, and Methodists, to name a few.

Recent history and current experience add to this testimony. Watchman Nee, the world-renowned Bible teacher and author and founder of the prolific "Little Flock" Chinese house church movement in the 1920s, spent much of his ministry teaching in house churches. And while many Christians today think Christ is properly worshiped only in public church buildings with traditional, Western-style, ecclesiastical architecture, millions all over the world—in China, India, Cuba, Korea, Europe, Africa, Canada, and, yes, America, too—still meet for worship, instruction, and fellowship in private homes.

Sometimes, especially in countries where Christians are actively persecuted, house churches are the only option. In other cases, believers worship in homes because they prefer a simpler, informal way of worship and warmer, more personal fellowship—two blessings that sometimes prove elusive in large congregations. But like conventional churches, house churches are not all alike.

Some are highly organized, others loosely. Some have pastors, others elders only. Some are linked to other house fellowships, others are independent. Some are accepted by their communities, others are summarily rejected and mislabeled a "cult." Some hold heretical teachings, others are soundly biblical. Some are rebelling against church authority, while others are meek, open-minded, courageous, and laudable for exercising their blood-bought liberty to worship in New Testament simplicity "from house to house."

Usually, these domestic flocks, like their ancient predecessors, are necessarily small in number.

A PREVALENT PASTORAL PREOCCUPATION

Regrettably, many pastors today are preoccupied with increasing their churches' numbers. There are several reasons for this.

Denominations, and even loosely knit associations of churches or ministers, tend to praise and favor larger churches and their pastors. Though unscriptural and unacceptable, this favoritism is understandable. The social argument, for one, is powerful: larger churches command more respect in the community. The financial argument is also strong: more worshipers mean more tithes and offerings with which to pay for salaries, mortgages, taxes, utilities, and church programs. So even when their churches are numerically and financially strong, some pastors still feel pressed to show increasing numbers. If not, they risk rejection or loss of respect from their parishioners, the public, other pastors, or their bishops or superintendents.

Conversely, if their numbers suddenly rise sharply, they risk falling into the snare of pride and self-deception. I remember one minister reminiscing of a time he was called to an "important pastorate." "Aren't they all?"

I wondered. When almighty God entrusts a minister with the overseership of even a few *eternally valuable souls* (the "true riches," Luke 16:11), how can that *not* be important? This minister was of course referring to pastoring a large, well-attended, well-funded, reputable church. Apparently, his pride in this very noticeable position caused him to overestimate its value to God and underestimate the worth of his other pastorates and ministerial assignments. The truth is, they were all important.

Another pastor told me how, at various ministers' conferences, the moment he mentioned that he pastored a "small, inner-city church," some ministers immediately lost interest and ignored him for the rest of the conference. That's sad but true. Any honest minister will acknowledge this scenario is repeated far too often. Why? Some pastors have never learned what God seeks and values in churches. Or they've forgotten it. Or, tired of standing for otherworldly goals among worldly churchmen, they've adopted popular but unspiritual viewpoints. So many of their peers and parishioners believe greater numbers equate religious success and ministerial perfection that they've just given in and bowed to the god of numbers, false though it is.

Once captive to this controlling idol, they can think of little else besides how to get more warm bodies seated in their sanctuaries come next Sunday morning or Wednesday evening.

THE REALLY IMPORTANT THINGS

The really important things in a church are few, and they are often neglected in our overriding lust for ever-bigger religion. Here are some of them:

- Is Jesus' presence sensed and voice heard, or is His nearness never felt and personal communication never discerned?
- Are God's Word and its timeless principles explained and applied accurately to daily living?
- Are the people coddled with religious sentimentality or challenged to walk in humility, holiness, kindness, faithfulness, and self-examination?
- Are the church's activities and ministries forged in prayer, or

are they chosen and pursued merely because they're popular?
- Are the church's methods of operation New Testament, "new cart" (2 Sam. 6:3), or New Age?
- Is the Holy Spirit dormant or active, hardly working or freely working—comforting, confirming, and convicting hearts in every meeting?
- Is the worship flowing or frozen, a reviving river of living praise or a dry branch of dead religious music?
- Are pastors and people alike bravely seeking and following God's guidance or blindly doing whatever is logical, economical, or traditional?
- Is the church weathering its storms of testing or withering? Evading or enduring the challenging rivers and hot fires God sends to grow and mature it?

These are the truly important issues and telling questions. They determine whether a local church is a spiritually progressive or stagnant flock, a growing or severed "member" of the worldwide body of Christ and an impertinent or integral part of His developing kingdom plan—whether their numbers are large, small, or medium, or they're rising, falling, or stagnant.

THE "CHURCH GROWTH" GOD SEEKS MOST

Other pastors and churches err due to their limited concept of "church growth."

To them this means only one thing: more people attending and joining the church. This is *numerical* church growth, and it is a blessing, but it is not the most important kind of increase. By far the greater growth is *spiritual*, the transformation of our characters into the image of Christ's character. This is the overriding divine "purpose" toward which the Holy Spirit is "working all things together" in our lives.

> We know that God causes all things to work together for good... [for] *His purpose.* For those whom He foreknew, He also predestined *to become conformed to the image of His Son...*
> —ROMANS 8:28–29, NAS

If through a church's faithful intercession, teaching, and counseling amid the tests of life, this transformation is progressing, vital *spiritual* church growth is occurring, even if more people are not attending meetings.

Spiritual church growth is a quiet, largely unnoticed work of the Holy Spirit. It doesn't make newspaper headlines, the evening news, Internet blogs, or even the lead articles in Christian periodicals. Yet it is underway and watched closely by God whenever faith is being fed, tested, and increased; biblical knowledge and insight are increasing; personal knowledge of God is on the rise; humility is blossoming; God's voice and guidance are increasingly recognized and obeyed; the various fruits of the Spirit are manifesting more steadily; and congregants seek "not to be ministered unto, but to minister and to give" (Matt. 20:28). This is the "church growth" God is most concerned with, that "Christ be [fully] formed in you" (Gal. 4:19), not that we impress each other and the world with big religion.

The Good Shepherd knows when, where, and how to call His sheep in every city and thus grow His one great worldwide flock: "The sheep hear his voice; and he calleth his own sheep by name, and leadeth them out... there shall be one fold, and one shepherd" (John 10:3, 16). It's unimportant to Him whether they gather in large or small local sheepfolds. That they hear His voice and follow is all that matters.

OUR UNREASONABLE PREOCCUPATION

How unreasonable, then, is our obsession with large numbers! "Come now, and let us reason together" (Isa. 1:18). And unbiblical! And unChristlike!

Does Jesus really care how large the churches are in which His children in a given town or community cluster to worship, feed on His Word, pray, and fellowship? All the believers in that locality are His whether they gather in forty churches with twenty-five members, twenty with fifty members, ten with one hundred members, five with two hundred members, or one with one thousand members. Nowhere does the New Testament reveal that larger congregations are specially blessed. Nor does it set a minimum number of worshipers for every church. For instance, first century A.D. Jewish tradition required that at least ten men be present at every synagogue service.[2]

If anything our inspired, infallible, written pattern (the Bible) hints, but stops short of declaring, that Jesus prefers smaller, more manageable groups to very large ones. When Jesus fed the five thousand He specified that His followers gather in groups of fifty or one hundred:

> And he said to his disciples, Make them sit down *by fifties* in a company. And they did so...and they did eat...
> —LUKE 9:14–17

> And he commanded them to make all sit down by companies....And they sat down in ranks, *by hundreds, and by fifties*....And they did all eat...
> —MARK 6:39–42

This well-known incident is a subtle allegory intimating Christ's preferred method for *feeding Christians spiritually*. He gathers His sheep in local flocks small enough for their shepherds to give them adequate personal attention (or in larger flocks with divisions headed by assistant pastors or teaching elders to give equally personal care). He gives these shepherds soul nourishment, timely spiritual "bread and meat" broken off from His Word, which they then pass on to their flocks. And though there are hundreds of millions of sheep in Christ's worldwide flock, not one little believing ewe lamb is left hungry or malnourished in the faith and knowledge of God.

Though He left us this allegory, Jesus never imposed minimum or maximum numerical requirements upon His churches. Why? Apparently it's not a priority to Him. If the Chief Shepherd has never declared a preference for large flocks, why should His undershepherds or sheep give it any thought?

CAUSES OF OUR UNREASONABLE PREOCCUPATION

Why are so many of the pastors and people of God preoccupied with large congregations? Seven reasons come to mind.

First, as mentioned earlier, we take pride in large numbers. Just as David counted his tribes and gloated, we tally our members and swell with a false and self-deceiving sense of religious superiority. Like the blind Pharisees we condemn in every sermon, we blindly trudge onward doing our righteous work, not to be seen and approved by God, but to be seen and saluted by men.

Second, we fail to realize that God loves, values, and uses small congregations as much as large ones. Contrary to popular opinion, the members of small churches are not second-class citizens in the body of Christ. Small churches often "despise" and endure the "day of small things," but God "rejoices" in it, eagerly observing, growing, and using His "mustard seed" congregations. "For who hath despised the day of small things? For they [the eyes of the Lord] shall rejoice and shall see [watch with interest]..." (Zech. 4:10).

Third, we easily forget that every congregant needs individual pastoral attention. How can one shepherd give adequate care to a huge number of God's sheep, who need not only Bible teaching but also personal counsel, correction, exhortation, and guidance on a regular basis? In ancient times, Middle Eastern shepherds stood over their sheep as they entered the door to the sheepcote (cave or walled enclosure for flocks) nightly, closely examining each one for signs of malnutrition, wounds, sickness, or parasites. God wants Christian shepherds to do the same for every "sheep" in their flock. This very personal "sheepcote care" is impossible in larger churches—unless the senior pastor is supported by a sufficient number of wise, caring, and vigilant associate pastors, elders, counselors, and mentors. We strive for and boast of small teacher-student ratios in our schools, realizing this usually results in a higher quality education. Why not in our churches?

Fourth, we fail to realize that excessive church-consciousness sometimes hinders Christ-consciousness. It is possible for believers to become so caught up with their church and its exciting ministries, programs, and buildings that they overlook and neglect their personal relationship to Jesus. Usually smaller churches offer no such distraction.

Fifth, many Christians seek church meetings that are large, exciting, rock-concert-type entertainment events rather than nourishing, corrective appointments with the Good Shepherd. These look for loud sounds, bright lights, and sparkling personalities, not simpler, calmer meetings marked by sound Bible teaching, soul-searching exhortations, and worshipful singing aimed at ministering to *Jesus*.

Sixth, we tend to judge our fruitfulness by immediate visible results. But sometimes God's plan is for our church to blossom later rather than sooner. He may cut back our church, or "purge" it, so it can bear "more fruit" two, three, or five years from now (John 15:2). Or He may let our work seemingly "fall into the ground and die" for a season, so it may rise again a decade later and bear "much fruit" (John 12:24). So, pastor, don't be discouraged if you stand before only a few disciples. Israel's greatest King, Jesus, came from one of its smallest villages, Bethlehem. (See Micah 5:2.) Who knows, one sheep in your "little flock" may grow to be a Luther, Wesley, Moody, or Graham through whom God changes the whole world!

Seventh, we easily forget that a church's real value is unknown until it's tested. Paul informs pastors, "Every man's work shall be made manifest; for the day [of testing] shall declare it…it shall be *revealed by fire*; and *the fire shall test every man's work* of what sort [quality, value] it is" (1 Cor. 3:13). This means that a pastor's rewards will be based primarily upon the quality, not the quantity, of his pastoral work (though a high quantity of high quality work is the goal; see 3:8b.) The quality of his teaching and counsel—excellent or erroneous, sound or shallow, spiritual or worldly—will be revealed by how well those who obey it endure the fires of testing. If his instruction enables his people to "abide" faithful and devoted, he will be rewarded (v. 14); if it causes their walk and work with God to fail and "burn," he will lose his rewards, though not his salvation (v. 15). (See Philippians 4:1; 1 Thessalonians 2:19.)

Many churches look great before they're tested: meetings are packed, faith is growing, zeal is strong, worship is heavenly, brotherly love abounds, donations flow in, and missionaries go out. But when "tribulation or persecution ariseth because of the Word," they're quickly offended (Matt. 13:21). Their faith and zeal wane. Their works wither. Their righteousness turns to corruption. Why? Their teaching prepared them for good times but not hard times; for God's blessing, but not His testing. So many, disillusioned, fall away. Ultimately, only a handful of the original church-full survive the fire: "I will bring the third part through the fire…" (Zech. 13:9). They are God's golden remnant hidden among the congregation's ore: "…and will refine them…and will test them as gold is tested" (v. 9).

That's sad but not surprising. Of the thousands that flocked to Jesus' meetings during His three-year ministry, only a hundred and twenty survived the fiery ordeal of His stunning betrayal, unjust crucifixion, and strange delays. (See Acts 1:15.) They were the true priceless remnant of His disciples. All the other thousands were sincere but untested; saved but of much less value and use to God in the "crunch."

Pastor, when hot fires of testing—controversy, slander, financial troubles, moral failures, heresy, betrayals, church splits, or public rejection—suddenly descend upon your large or small "tabernacle," rejoice! You're about to discover the true worth of your church and your teaching, whether it's pure gold or painted tin; or worse, wood, hay, and stubble. Sometimes very big churches are reduced to ashes by testing; they melt, collapse, and burn. And sometimes small ones appearing to have only stubble prove instead to have surprising amounts of "gold tried in the fire"—after testing!

Watch for Reverse Prejudice!

We must also guard against reverse prejudice—rejecting or devaluing large churches merely because they are large. Demonizing big religion is just as wrong as deifying it. Why?

Congregations are just as unique as individuals. Granted, some megachurches have grown enormous because they've compromised the gospel, carefully omitting, denying, or altering the harder truths of discipleship to draw the mixed multitudes and keep them pacified with lukewarm religion. But others have not diluted the good news. Their large numbers are entirely of God. This was the case in Jerusalem when "the Lord added to the church daily" (Acts 2:47) and "believers were the more added to the Lord, multitudes both of men and women" (Acts 5:14). This was also the case at Antioch when "the hand of the Lord" worked powerfully through lay evangelists and "a great number believed, and turned unto the Lord," founding a new, large, and committed congregation (Acts 11:21). The same invisible, divine "hand" was working at London's Metropolitan Tabernacle, where the Spirit led hungry thousands to feast on Charles Spurgeon's sumptuous, uncompromisingly biblical sermons—while thousands more waited hungrily outside!

And while some large churches and prominent pastors look down on small ones, others do not. Because many Christians take pride in numbers, it does not follow that all those in large churches are proud. To the contrary, some are very spiritually minded, humble, and Spirit-led. Nor should we conclude that because it is more difficult for large churches to give personal attention to believers, they do not serve their people's spiritual needs well. To the contrary, some are very conscientious to watch over, teach, counsel, and support by intercession and fellowship every soul God gives them. And let's not forget, pastoral negligence can occur in small churches just as easily as in larger ones.

WWJW—Where Would Jesus Worship?

Here's a thought-provoking question: if Jesus visited your fair city, what church would He worship in next Sunday morning?

As explained in chapter seventeen, Jesus' words state definitively what He wants most from any local church:

> The *true worshipers* shall worship the Father *in spirit and in truth*; for the Father seeketh such to worship him…they that worship him [acceptably] must worship him *in spirit and in truth*.
>
> —John 4:23–24

In Christ's mind, therefore, it is most vitally important that churches live, work, and worship in the "Spirit and truth" of God. Such assemblies are His "true worshipers"—and the places He would likely choose to worship in if He came to your city.

On the other hand, many campaigning politicians would choose the church with the most registered voters or highest public profile. Some bishops or superintendents would visit the one with the largest congregation or best-known pastor. Some singles would visit the one with the most appealing singles ministry or divorce recovery program. Many parents would select the assembly with the best children's church, youth programs, or school. Materialistic Christians may be drawn to the church with the most prosperous congregants or newest, largest buildings. Computer-loving Christians may favor the church with the best Web site or blog. "Techy" believers might opt for the church whose sanctuary is wired with all the very latest technological wonders of sight, sound, and motion. Gospel musicians might select the church with the largest or most skilled choir, orchestra, or worship team. And we could go on describing Christians who choose churches merely to suit their strongest individual interests.

But if the New Testament describes Him accurately, and it does, Jesus would choose a church not based on His personal preferences but rather on His spiritual priorities. He would opt not for big religion but for best religion—the church having the *best spirit* and *most truth*, whether its numbers were soaring, sinking, or stuck. Such a church is and has spiritual gold, even if it doesn't glitter.

~

If you pastor or attend a small church, don't be doubtful, discouraged, or ashamed. Be ashamed only if your church is not walking in spirit and truth, but never because your numbers are small!

And resolve never to envy or criticize pastors or churches just because they have more people than you do. Never object to what *God* has done for them: "A man can receive nothing, except it be *given him from heaven [by God]*" (John 3:27). And never despise what He has given you: "All wait upon thee . . . [and] *that which thou givest them*, they gather" (Ps. 104:27–28). Instead praise God for what He has given them—and for what He has given you! Earnestly remember what is and is not important to God: quantity of worshipers never determines quality of worship. Understand that a church's favorable ecclesiastical or social standing doesn't increase its spiritual power, nor does lacking them decrease it. When in seasons of persecution or strong testing a small but faithful church is ignored, it may still play a big part in God's plan if it stays close to Christ and prayerful. Why? He knows all about small flocks, and He loves them.

Though multitudes thronged Jesus relentlessly, He personally pastored only twelve people during His three-year ministry. Only twelve! And only eleven survived testing! Therefore, as one of their own, Jesus says to the pastors and people of small churches:

> Fear not, *little flock*; for it is your Father's good pleasure to give you the kingdom.
>
> —LUKE 12:32

So be hopeful about your "little flock"—and your little ones!

Chapter Twenty

HOPE FOR THE PARENTS OF CAPTIVE CHILDREN

I will contend with him that contendeth with thee,
and I will save thy children.

—ISAIAH 49:25

*C*hristian parent, if one or more of your children are captive to anyone or anything, there is strong hope for you and for them in God.

Isaiah 49:24–25 spells out that hope. There the Lord promises to release His people's children from even the most hopeless captivities, even as the prophet foresees a very ugly sight indeed: God's people suffering in the seventy-year Babylonian captivity.

> Shall the prey be taken from the mighty, or the lawful captive delivered? But thus saith the LORD: Even the captives of the mighty shall be taken away, and the prey of the terrible shall be delivered; for I will contend with him that contendeth with thee, and I will save thy children.
>
> —ISAIAH 49:24–25

Judah and Jerusalem first fell to, and its people were deported by, the Babylonians in 605 B.C. Subsequently Judah remained subject to Babylon's will for nearly twenty years, its rulers appointed and removed at the whims of Babylonian regents. A second major defeat and larger deportation followed in 597 B.C. With Jerusalem's third and final defeat in 586 B.C., and the deportation of all but Judah's poorest citizens, the captivity was officially fully underway. As alluded to in our text, the militarily superior ("mighty") and barbaric ("terrible") Babylonians had finally crushed Judah, the lone remaining Jewish state, and forced its people ("captives of the mighty" and "prey of the terrible") into a long, sad period of exile. It was a time of anguish. For at least the first few years, the Jews' psychological pain was intense and unrelieved.

The sons of the deposed Judean king, Zedekiah, were executed in his presence. Zedekiah's eyes were then put out and he was imprisoned! Thousands of Jews were slain in the battle of Jerusalem, as the streets turned red with Jewish blood. All the major cities of Judah were burned and thousands of Judeans were led off against their wills on an approximately 500-mile forced march to Babylon.[1] Though many Jews eventually lived comfortably in Babylonian culture—some, such as Daniel, rising to prominence and others becoming successful merchants—the Jewish people as a whole suffered greatly. They were denied the possession and autonomous rule of their homeland. They could not worship their God in their national temple, which had been thoroughly sacked, destroyed, and burned by the Babylonian armies. Their once-proud capital, Jerusalem, with its inner city and stronghold of David, Mount Zion, lay in ruins. Their formerly impervious sense of national security was brutally shattered, leaving them tormented by fears of vulnerability to other hostile nations. And, most humiliatingly, they had to endure the constant needling of their Babylonian captors, who gloatingly claimed that Judah had fallen because its deity was inferior to and impotent before Babylon's gods. They even taunted them to sing Jewish worship songs for their amusement.

An anonymous psalmist vividly describes this painful mockery:

> By the rivers of Babylon, there we sat down, yea, we wept, when we remembered Zion. We hung our harps upon the willows in the midst thereof. For there they that carried us away captive required of us a song; and they that wasted us required of us

mirth, saying, Sing us one of the songs of Zion. How shall we sing the LORD's song in a foreign land?

—PSALM 137:1–4

The most depressing fact about this stunning defeat and dispersion of God's people was that it was all, as our text states, "lawful." "Shall the...*lawful* captive [be] delivered?" (Isa. 49:24). It was executed in exact accordance with not only Babylon's heathen ordinances but also, more importantly, *God's* holy law.

In the Pentateuch, God had clearly forewarned His people, not once but twice, that He would punish them with foreign invasion and captivity if they turned from Him to worship other gods. His first explicit caveat was duly recorded in Leviticus 26:23–39. As if sensing the first warning was ignored, the second screams out from the pages of the Book of Deuteronomy:

Because thou servest not the LORD thy God...the LORD shall bring a nation against thee from far...whose tongue thou shalt not understand; a nation of fierce countenance, who shall not regard the person of the old, nor show favor to the young. And he shall eat the fruit of thy cattle, and the fruit of thy land....And he shall besiege thee in all thy gates...And ye shall be plucked from off the land....And the LORD shall scatter thee among all people, from the one end of the earth even unto the other....And among these nations shalt thou find no ease, neither shall the sole of thy foot have rest...

—DEUTERONOMY 28:47–65

So, after bearing with Judah's recurring and increasing idolatry for over 350 years, God performed exactly what He had preached. Merciless foreign invaders, swords, siege, famine, destruction, dispersion, all of these envisioned evils materialized before the Jews' disbelieving eyes and fallen faces.

With their national destiny and individual lives seemingly ruined beyond repair, many surviving Jewish parents in Palestine despaired of ever seeing their deported children's faces again. Actual realities gave them no hope. Yet in His great faithfulness God gave hope to hopeless parents, a very sure hope conveyed by a very clear promise to reunite their dissected families: in His time and way, all His captive children, and theirs, would return, forever free!

Paraphrased, God's comforting promise reads:

> Who has ever heard of spoil being recovered from powerful conquerors? What are the chances of legally held prisoners being released? But God says, THIS WILL HAPPEN! Even the prisoners of the strongest captors will be recovered and victims of the cruelest oppressors released! Why? Because I will personally see to it. I will fight against [literally, *toss, grapple with*] those who have fought against you, and are still fighting, and I will rescue [and return] your children [and mine].
>
> —ISAIAH 49:24–25, AUTHOR'S PARAPHRASE

This paraphrase of our text is based in part on the meaning of the Hebrew word *riyb* (roob), which is translated "contend" in the Authorized Version (KJV). This word means "to toss," that is, "to grapple." Figuratively, it means "to wrangle" or hold a controversy.[2] To "toss and grapple" is language most specifically associated with wrestling.

As it is today, wrestling was a popular sport in ancient times. The Greeks made it a part of their Olympic games around 708 B.C.[3] The Romans later modified certain aspects of Greek wrestling to forge their own "Greco-Roman" style wrestling, which along with "freestyle" wrestling is still used today in international and Olympic wrestling. Isaiah, a very cultured, courtly, knowledgeable, and observant man, would have been familiar with Greco-Roman wrestling and basic terms associated with it. It is entirely congruous, then, that he may have selected his words intending to allude to the intense struggles of ancient wrestlers.

Our text from Isaiah 49:25 envisions an ancient Greco-Roman wrestling match in which two opponents grapple with one another—grasping, pulling, pushing, holding, switching positions, using leverage, and so forth—until one outmaneuvers or overpowers the other, "tosses" him to the ground, and "pins" his shoulders, terminating the contest by a "fall." Isaiah's use of the word *riyb* intimates as much. Thus God uses very graphic wrestling terms—"grapple and toss"—to describe what He will do to those who stubbornly wrestle (or contentiously wrangle) with His people over their children in an attempt to exert harmful control or influence over them with spiteful, vengeful, or purely selfish intent.

A Greco-Roman wrestler's paraphrase of God's promise might read:

I will *grapple with and toss* him that has grappled with and tossed you.

History confirms that, indeed, God kept His promise to His Jewish captives. In October of 539 B.C., He sent the Persian forces to the gates of Babylon with brilliant tactics in hand. Babylon's massively thick and high double walls, with their eight fortified gates, were truly impenetrable by all conventional means of assault. But the Persians noted one possible means of entry: the Euphrates River flowed under the walls, through the middle of the city, and out the other side. In one of the most ingenious military maneuvers in history, the Persians temporarily diverted a large volume of the Euphrates' waters into a marshy area upstream so that, when the river's depth was significantly reduced, their soldiers could wade into it, go under the walls spanning the river's entrance to and exit from the city, and enter both sides of Babylon simultaneously.[4] Once inside, the fighting was comparatively easy, since the Persians had chosen to attack on a night when many Babylonians, including King Belshazzar (Dan. 5), were celebrating a national holiday and were either satiated with banqueting, hopelessly drunk, or asleep. Thus the Persians militarily overpowered, or "grappled with and tossed," Babylon's stunned defenders.

The Persian king Cyrus' ensuing decree of liberation (538 B.C.) permitted all the *children of Judah* (Jewish captives and their children of all ages) to return to Palestine to rebuild their temple and reestablish their worship and way of life (Ezra 1:1–4). So after approximately seventy years (605–538 B.C.) God kept His promise to "contend" with those who had "contended" with His people—and all His children who wished to do so, and their children, returned home.

It was a sudden, sweet, and satisfying end to a long, sad, and painful season of captivity. The heavenly Father, and every father and mother in Judah, rejoiced! The Jewish "captives of the mighty" were free at last! But their liberation didn't fully end the story of captive children.

Today many Christians have children who are "captives of the mighty" and "prey of the terrible" in urgent need of liberation.

CAUSES OF MODERN CHILD CAPTIVITY

Are any of your children captives, my friend? By "children" we mean *not only young but also adult children and grandchildren*. By "captives" we mean not only child hostages, refugees, or prisoners but also *children whose spiritual or natural welfare is being harmed or limited in any way*, usually by the control of personal enemies, bad influences, or demonic forces.

There are many causes of such modern child captivity. I offer this brief listing only because these are fairly common.

Unhealthy habits

Maybe your child is ensnared by unhealthy personal habits, such as laziness or overeating. Inaction and indulgence are helping obesity put its shackles on thousands of children across America today.

Or he (or she) may be bound by an obsessive interest with television, the Internet, video games, or cell phones. Too much wondering at these wonderful technologies leaves one's work undone, body unexercised, and mind undeveloped.

Destructive habits

Perhaps your child has formed clearly self-destructive habits, such as smoking, drinking, pornography, or fornication. These in no way help and in every way harm the mind and body.

Maybe lying, cheating, and stealing have become his new "work ethic" instead of working, paying his bills, and giving to the needy.

He may be ensnared in criminal activities—such as the production, sales, or use of illegal drugs; prostitution; or the burgeoning pornographic industry—and already showing signs of an abnormal lifestyle, altered personality, infirm body, or paranoid mind.

Or, as so many today, his mind may be gripped by the demonically inspired, sexually debased lyrics to the mesmerizing, hellish, unmusical "music" CDs being produced and sold today by the millions, often by "recording artists," who, I'm sad to report, often don't know sharps from flats, melodies from monstrosities, or musical greatness from mad graffiti.

The truth be told, I believe Satan is using the female-debasing, profanity-laced perversion of rhythm and rhyme known as "hip-hop" (especially crime-glorifying "gangsta rap") to bind, twist, and harm the eternal souls of youth today. It's the same thing he did in the 1960s through the wicked words and wild shrieks of hard rock music, with its superficial and subliminal calls to rebellion, sexual promiscuity, and illicit drug use. (I'm not condemning any decently worded hip-hop or pop music. Nor do I condemn as hopeless anyone presently caught in the above-described snares; I rather pray for them.)

Emotional, mental, or nervous troubles

Possibly your child is bound by emotional, mental, nervous, or physical problems that hinder his personal growth or happiness.

His (or her) anger may be volcanic and a constant source of self-opposition in relationships, school, work, or church.

He may be hindered by recurring thoughts of inability or ignorance or paralyzed with fears of failure when facing new tasks or challenges.

He may be bound by envy—anger at others having what he wants—and so discontent, discouraged, or driven to imitation or competition every time his friends or associates are promoted, blessed, prospered, or favored.

He may suffer from some form of mental or nervous disorder: anorexia nervosa, anxiety disorders, autism, bipolar disorder, depression, epilepsy, hyperactivity, learning disorders such as dyslexia, and so forth.

Physical hindrances

Your child may be shackled by blindness, deafness, muteness, or stuttering. These physical conditions may severely limit his perception of and reaction to people, conversation, and circumstances.

Or he may suffer from a chronic physical illness, debilitating injury, or another physical handicap.

Mischievous friends

Your child may be yoked and led astray by the bad influence of mischievous friends who repeatedly draw him into trouble. The apostle Paul had it right when he asserted, "Be not deceived: Evil company corrupts good morals" (1 Cor. 15:33). Or, "Don't be fooled…bad company corrupts good character" (NLT).

A rebellious attitude

Your son or daughter may be bound with a spirit of rebellion. He (or she) won't even listen to, much less obey, your parental instructions. He clashes regularly with authorities at school, work, church, or in society. Shackled with stubbornness, he hinders his education, occupation, and spiritual and human development, and is unable to function productively within any chain of command.

A broken home

With unscriptural divorce rampant and rising in the American church, increasing numbers of believing parents find themselves locked in bitter child custody disputes or unpleasant custody arrangements with covenant-breaking spouses and estranged in-laws. Consequently, the seed of the righteous are subjected temporarily to the rod of the unrighteous—the court-ordered custody or visitations of relatives hostile to you or your faith.

If your children are presently in the sole or joint custody of a hostile or hypocritical ex-spouse, Isaiah's promise is particularly addressed to you. God can do what looks and feels impossible—free your children from the influence of uncaring parents or vengeful relatives who mislead them with worldly values or trouble them with slanderous lies. And He'll do so, if you trust and obey Him.

Gangs or human trafficking

Possibly your son or daughter is caught up in one of the many dangerous youth gangs that are increasingly troubling cities across this nation.

He (or she) may be brainwashed with the foolish thinking of demonic gang leaders, surrounded by violent behavior, and allured by the false bravado and thrill of criminal activity.

Girls and young women particularly may be ensnared in the growing human trafficking (slave) business, held by their captors' threats to perform manual labor or for sexual abuse or prostitution.

Jail or prison

Your child may have been justly convicted of a crime and therefore be a "lawful captive" in a county jail or state or federal prison.

Once in prison, he risks captivity to the various dangers unique to prison life and culture: despair, drug use, riots, gangs, and vicious sexual or physical assaults.

False religions, churches, or cults

Your child may be bound by false beliefs, teachers, religions, or cults.

He may be under the influence of transcendental meditation, yoga, or other mystical Eastern beliefs or practices.

He may be captivated by the charm, intelligence, or exceptional abilities of a cult leader and the false peace and prosperity of his (or her) deluded followers.

He may be convinced that false religions—Mormonism, the Watchtower Society, Christian Science, Islam, Buddhism, Hinduism, Satanism, the Unification church, indigenous religions, and so forth—are true and Christianity is false.

Or he may have joined a lukewarm Christian denomination that embraces liturgy, ritual, and sinner-friendly values and jilted Bible-believing evangelicalism.

Or he may be enthralled with a Bible-professing pastor and church whose key doctrines and practices are actually *unbiblical*—errant, unbalanced, or corrupt.

Astrology, witchcraft, occultism, psychics, or secret societies

Your child may be entangled in one of the many popular and prospering works of spiritual darkness that are thriving in the Western world today.

He may be convinced that the oldest form of satanic deception and bondage—astrology—is actually new divine light and liberty. Thus he may unintelligently submit his intelligence to the purported power of celestial bodies to control human events and destiny.

The growing Harry Potter craze has fed on public interest in Wicca and boosted witchcraft-related activities. Your child (or grandchild) may be under the influence of this dark covering or other related works of occultism.

Or he may regularly consult New Age channelers (spiritualists), clairvoyants, necromancers, psychic hotlines, or other demonic mediums and put more faith in the readings of the psychics than in the writings of the prophets.

Or your son or daughter may be spiritually snared by membership in secret societies offering darkness disguised as light and unbiblical beliefs and rituals cloaked by a façade of good works. Among these are the Shriners, Freemasons, and Eastern Star, to name a few.

If your child is caught up in these or other literal, figurative, or spiritual captivities, our God, the Liberator of believers worldwide, Jewish and Christian, has a word for you. It is a word of irrepressible, undefeatable hope: "I will contend with him that contendeth with thee [or grapple with and toss him that has grappled with and tossed you] and *I will save thy children*" (Isa. 49:25).

EIGHT EFFECTIVE BIBLICAL RECOMMENDATIONS

What should you do to ensure that you qualify for, and hasten, God's promise in Isaiah 49:25? Here are eight effective biblical recommendations.

1. Give thanks

If you have other children who are *not* captives, *give thanks* to your heavenly Father for their liberty: "In everything give thanks," or, as described earlier, offer "the sacrifice of praise to God...that is, the fruit of our lips giving thanks to his name" (1 Thess. 5:18; Heb. 13:15).

If you don't have other children, thank God for all your other bless-ings.

2. Fully believe God

Choose to completely *believe* God's promise just as He has stated it: "I will contend…I will save [rescue, release] thy children." Hope for nothing less than a full release from captivity. Yes, God is graciously and abun-dantly able to preserve and protect them in captivity. But here He promises not to preserve but to release them. Fully believe Him.

3. Abide close to the Liberator

Determine to *abide close* to your loving Liberator and His living words. He promised, "If ye abide in me, and my words abide in you, ye shall ask what ye will, and it shall be done unto you" (John 15:7). So realize with delight that *your* walk with God is the key that will, through your steady intercession, unlock your child's captivity.

4. Pray—persistently, in faith, in agreement, and reminding God

Persistently *pray* "without ceasing" (1 Thess. 5:17) for your child's deliverance, in faith, in the Spirit, binding and loosing (Matt. 18:18), and agreeing with prayer partners (v. 19). And also remind God respectfully but persistently of His wonderful promise in Isaiah 49:25. Why? He instructs us to do so: "*Put me in remembrance* [of My covenant promises]; let us plead together [in full agreement]; declare thou [My promises], that thou [your petition] mayest be justified [as worthy of a response]" (Isa. 43:26).

5. Speak to the "mountain"

In faith *speak to the "mountain,"* or imposing coalition of human and demonic antagonists, standing in the way of your child's liberation. This is not praying but *saying*. It is not a plea but a *command*. It is not speaking in your authority but *Christ's*: "Be thou removed…be thou cast into the sea" (Mark 11:23).

6. Reject all doubts

With conviction *reject all doubts* regarding your child's deliverance and turn your thoughts instead to Christ's promise: "Whosoever shall say unto this mountain, Be thou removed...*and shall not doubt in his heart*, but shall [continue to] believe that those things which he saith shall come to pass, *he shall have whatever he saith*" (Mark 11:23). Hold firmly your confidence that what you have commanded in Christ's name and will must come to pass in His time and way.

7. Offer anticipatory worship

Offer anticipatory worship to God, expressing loving adoration to the Lord for your child's deliverance before you see it. This seemingly small act releases God's awesome power.

King Jehoshaphat ordered his people to worship God for their victory *before*, not after, they joined the battle with their enemies: "He appointed singers unto the LORD, who should praise...*as they went out before the army*...[singing] Praise the LORD; for his mercy endureth forever" (2 Chron. 20:21). At once, the Lord began "grappling with and tossing" their enemies and their resistance imploded: "When they began to sing and to praise, the LORD set an ambush against [their enemies]...and they were smitten...everyone helped to destroy another" (vv. 22–23). Perhaps the Lord will do the same for you as you offer anticipatory worship in the full expectancy of faith.

8. Wait patiently

Wait patiently for God's time and way of release. "He hath made every thing beautiful in its time" and ugly out of its time (Eccles. 3:11). God appointed a time for Judah's release and will also appoint a time for your child's deliverance. We may wait patiently or impatiently for God's time, but wait we must. Impatient (rebellious) waiting disqualifies us from receiving God's help—and "He will *not* save thy children!" So we must learn to wait patiently for God: "I waited *patiently* for the LORD, and he inclined unto me" (Ps. 40:1).

God has kindly given us two things to help us wait patiently: a word and a work.

The word is Romans 8:28. We *don't* know when, where, or how God will deliver our children, because "it is not for you to know the times or the seasons, which the Father hath put in his own power" (Acts 1:7). But here's something we know: "*We know* that God causes all things to work together for good to those who love God…who are called according to His purpose" (Rom. 8:28, NAS). Translation? God is making every single day of our children's captivity serve some good purpose! When it's over, we'll understand clearly how the enemy's woeful work has only served the Almighty's wonderful plan! Believe this!

And since we wait best when busy, God always gives us work: secular employment, church work, ministry, missions, volunteer work, charitable works, prayer, and so forth. As we faithfully work "heartily [wholeheartedly], as to the Lord, and not unto men" (Col. 3:23), God faithfully works deep peace and confidence—pure spiritual gold—into our hearts, while He works every circumstance and event "together" for our, and our children's, ultimate good.

Such steadfast trust and obedience can lead to only one thing: at His appointed time, in His chosen way, at His designated place, the Lord will step onto the mat of your circumstances and will "grapple with and toss" the forces and people who have grappled with you concerning your child's welfare and, at times, have tossed you into discouragement and despair. Working powerfully by His Spirit and providentially by human agents, He will outmaneuver, overwhelm, and "pin" them with either repentance or ruin. Whichever the case, they will "fall," defeated, and you will rise, victorious. Their cruel plans will fail and God's kind promises prevail. Your grueling wrestling will end and your child's homecoming begin—with joy and singing!

> The ransomed of the LORD shall return…with songs and everlasting joy.
>
> —ISAIAH 35:10

And for winning your match in the "Overcomers' Olympics," you will win a "gold medal" at the judgment seat of Christ.

We see this foreshadowed in Joseph's life: "And Pharaoh…put *a gold chain* about his neck" (Gen. 41:42). It is also intimated in Daniel's experience: "Then commanded Belshazzar, and they…put *a chain of gold* about his [Daniel's] neck" (Dan. 5:29). And it is symbolized in the golden crown God, through the elders of Israel, awarded David at his coronation: "Thou settest a *crown of pure gold* on his head" (Ps. 21:3). Why did God order that Joseph and Daniel be given gold chains and David a golden crown? He saw that they not only possessed "gold tried in the fire"—a priceless, proven trust in God and knowledge of Him—they also embodied it. So they won what they were: gold medals and gold crowns!

That's your hope, Christian parent, and your reward for your enduring loyalty to your children and your God.

Chapter Twenty-One

About Loyalty to God

Who is on the Lord's side?

—Exodus 32:26

Our loyal support of our children springs from an even more fundamental and vital source of fidelity: our loyalty to God.

Though the word *loyalty* is not found in the Authorized Version (KJV) of the Bible, it is the theme of many of its historical accounts, psalms, proverbs, precepts, parables, and epistles. In these passages, "faithfulness" is the biblical synonym most often used to describe loyalty. For instance, God promised loyalty to David with these words: "My faithfulness and my mercy shall be with him" (Ps. 89:24).

By definition, *loyalty* "implies a sense of devoted attachment to something or someone."[1] It is our *devoted attachments* to people and things that we wish to examine in this chapter.

Loyal to Whom and to What?

As born-again Christians, to whom and to what should we be loyal? We have both primary and secondary loyalties.

Our first loyalty should be to *God* Himself. He who has created us and given all to redeem us deserves our "devoted attachment" more than any other being or entity. From this prime loyalty spring secondary loyalties.

Our secondary, or *Christian loyalties,* are all natural expressions and extensions of our prime and abiding loyalty to God. Let's identify them and briefly describe them.

Our Christian loyalties

Christians should be loyal to *God's Word* (the Bible) above all other philosophies, ideals, codes, manifestos, creeds, and dogmas. This is not merely because the Bible is authoritative, but because it is accurate. It reveals to us God's true heart—His personal viewpoint, will, plan, and values—without any misrepresentations, deviations, or omissions. We may safely trust its revelation. Confidently and correctly, the psalmist declared:

> I esteem all thy precepts concerning all things to be right, and I hate [by comparison] every false way [biblically contradictory teaching].
>
> —PSALM 119:128

We should also be loyal to *God's people*—spiritually reborn Christians who share our vital affection for and attachment to God—because they are His dear children and He remains utterly faithful to them. The apostle John urged us to nurture and exercise our loyalty to God's people: "Everyone that loveth him that begot loveth him also that is begotten of him. By this we know that we love the children of God, when we love God" (1 John 5:1–2).

Additionally, we should loyally support *God's anointed leaders*, for it is His express will that they teach, correct, and guide us in life: "ministers...[whom] the Lord gave to every man" (1 Cor. 3:5). Paul wrote, "We beseech you, brethren, to know them who labor among you, and are over you in the Lord, and admonish you, and to esteem them very highly in love for their work's sake" (1 Thess. 5:12–13). Or, "Brothers and sisters, we ask you to appreciate those who work hard among you, who lead you in the Lord and teach you. Respect them with a very special love because of the work they do" (NCV).

Furthermore, we should loyally prepare for and pursue *God's call* on our life. For every Christian, God has preplanned and reserved a holy calling, a specific course of work or ministry with attending gifts:

"good works, which God hath before ordained that we should walk in them" (Eph. 2:10). This vocation or calling is our primary means of blessing His people and advancing His plan on earth. Paul described Christians as people who not only love God but who are also distinctly "called according to his purpose" (Rom. 8:28). He acknowledged that he was called as an "apostle," or sent-forth one, or special messenger: "Paul...called to be an apostle" (Rom. 1:1). And he urged us to remain loyal to our callings: "Let every man abide [loyally] in the same calling in which he was called" (1 Cor. 7:20).

And finally, we should loyally honor and uphold *God's institutions*—marriage, family, church, and government (the rule of law). Why? God has wisely and lovingly placed these social "foundations" in society for the good of all.

True (heterosexual, monogamous) marriage is a holy, safe haven for sexual love and human procreation and the sole historic nucleus of stable family life. Families provide personal security and lasting social stability and structure. The church provides spiritual life, nurture, and guidance to our souls, without which individuals and nations cannot thrive, no matter how excellent their educational system or governmental infrastructure. And government sits atop society providing (ideally) peace, law and order, social justice, and equal opportunity for its constituents to pursue their livelihoods and happiness. Whenever any or all of these divinely established institutions ("foundations") fail, we suffer trouble, loss, or harm: "If the foundations [institutions of society] be destroyed, what can the righteous do?" (Ps. 11:3). Therefore, we should loyally support them, as far as possible, just as we loyally serve God.

By our "devoted attachment" to these secondary or Christian loyalties—God's Word, people, anointed leaders, call, and institutions—we demonstrate our primary "devoted attachment" to God who ordained them.

Biblical Examples

Throughout the Bible we find people who were devotedly attached to God and others who clearly were not. Please ponder these examples of God's loyalists and God's disloyalists.

God's loyalists

When the rebellious archangel, Lucifer, and one-third of the lower angels decided to overthrow the rule of the Father of Spirits, two-thirds of the angelic hosts chose to remain loyal to their Creator.

Abraham grew so attached to God in Ur that, when God called, he forsook his sin-darkened country, culture, tribal family, and home to follow his new dominant loyalty. And he "went out, not knowing whither" (Heb. 11:8, KJV) He would lead him.

On Mount Moriah Isaac literally laid down his life in loyal devotion to his father's God. When it became clear that Abraham meant to bind and slay him as a human sacrifice, Isaac, in amazing submission foreshadowing that of Christ on Calvary, offered no resistance. His was a "devoted attachment" even unto death.

When the Israelites began cutting their ties with Jehovah to join themselves to Canaanite idols, Joshua decried their sin and declared his unswerving loyalty to Jehovah: "As for me and my house, we will serve the LORD" (Josh. 24:15).

Ruth remained faithful to the only true believer she knew—her mother-in-law, Naomi—vowing amid the worst adversity to stay by her side come what may. Her memorable words are the quintessential expression of loyalty to God's people:

And Ruth said, Entreat me not to leave thee, or to turn away from following after thee; for where thou goest, I will go; and where thou lodgest, I will lodge: thy people shall be my people, and thy God, my God. Where thou diest, will I die, and there will I be buried; the LORD do so to me, and more also, if anything but death part thee and me.

—RUTH 1:16–17

Ittai the Gittite and his men stood by King David through adversity and prosperity. When Absalom's rebellion forced David from his throne, Ittai refused to abandon God's anointed leader, choosing instead to follow David into exile. His loyal declaration echoes Ruth's: "Surely in what place my lord, the king, shall be, whether in death or life, even there also will thy servant be" (2 Sam. 15:21).

When King Nebuchadnezzar demanded that Meshach, Shadrach, and Abednego bow to his golden image or be executed, the three Jews responded with an unequivocal *no*. Live or die, they would remain steadfastly dedicated to the only true God and His trustworthy Word.

When many of Israel's prophets and people strayed from God to serve Baal, Elijah remained unmoved. He chose to suffer anything—abandonment, misunderstanding, hatred, deprivation, false allegations, expulsion from his country—rather than be disloyal to the one true God.

When at Sinai the Israelites made a golden calf and reveled in their sins, Moses issued a crucial clarion call to the remnant of God's loyalists: "Who is on the LORD's side?" The Levites alone responded: "And all the sons of Levi gathered themselves together unto him" (Exod. 32:26). For standing with God at great cost—against even their own family members who continued rejecting God by practicing sin—He awarded them the priesthood. (See Deuteronomy 33:8–11.)

When Jesus was suddenly betrayed, condemned, and led away to crucifixion, all His disciples forsook Him and fled—but one, John, who devotedly "stood by" Jesus' side till the end: "Now there *stood by* the cross of Jesus…the disciple…whom he loved [John]" (John 19:25–26).

For approximately ten years, Saul (Paul) lived humbly in his hometown of Tarsus, steadfastly preparing himself to fulfill his apostolic call though his prospects for apostolic ministry seemed nil.

The coming Jewish Christians of the Tribulation—the 144,000 evangelists, the martyrs, the hidden remnant, and the two witnesses—will remain devotedly attached to their newly acknowledged Anointed One, Jesus, while the rest of the Jews and the world increasingly idolize and follow the false messiah, the Antichrist.

God's disloyalists

Interestingly, in the very circumstances or periods in which God's true servants demonstrated their "devoted attachment" to God and to Christian loyalties, others distinguished themselves for breaking with Him and His interests. Consider these, God's disloyalists.

When two-thirds of the angels stood true to God, one-third abandoned Him to believe, serve, and follow Lucifer. Thus they severed their divine attachment to forge a new, diabolical, and disastrous one.

While Abraham wholly followed God's call, Lot turned aside to seek prosperity and power in Sodom, though Scripture implies that he knew of its notoriously corrupt lifestyle: "Lot...pitched his tent toward Sodom. *But [as he well knew,] the men of Sodom were wicked and sinners before the* LORD *exceedingly*" (Gen. 13:12–13).

When without regard for her personal desires or needs Ruth clung devotedly to Naomi and her God, Ruth's sister-in-law, Orpah, returned to Moab to pursue selfish desires—a husband, home, and children among the worshipers of false gods. Naomi observed, "Behold, thy sister-in-law is gone back unto her people, and unto her gods" (Ruth 1:15). Orpah seemed to show loyalty when she "kissed her mother-in-law" (v. 14), but her subsequent departure proved her disloyalty.

While Ittai and his men declared and demonstrated their unswerving dedication to David, Ahithophel, David's close friend and chief adviser, quietly sided with Absalom. A painful dagger of disloyalty pierced David's soul when he heard, "Ahithophel is among the conspirators with Absalom" (2 Sam. 15:31)—and their long, sweet friendship was permanently severed.

While Elijah sat alone by the brook Cherith, many prophets conveniently shifted their allegiance to Ahab and Jezebel's religion. Soon they were preaching Baal's gospel and feasting at Jezebel's table. And when Elijah later challenged his fellow Israelites to declare their loyalty to Jehovah, "The people answered him not a word" (1 Kings 18:21). Clearly, Israel's prophets and people alike were "devotedly attached" to their self-interest and self-preservation, not to Jehovah and His truth. Whatever for the moment kept them out of trouble, they did.

When the Levites boldly stepped forward to stand with God, His Law, and Moses against the golden calf, the other eleven tribes of Israelites remained comfortably as they were—grossly disloyal to their deity, Decalogue, and dedicated leader.

While the apostle John faithfully followed Jesus down the *Via Dolorosa*, the perfidious apostle turned apostate Judas stood with the enemy, thirty pieces of silver in hand. Notwithstanding his deceptive kiss in the garden, Judas' abiding loyalty remained with his covetousness, not his Christ.

While the apostle Paul remained loyal to God's apostolic call despite suffering persisting perils, pains, and persecutions, Demas forsook his ministry of helps to seek satisfaction in the things of this present life. Paul lamented his disappointing disloyalty in his letter to Timothy: "Demas hath forsaken me, having loved this present world" (2 Tim. 4:10).

While many Jews will serve Jesus "unto death" during the Tribulation period, other Jews will reject the emerging gospel of Messiah Jesus, believe the Antichrist's deceptive diplomacy (Dan. 9:27), and "devotedly attach" themselves to him, ultimately taking his mark and worshiping his image. Jesus foresaw and sadly decried this ultimate and terminal Jewish treachery: "I am come in my Father's name, and ye receive me not…another shall come in his own name, *him ye will receive*" (John 5:43).

WHY THE DISLOYALTY?

Just as the creation is not the result of random forces, disloyalty to God doesn't just arbitrarily happen. Our open betrayals of the Most High are always prompted by hidden causes. What motivated the disloyalties described above? *All these disloyal ones were moved to break their devoted attachment to God by some form of sin or self-will.*

The fallen angels apparently had their own susceptibility to pride, inclination to envy God, and aversion for His divine authority. So when Lucifer called for insurrection, they readily and willingly answered.

Though we know Judas was convicted of and corrected for his love of money on at least one occasion (John 12:1–8, esp. v. 6), he refused to forsake his besetting sin. So when the thought of selling out Jesus for gain quietly appealed to his mind for entry, it proved irresistible.

Wise as he was, Ahithophel calculated that following David into exile would probably cost him demotion, humiliation, and impoverishment. (Yet, foolishly, he overlooked that God could intervene in judgment at any moment.) So, self-interested, he held to his power, prestige, and prosperity, even if that meant siding with a despicable rebel like Absalom—and abandoning his long, loyal friendship with David.

The weight of biblical evidence suggests that Orpah loved her mother-in-law, Naomi, and perhaps even her God. But she loved the security, pleasure, and maternal fulfillment she hoped to find in a Moabite husband even more.

Secret sins, self-preservation, self-interest—these are the hidden forces that arose to spoil their fidelity to God and Christian loyalties. And they will spoil ours too if we don't deal with them.

What Tests Our Loyalty to God?

The strength of our devoted attachment to God is tested by any situation that challenges us to fully deny our besetting sin or self-will, or to suffer adversity, for our loyalty to God and Christian loyalties.

For instance, God's demand for holiness—requiring us to abandon *all* known sins—tests our loyalty to His high standards: "As he who hath called you is holy, so be ye holy in all manner of life, because it is written, Be ye holy; for I am holy" (1 Pet. 1:15–16). Are we more attached to God or to the besetting sins we cling to? To biblical integrity or bodily indulgence? To serve our Lord or our lusts?

The Spirit's guidance tries our loyalty to God. Will we steadfastly follow the Holy Spirit when we do not understand or like the way He leads? Will we "trust in the LORD with all thine heart" (Prov. 3:5) and follow His lead, or will we turn from the Lord to follow our heart's desires or reasoning?

The apostasy of our Christian friends further tries us. When our believing friends or relatives forsake the Lord, we must decide: Will we go back with them or go on with the Lord? Will we stand by our unfaithful brethren or our faithful Friend who is closer than a brother?

Popular but unbiblical trends test us. When we recognize the error of a popular teaching, practice, movement, or trend, will we for fear of being different run with the Christian herd, or will we stay loyal to Christ's biblical teachings, works, methods, and kingdom goals?

If in such cases we stop doing God's will, depart from His ways, or deny His truth in order to spare ourselves displeasure or rejection, we compromise our loyalty to God and Christian loyalties. That we find reprieve for the moment is no lasting consolation. Why?

Compromisers evade trouble for the present, but they do so at the high price of disqualifying themselves from being overcomers.

God's Loyalists Are Overcomers

Overcomers distinguish themselves by remaining consistently loyal to God and Christian loyalties *regardless.*

They always preserve their vital union to Christ, ever seeking His approval, whether advantageous or adverse consequences follow. Wisely, they adopt Esther's brave attitude toward the potentially undesirable consequences of their loyalty to God or Christian loyalties. When it became clear to Esther that she could not preserve herself from trouble and also preserve her relationship to God, she chose to protect the latter, putting her spiritual loyalties before her self loyalties: "So will I go in unto the king, which is not according to the law. And if I perish, I perish" (Esther 4:16). Like Esther, overcomers don't desire to lose, suffer, or die. Yet they would rather lose than be lukewarm, suffer than sellout truth, and die than be disloyal to God and their Christian loyalties. Are we following Esther's example? Are we becoming overcomers?

Why is this important? While all born-again Christians will live in Christ's kingdom, only overcoming Christians will rule with Him.

The apostle Paul revealed this:

> *If we suffer* [for loyalty to God and Christian loyalties], we shall also reign with him; [but] if we deny him [to avoid suffering], he also will deny us [the right to rule with him].
>
> —2 Timothy 2:12

Jesus confirmed Paul's revelation, when, in His challenges to the churches of Asia and the entire church age, He promised kingdom rulership only to overcomers:

> *He that overcometh,* and keepeth my works unto the end, *to him will I give power over the nations; and he shall rule them* with a

rod of iron [unbreakable Christlike authority].

—REVELATION 2:26–27

To him that overcometh will I grant to *sit with me in my throne...*

—REVELATION 3:21

This way of *rulership through overcoming* is the way Jesus went. He asserted that He rules today at the Father's right hand only because He overcame and remained loyal to His Father to the end:

...even as *I also overcame, and am set down with my Father in his throne.*

—REVELATION 3:21

Many believers have followed Jesus' example and exhortation to become loyal overcomers.

Of the seven churches of Asia in A.D. 95, those at Smyrna and Philadelphia are the best examples. Despite being imprisoned and threatened with execution for their witness and works, the believers in Smyrna remained "faithful [loyal] unto death" (Rev. 2:10). The Philadelphians chose to patiently endure reproach and oppression from their Jewish enemies rather than deny Christ's deity or teachings. Pleased, Christ commended their brave loyalty: "I know thy works...for thou...hast kept my word [teachings], and hast not denied my name [deity]" (Rev. 3:8). When tempted to be disloyal, the believers of Smyrna and Philadelphia quietly and persistently chose to maintain their devoted attachment to Jesus whatever the cost. For this Jesus distinguished them as "overcomers," promised them rewards, and honored them by lauding their loyalty in the Holy Scriptures.

For first-century Smyrnean and Philadelphian Christians, their tale is told. Forever they are God's loyalists. Forever they will rule with Jesus. Forever they will live close to Him in the city of ultimate honor and blessing He is preparing for all His loyalists, New Jerusalem.

But our loyalty is not yet proven nor our story written. Will we follow the brave and glorious example of the overcomers of Asia Minor, or will we turn back and join the long, shameful column of God's disloyalists?

In these last days, God will test not only our faith and patience but also our loyalty. Why? He wants it, passionately! And so does the enemy, persistently! In many trying situations, Satan will use any remaining remnants of our worldliness and carnality to probe and test the strength of our loyalty to God. And God will stand back and let him do this because He wants an answer to this question: Is our "devoted attachment" to God and Christian loyalties stronger than our attachment to sin? To self-will? To self-preservation?

In those trying times, various pressures will attempt to separate us from God and bind us to new, lower loyalties. Will we continue steadfastly loving God first when human loves pull our heartstrings? Will we remain committed to the integrity of God's Word when scientific theories, new philosophies, and cultural changes mock its inspiration, credibility, and relevance to our culture? Will we stand by and assist committed Christians when the paganized public misunderstands, misrepresents, mocks, and persecutes them? Will we continue faithfully supporting anointed leaders when acrimonious liars willfully slander them and crucify their good name? Will we devotedly follow God's call on our life when the way the Spirit leads grows harder and more perplexing by the day? Will we continue respecting God's institutions when the twisted devotees of secularism laugh them off the world's stage as foolish relics from the human race's unenlightened past? Such tests will tell our loyalty—and our tale.

So keep a close eye on your loyalties, my friend. Let nothing and no one break your devoted attachment to God and Christian loyalties. May the immovable Rock of Ages personally help you never be moved.

Chapter Twenty-Two

Don't Be Moved!

But none of these things move me.

—Acts 20:24

No matter how loyal we are to God, at one time or another, everything and everyone in this satanically influenced world will try to "move" us from God. So we must learn, as the apostle Paul did, to not be moved: "But none of these things *move* me" (Acts 20:24).

To "move" something physically is to *change, shift, reposition, or relocate* it. Such a change in physical place or position inevitably creates a separation from other things previously close or united.

A Christian is "moved" spiritually when he (or she) yields to satanic pressure to make wrong and harmful changes in his belief, daily living, or service. This speaks of a *detrimental spiritual shift* away from Jesus—closeness to Him, confidence in Him, and conscientious compliance with His will for our personal life. Such a "move" leaves us, Christ's earthly branches, separated from Him, our heavenly Vine, with whom we've previously been united, through whom alone we receive spiritual life, and by whom alone we produce spiritual fruit.

Thus "moved," we immediately begin degenerating. (No one stands still spiritually; the day we stop walking forward, we start sliding back.) Spiritual *degeneration* is the opposite of spiritual "edification." Instead of "building up, strengthening, and improving" our soul daily in faith, knowledge of God, and spiritual fervor, we gradually weaken and wear down.

Instead of moving steadily forward in our relationship with God, we step back from seeking, loving, and serving Christ and incrementally return to "carnality"—unspiritual thinking (the reasoning of the old, unregenerated, "fleshly" nature), unbiblical living, and worldly values, interests, and preferences. (See 1 John 2:15–17.) Degeneration is a very serious matter. Why? It leaves us unwilling to draw near the Lord, unfit for His use, and unable to detect the tempter's traps. And, if continued, degeneration leads to full-blown *apostasy*, or a spiritually disastrous "defection from truth." We completely fall away from living in the truth, faith, righteousness, fellowship, and ways of God. Scripture warns us repeatedly of this ominous failure of faith.

As stated earlier, Paul's trusted assistant, Demas, fell away: "Demas hath forsaken me, having loved this present world" (2 Tim. 4:10). So did many of Jesus' original followers: "From that time many of his disciples went back, and walked no more with him" (John 6:66). Peter wrote sadly of apostate teachers, "who have forsaken the right way, and are gone astray" (2 Pet. 2:15). And Paul somberly prophesied that in these last days many faithful Christians would turn and become apostates: "And they shall *turn away* their ears from *the truth*" (2 Tim. 4:4).

So we conclude that being "moved" leads to degeneration and that leads to apostasy.

THE WAYS SATAN TRIES TO "MOVE" US

To defeat an enemy, one must discern his strategy, or plan of attack. So to avoid being moved by Satan, Christians must recognize the various ways he tries to move us. Here are some of them.

Moved to doubt

Satan tries to move us to doubt by exposing our minds to apparent contradictions to God's Word. Peter walked stably on Galilee's stormy waters until he began rethinking his trust in Jesus' promissory command to "come" (Matt. 14:29). Then he quickly began sinking, prompting Jesus' probing question, "Why didst thou doubt?" (v. 31).

Doubts may be provoked by anything that makes us worry that God may not really be what the Bible, the Spirit, and our faith all agree He is:

true, loving, fair, all-knowing, all-powerful, present everywhere at once and yet always near, attentive to our prayers, and in full, unchallengeable control of our personal lives and the whole world. Oh, and *just like Jesus,* as He is so adequately described in the New Testament: "He that hath seen me hath seen the Father" (John 14:9).

If we don't guard our minds closely, any one of many mental stimuli may cause us to doubt God. For instance, things such as: seeming or actual unanswered prayers; delayed divine help; disappointed hopes; very long trials; Christian sufferings (crosses of rejection for Christ's, ministry's, or the Word's sake); the triumphing and prosperity of the wicked; unexplainable archaeological or paleontological finds; unproven yet widely accepted scientific theories; physicists' plausible but unbiblical projections of future astronomical, geological, or oceanic catastrophes or humanly induced doomsday scenarios; the growing influence of false religions or unbiblical philosophies and ideologies; the rise of false teachers, teachings, and movements in the church; deluded but confident secular talk show hosts, journalists, or Hollywood celebrities who hold smug, head-shaking contempt for our seemingly archaic biblical faith, morals, and world view; and so forth.

These are just a few of the sharp, potentially deadly "arrows" of misgiving Satan shoots at his favorite target: our confidence in God's unfailingly faithful character and Word.

Moved to fear

The enemy tries to move us to fear by luring us to focus our attention on dreadful or terrifying personal prospects.

For instance, rejections tend to intimidate us. When people turn away from us, we may forget that God still stands by us—"I will never leave thee, nor forsake thee" (Heb. 13:5)—and become afraid. Unexpected defeats may temporarily stun and destabilize us. When we first run headlong into "the triumphing of the wicked" (Job 20:5), our naïve assumption that "God would never let bad people win" is badly shaken. When we hear reports of Christians failing in their faith, duties, relationships, or ministries, Satan may try to suggest to us a false corollary—that because they failed, we will too. Slander may put a scare into us. Our heart may sink when we hear an enemy has misrepresented us—and people are *believing*, not dismissing, their lies. Threats made by crude and violent enemies are another cause of trepidation. God let Jesus, Paul, Stephen, and countless Christian martyrs suffer physical attacks; will He let us also? When we're weak, sick, or weary with well-doing, Satan may try to flash-flood our minds with negative, self-denigrating, debilitating thoughts—vivid flashbacks of all our failures and follies, but none of our faithfulness and fruitfulness—to make us feel condemned, inferior, and worthless.

Or, if these personal dreads don't shake us, the enemy may try to make us afraid for our loved ones or friends. Their financial crises, career challenges, business failures, or marriage problems may tempt us to fret or worry rather than pray and believe.

If we don't quickly and efficiently cast down these intimidating imaginations, they will quickly and effectively move us from faith to fear—and failure!

Moved to sin

The tempter tries to move us to sin by placing before our eyes or ears the alluring sights and sounds of wickedness or worldliness.

Through television or movie images he may invite us to entertain sinful pleasures rather than enjoy sacred joy: "In thy presence is fullness of joy" (Ps. 16:11). When talking with people who are covetous, he may urge us to follow their lead and greedily seek "mammon"—deposited securities, or monetary or material wealth trusted in—rather than seek to stockpile the real "gold," the invaluable faith, truth, and wisdom of God. After listening to boasters, we may decide to stop seeking the honor that comes from God only and start striving for the praises and prizes of men. When we see non-Christians experiencing great success or celebrity, we may begin envying their prosperity and despising our hidden but happy walk with Jesus. When our personal enemies seem to evade God's justice, we may succumb to the spirit of vengeance and secretly hope for retribution rather than pray for their repentance.

In short, the devil tries to move us to commit or harbor *any* sin—disobedience to God's Word or will—knowing that sin separates us from our Savior.

Moved to pride

As surely as the sun sets daily, the father of pride will try to move us to pride, the original, worst, and most despiritualizing sin.

He may prompt us to belittle or condemn those who are ignorant, poor, or uncultured and swell with a false sense of superiority. He may flood our minds with self-important thoughts—self-serving plans, self-aggrandizing ambitions, self-exalting imaginations, or self-congratulatory memories of past accomplishments and honors. Among these self-focused cerebral impulses there is little or no gratitude to God or to others. They're all about the "big three"—me, myself, and I. These prideful rushes of inflated thoughts are often accompanied by the onset of another cerebral disease: total amnesia regarding our past sins, follies, and failures.

Combined, these internal forces of conceit move us from the God who, as discussed previously, loathes pride and loves humility.

Moved to neglect our time "with Him"

The enemy may try to move us to neglect our personal fellowship with Jesus.

Christ called His original followers to "be with him" daily before sending them to work for Him: "He appointed twelve, that they should *be with him*, and that [later] he might send them forth to preach" (Mark 3:14). He still calls Christians to establish regular private fellowship "with Him" every day: *Come unto me* all ye that labor and are heavy laden, and I will give you [soul] rest" (Matt. 11:28). Some wisely hear and heed His call, sitting at His feet daily.

But the spirit of *anti*-Christ is determined to change this. He convinces some that because popular Christianity has changed over the centuries, personal devotion is no longer necessary. God is no longer "a rewarder of them that diligently seek him" (Heb. 11:6). So they stop seeking Jesus' face. Some turn away when other believers, ministers, and churches *seem* to prosper without emphasizing the devotional life. Others simply let the engaging interests and pressing cares of this frenetic world gradually draw them away from their discipline of taking time for God.

So a distinct shift occurs in their daily priorities: instead of nurturing their private time at Jesus' feet, they neglect it.

Moved to bitterness

The adversary tries to move us to bitterness by various provocations.

He tries to stir us to envy people, knowing envy will move us from the tenderness of God's love to the agitation of human strife: "If you have *bitter envying and strife* in your hearts..." (James 3:14). He sends offensive people our way hoping we will take offense at them and nurse a bitter spirit of unforgiveness. This separates us from the One who commanded, "Forgive, if you have anything against anyone," and warned, "But if you do not forgive, neither will your Father who is in heaven forgive your transgressions" (Mark 11:25–26, NAS). When long oppressed by cruel leaders or corrupt governments, we may grow bitter at God for delaying relief. Or we may grow bitter toward Him when we experience large losses, lengthy sicknesses, or separations from loved ones. Satan hoped this would embitter Job: "[Just] touch all that he hath, and he will curse thee to thy face" (Job 1:11). We may grow deeply disappointed because, despite our fervent prayers and hopes, our nation grows more sinful, our church more lukewarm, or our home life more dysfunctional, and, unless checked, this disappointment may turn into poisonous cynicism.

These or any "root of bitterness" will separate us from the sweet Root of David, whose spirit is always soft, gracious, and full of living water—and through us, embitter and move others: "lest any root of bitterness springing up trouble you, and by it many be defiled" (Heb. 12:15).

Moved to abandon duty

Satan tries relentlessly to move us to abandon our God-assigned duties or ministries. To achieve this, he pummels our minds incessantly with various circumstantial hammer blows, intending to render us dizzy, numb, or preferably paralyzed, with a sense of futility.

For instance, our enemies repeatedly vex, oppose, or slander us. Their hateful opposition seems as insurmountable and unmovable as a mountain. Individuals at home or work change their attitudes and become painful "thorns" in our sides. Despite these adversities we persevere in our duties, only to see our best efforts fail to succeed as we hoped. Bodily weariness sets in or sickness visits, adding physical burdens to our already heavy psychological ones. Troubled and confused, we pray, and God quietly blesses us with His Spirit, strengthens us with His Word, and encourages us to keep working—yet sends little tangible help for long periods of time. Under these heavy "blows," we get discouraged and wonder if it's worth it to go on. "All this misery is from the LORD! Why should I wait for the LORD any longer?" (2 Kings 6:33, NLT).

The adversary reasons, "Why are you working so steadily? Give it up! Get a life!" Well-meaning Christian friends "minister" to us: "Face facts; your work has failed. God will never bless it. It's time to move in a new direction." So, under this enormous pressure, we "move in a new direction"—*away* from God's call, our kingdom destiny, and our eternal rewards.

Moved to abandon God's ways

The tempter tries to move us to abandon God's "ways"— distinctively biblical ways of living, working, and ministering. Our tendencies to compare and conform are two tools he uses to achieve this spiritual shift.

When we compare God's ways of living and working with those of modern society, the differences are large and glaring. Modern ways are sophisticated, while God's are simple. Modern ways are novel, while God's are old, even ancient. Modern methods are constantly innovating, while God's remain basically unchanged. Modern ways are conceived by human intelligence, while God's are born of eternal wisdom. Modern ways are quick developing, while God's are slower to reach their goals. Modern ways rely upon human energy, while God's rest on divine faithfulness. Modern ways thrive on popular support, while God's endure by His approval. These antipodal differences make it clear that if we live and work in God's ways, we'll be glaringly different from secular society and many Christians and churches that conform to it. Are we willing to be different?

If we're not, the pressure to conform to this world's ways will move us to conduct our lives, handle our problems, run our churches, and pursue our ministries by its methods, not God's.

Moved from our appointed places

Satan tries to move us to forsake the places in which God has chosen for us to live, work, attend church, or minister.

When God calls us, He leads us to reside, learn, worship, fellowship, and labor in specific locations He has prepared just for us: "Behold, I...bring thee into *the place which I have prepared [for you]*" (Exod. 23:20). These places (dwellings, jobs, churches, and ministries) often change with the seasons of our lives. We receive the full, inward blessing of God's Spirit daily only if we stay in our places until God changes our seasons. So Satan's plan is simply to use any means possible to move us from our appointed places.

He may create disheartening "famines," or absences of outward fruitfulness and success. He may cause stressful firestorms of controversy to swirl around us. He may release overwhelming floods of slander against our good name. He may incite bitter or violent attacks of persecution against us. Or he may needle, frustrate, or exhaust us with the constant problems of our companions. Whatever their natural reasons, the spiritual causes for these pressures are one: to force us to leave the places God has put us in. Our determination must also be one: to stay where God puts us until He changes the season and sends us elsewhere.

When after years of patiently waiting for God in the Judean wilderness David relocated in Ziklag—a place outside of God's plan for him—Satan succeeded in moving an anointed person from his appointed place. It took a harrowing crisis to get David back in place. If we're not very determined to remain in our appointed places, like David, we'll be driven from them.

As we consider the courageously unmoved Christian life, the devil may challenge us with the same lie he has used to spiritually "move" many a good Christian: "This just can't be done! It's impossible to never be moved!" But the Bible asserts the contrary: "With God all things are possible" (Matt. 19:26). That is, by God's grace, we can live a spiritually unmoved life.

Consider this impressive list of unmoved ones taken from biblical and church history.

UNMOVED BIBLICAL CHARACTERS

Moses refused to be moved from his sweet personal fellowship with I AM despite the bitter, full-blown hatred and denunciation of the Egyptian state and its stubborn head, Pharaoh.

Isaac was not moved from the place to which God called him even though his Philistine neighbors treated him rudely, even violently, over water rights.

Hezekiah and his peers were not moved to fear and panic, though, when surrounded by Sennacherib's massive undefeated armies, they seemed to be staring disaster in the face.

Nehemiah was not moved from his duty to rebuild Jerusalem's walls by the mockery, threats, and plots of his enemies or the gross disloyalty of some of his Jewish brethren.

Joseph was not moved to immorality despite his natural desires, his single state, and the lustful advances of Potiphar's undoubtedly attractive wife.

Jesus was not moved from His heavenly Father's will, ways, and times. When the devil offered Jesus the *kingdom now*—his way and time for Jesus to exert spiritual power, religious authority, and political governance over all nations, without the cross or the church—He declined.

The early Christians refused to be moved to offense at the Good Shepherd, even when their Christian friends and relatives were publicly condemned, deprived of property, imprisoned, tortured, or horribly executed by the unfair decrees of callous Roman emperors and governors.

Nor were the now famous (but then infamous) Bible translators, reformers, and revivalists, such as William Tyndale, John Hus, and Charles G. Finney, offended when their good names were viciously disparaged by unenlightened, envious, or apostate religious leaders.

～

You may wonder, "How did they do it?" Or more to the point, "How can I pass through this life unmoved?"

TIPS TO LIVING A SPIRITUALLY UNMOVABLE LIFE

Here are five tips sure to help you become and remain spiritually unmovable.

First, study the ways Satan uses to move Christians, as discussed earlier, and ask the Lord to help you discern his strategies when you meet them.

Second, study the lives of the unmoved biblical characters listed above and practice the godly habits and traits that made them strong in spirit.

Third, "set" the Lord before you at all times. The psalmist identified this key to spiritual stability: "I have *set the LORD always before me*; because he is at my right hand, *I shall not be moved*" (Ps. 16:8). We "set" the Lord before us by turning and fixing our thoughts on Him, specifically His Word, in every new circumstance. So to set the "Lord" before us is to set the "Word" before us. We read, study, and meditate in the written Word regularly. And we commune with the living Word, Jesus, in prayer regularly. Also, we obey the written and living Word, Jesus' teachings and His Spirit's guidance, in daily circumstances. This keeps us Word-filled and Spirit-filled—and divinely fortified. The diabolical one can't move a divinely fortified believer.

Fourth, trust the Lord in all circumstances. The psalmist asserts that trusting God makes us immovable: "*They who trust in the LORD* shall be as Mount Zion, which *cannot be removed*, but abideth forever" (Ps. 125:1). Trusting God means choosing to rely on Him to keep His promise to help us when we see no way for our present pressing problems to be resolved.

Fifth, receive God's faithful correction. If by failing to practice these tips we let the enemy begin moving us, we still have a strong safety net: God's unfailing faithfulness! When quoting Psalm 16:8 on the Day of Pentecost, Peter cited God's faithfulness as the key reason for our stability: "I foresaw the Lord always before my face; for *he is on my right hand, that I should not be moved*" (Acts 2:25). Indeed, not our diligence alone but, more importantly, God's faithful watchfulness and assistance enable us to remain steadfast. Our part is to "set the Lord always before me [us]" (Ps. 16:8); as we do so, the Lord stands by us, "on my right hand" (Acts 2:25), to faithfully warn us whenever we are being moved.

But our response to Him is crucial. Psalm 62 differentiates between being "moved" and "greatly moved." "I shall not be *greatly moved*...I shall not be *moved*" (vv. 2, 6). If after being "moved" a little by brief spiritual degeneration we humbly and wisely receive God's correction, we will not be "greatly moved"; spiritual degeneration will not set in. If through pride, however, we reject God's correction, we will be "greatly moved"; spiritual degeneration will continue and grow into full-blown apostasy. We will experience a *lasting detrimental, spiritual shift away from Jesus*—confidence in Him, closeness to Him, and conscientious compliance with His will.

It is vital that we not let ourselves be moved, because many people depend on our spiritual stability: our spouses, children, fellow believers, and only God knows how many others whom we will meet and influence over the course of our lives. If our "houses" of Christian character stand firm when hostile satanic forces come storming down on them—"the rain...floods...wind blew and beat upon that house, and it fell not" (Matt. 7:25)—our example of spiritual steadfastness will convert unbelievers and strengthen believers. But if we're moved, just the opposite will occur. The collapse of our "house" will have far-reaching effects: "And it fell; and [of] great [effect or fallout] was the fall of it" (v. 27). Many unbelievers, seeing our instability, will remain unconvinced of Christ and unconverted to the faith: "This man began to build, and [but] was not able to finish" (Luke 14:30). And the faith of many Christians will falter—and their houses of Christian character collapse.

And one more thing: we will grieve the Lord. When Mary and Martha let their brother's untimely death move them to unbelief, Jesus was moved to tears: "Jesus wept" (John 11:35). To avoid grieving Him again, ponder and practice the truths in this chapter. Begin by making this confession:

None of these things shall move me!

Then nothing in this world will move you—even deep waters.

Chapter Twenty-Three

THE DEEP IS CALLING

Deep calleth unto deep at the noise of thy waterspouts...
—PSALM 42:7

While lamenting his ongoing exile in Babylon and the absence of God's tangible help, the writer of Psalm 42 turned his thoughts to the Upper Jordan river, located between the base of Mount Hermon and the Sea of Galilee: "Deep calleth unto deep at the noise of thy [Jordan's] waterspouts" (v. 7). Something he had seen there in the past comforted him in the midst of his most discouraging present circumstances.

Apparently, he discerned a parallel between his own experiences and the way of a river. Unlike the constantly roaring, pounding waves of the ocean surf, a river is normally a peaceful, quiet body of water. But at its rapids and waterfalls this changes.

There a river generates its own excessive noise, as its rushing cataracts fall and pierce its depths, eroding the riverbed beneath and creating pools holding new depths of water. To confirm this, go stand beside a river equidistantly between two waterfalls. All other creatures of forest and field being quiet, the silence of the river before you will be broken only by the sounds of the rapids nearest you, upstream and downstream. From these opposite directions you will hear the river's "deeps" (its deepwater pools) calling to each other—the deep calling to the deep, one waterfall raising its "voice" to speak to the next, one deep pool reaching out to connect, if only audibly, with the next downstream, and so on. It was this *way of a river* that the psalmist had in mind when he wrote, "[Roaring] deep calls to [roaring] deep at the thunder of Your waterspouts" (Ps. 42:7, AMP). Apparently this lasting impression resulted from an earlier visit to the cataracts of Palestine's largest water flow, the river Jordan.

Appropriately named in Hebrew, *Yarden* (yar-dane´), meaning *the Descender*, the Jordan falls approximately 1,500 feet in elevation over its estimated 210-mile total length from its headwaters on Mount Hermon's southwestern base (230 feet above sea level, near the Huleh basin) to its terminus at the lowest elevation on earth's surface, the Dead Sea (1,292 feet below sea level). In the 10-mile gorge between its headwaters and the Sea of Galilee, the Upper Jordan descends nearly 700 feet and creates so many rapids (27) and waterfalls that it is unnavigable.[1] There also, where its cataracts have created a number of pools, the Jordan's deepest waters (about 10 feet) are found. In the relatively peaceful Lower Jordan, which extends from the southernmost point on the Sea of Galilee to the Dead Sea, the depth rarely exceeds five feet, except in flood season (March).

Clearly, then, it was the Upper Jordan region that captivated the psalmist's thoughts: "Therefore will I remember thee [your ways, Lord] from the land of Jordan [its upper course], and of the Hermons [Mt. Hermon], from the hill, Mizar [believed to be near Hermon]" (Ps. 42:6). And his attention was focused mainly on the deepwater pools created by Jordan's rushing cataracts. Why? Figuratively speaking, that was where he and the faithful remnant of Israel were at the moment. Actually, they were in defeat and exile in Babylon, cut off from their homeland, capital city, and most importantly, their temple and its joyful worship of God. He describes his grief and desire for restoration in verses 1–4. But figuratively, they were struggling in spiritual "deep waters"—caught in the grip of a deep, swirling, pitiless "river" of trouble, being pummeled, pulled along, and pushed under at will by unrelenting "rapids" of opposition, "waterfalls" of defeat, and "whirlpools" of terror.

In biblical symbolism, "deep waters" speak of *deep troubles that greatly try our faith, patience, and loyalty to God*. David's opening statements in Psalm 69 make this evident:

Save me, O God; for *the waters* are come in unto my soul. I sink...where there is no standing; I am come into *deep waters,* where *the floods overflow me.*

—PSALM 69:1-2

The balance of Psalm 69 gives us a full and graphic description of the basic features of "deepwater" trials. They are:

- We are HATED without a cause: "They that *hate me without a cause*...let me be delivered from those who hate me...out of the *deep waters*" (vv. 4, 14).
- We are REPROACHED for our Christian faith, decisions, lifestyle, or ministry: "For thy sake I have borne *reproach*...the *reproaches* of those who reproached thee *are fallen upon me*" (vv. 7, 9).
- We are ALIENATED from one or more relatives: "I am become a *stranger* unto my brethren, and an *alien* unto my mother's children" (v. 8).
- We have numerous ENEMIES: "They that hate me...are *more than the hairs of mine head...mine enemies*" (v. 4).
- We suffer INJUSTICE: "Then I restored that which I took *not* away" (v. 4).
- We suffer SHAME: "*Shame* hath covered my face" (v. 7).
- We are treated with CONTEMPT and MOCKERY: "I became a proverb to them. They that sit in the gate speak against me, and I was the *song of the drunkards*" (vv. 11–12).
- We experience HEAVINESS of spirit: "I am full of *heaviness*" (v. 20).
- We experience BROKENHEARTEDNESS: "Reproach hath *broken my heart*" (v. 20).
- We grow WEARY of waiting for God's help: "I am *weary* of my crying...while I *wait for my God* [to deliver me]" (v. 3).

During seasons in which God requires us to endure these kinds of afflictions—all, most, or even some of them—for His sake, we may be said to be in "deep waters."

That's exactly where the writer of Psalm 42 found himself and his Judean brethren. Their foreign captivity reminded him of the Upper Jordan, where deep and turbulent waters seemed to never end. He wondered openly if God would ever end his trials: "I will say unto God, my rock, Why hast thou forgotten me?" (Ps. 42:9). Indeed, to him one experience of deep and overwhelming difficulty seemed to call to, and so link up with, yet another. And another. And another still. Discouraged and frightened by his recurring deep adversities, he felt as if he would never live to see the end of his spiritual turbulence. One commentator notes, "The floods and cataracts of the headwaters of the Jordan illustrate the waves of sorrow that overwhelm the writer."[2] Or, as the psalmist put it, "All Your breakers and Your rolling waves have gone over me" (Ps. 42:7, AMP). Paraphrasing, he was saying, "Lord, every kind of trouble there is has poured over me, pummeled me, pushed me under, and pulled me downstream again, and all I see ahead is more white water."

Then, in the depth of his trial, the Spirit spoke to the psalmist's heart, reminding him of God's unfailing faithfulness to His children. And he said, "Yet the LORD will command his loving-kindness in the daytime" (Ps. 42:8). With his confidence in God's utter reliability restored, he twice exhorted himself, "Hope thou in God" (vv. 5, 11), sure now that God would one day bring him out of his "deep waters"—that is, end all his trials and openly restore His favor: "I shall yet praise him for the help of his countenance [face, smile of approval]" (v. 5). Why, God promised to end every trial: "Surely there is an end, and thine expectation shall not be cut off" (Prov. 23:18). Even the roaring whitewaters of the Upper Jordan have an end!

Indeed, just before it enters the north end of the Sea of Galilee, the Jordan calms down, vastly decreasing its rate of descent, and gently, peacefully, and deceptively flows into Galilee as if it had never churned out any white waters. Recalling this, the psalmist reasoned his distressing trials would do the same. In His appointed time and way, God would intervene and speak peace upon his distressing deeps: "Peace, be still." Then all his troubles would merge into a peaceful lake of fulfillment. And Manasseh—the psalmist would forget all his deep waters just as Joseph forgot his: "…Manasseh [lit., forgetting]: For God, said he, hath made me forget all my toil" (Gen. 41:51).

This saving faith, inspired by the memory of Jordan's deep waters, buoyed the psalmist's burdened soul with fresh hope. It even restored a smile to his saddened face! "I shall yet praise him, *my face-healer*" (v. 11, MLB); or "the salvation of my countenance" (YLT). So he endured and so he prevailed over "the deep."

The same "deeps" are calling to you today: "Deep calleth unto deep at the noise of thy waterspouts" (Ps. 42:7). Are you struggling in turbulent, deep waters of affliction and trial? Is your soul "cast down" (v. 5) and "disquieted" (v. 11), or discouraged and anxious, because God has seemingly forgotten His promises to you for a long, long while? Is your "countenance," or face, fallen and frowned and in need of "healing"?

Then consider these lessons from "the deep." Though distressing, "the deep" will do four wonderful things for you that nothing else can do:

1. It will compel you to seek the deeper truths of God.
2. It will drive you to a deeper commitment to God.
3. It will produce in you a new depth of character.
4. It will create new depths of power in your work or ministry.

LESSONS FROM THE DEEP

Deeper truths

"Deep waters" call for deep truths. "Deepwater" trials summon us to learn and walk in the deeper truths of God's Word. No casual appeal, this summons is an urgent *demand!* Why? The pressure of relentless spiritual turbulence forces us to launch out into a new depth of Bible study—or drown in a watery grave of spiritual ignorance or shallowness described by the prophet Hosea: "My people are destroyed for lack of [deep, wide biblical] knowledge" (Hos. 4:6). Thus driven, we go deeper.

No longer content with our fifteen-minute morning devotional, we now give much more time to prayerfully reading, studying, and pondering God's Book, running references from cover to cover. Compelled by our difficulties, we seek not only the letter but also the spirit of the Word; we now want to know not only what prophets and apostles advised Jews and Christians long ago but also what God is saying to us in our deep dilemmas. Therefore we turn from teachers and counselors who tell us only what we want to hear to those who dispense the deeper insights and knowledge we need to hear, those who have faced their own raging rapids and will frankly tell us the full truth, or "all the counsel of God" (Acts 20:27). We don't want our ears tickled any more. We want the very depths of our soul strengthened, restored, and infused with spiritual iron. Consequently, we also turn from shallow churches, which offer large amounts of religious entertainment and brief sermons, to those offering real solid spiritual edification—sumptuous "feeding" sessions of Spirit-led Bible teaching, stimulatingly Spirit-filled congregational praise, godly correction, and wise counsel. And we now seek pastors who minister not what's popular but what's pertinent; not what's trendy, but what's truthful. Like the prophets of old, they walk closely with God, live in His Word, listen carefully to His Spirit, and relay faithfully what He's saying to us. Why? They know the "deeps" demand it.

Truly, if we are to ride the perilous spiritual rapids, and avoid being overwhelmed in their yawning depths of despair or vortexes of confusion, we must move beyond the lighter truths and lay hold of the "weightier matters" (Matt. 23:23). Only deep biblical truths see us through "deepwater" testing. But are we ready for this?

Are we willing to "go on unto perfection," to stop delighting in the correct-but-shallow truths of Christianity and start cultivating a passion for its deeper, more demanding truths? "Therefore, leaving the principles of the doctrine of Christ, *let us go on unto perfection* [spiritual maturity], not laying again the foundation [shallow, elementary Christian truths]" (Heb. 6:1–2).

A deeper commitment

"Deep waters" call for deeper commitment to God. They require partially committed Christians to abandon any remaining lukewarmness and fully surrender themselves to the Lord and faith they profess.

When new and stronger "waterfalls" of trouble overflow us, to survive we must not only know the deeper truths of Christianity, but we must also walk steadily in them—daily, hourly, minute by minute. To do this, we must increase our spiritual self-discipline.

Because our challenging new circumstances bring many unpleasant choices, we must surrender our self-will more often. Because our trials are more difficult and threatening, we must put our trust in the Lord more frequently and fully: "Trust in the LORD with *all* your heart" (Prov. 3:5). Because our adversaries are more adamant, we must be more determined to prevail over their inspirer, *the* adversary, God's way. Because more circumstances are conspiring to render us unfaithful, we are constrained to focus more on being faithful. Soon our commitment to every essential Christian duty—seeking God, studying His Word, interceding, confessing our sins, walking in love, discharging our job, helping our church, or pursuing our ministry—grows stronger and more abiding. As a result, we dig deeper in God and build our spiritual foundations more firmly, broadly, and immovably on the rock of doing God's will.

This deeper obedience transforms us from ordinary to extraordinary believers, or in Jesus' words, "disciples indeed"—student-followers of Jesus who are deeply serious and irrevocably committed to Him. While shallow Christians will obey God if it costs them little or nothing, "disciples indeed" obey Him at all times, even when it brings strong rejection or great losses. Why? Their "deepwater" trials have created in them a deeper commitment to Christ. Now they know that, come high honors or "deep waters," their dedication to Him is fixed and sure: *They will do His will!* He knows it too.

Assured of their deeper devotion to Him, the Lord gives them a deeper assurance of His protecting presence: "When thou passest through the waters, I will be with thee; and through the rivers, they shall not overflow thee" (Isa. 43:2). Now they too are sure: *He is with them!*

New depths of character

"Deep waters" call for deeper character. They summon, or produce in our lives, a new, deeper character-building process.

As we seek and study the deeper truths of God and walk daily in deeper commitment to His ways, a rare and wonderful transformation occurs inside us. Just as the Upper Jordan's waterfalls pierce its waters, erode its riverbed, and create deeper pools of water, so God uses "deep-water" trials to pierce our spiritual shallowness and plumb new depths of integrity and godliness in our souls. As a result, our decisions and actions become more consistently like Jesus, the Lord of "the deep."

Gradually, distinctly more profound Christian character traits—lamb-like meekness, holy boldness, unshakable faith, unfailing patience, sacrificial love, effective peacemaking, long-suffering with kindness, unquenchable joy—begin manifesting in us. These large, lush "fruit of the Spirit" are undeniable evidences of Christlikeness, or the Spirit conforming our characters to the image of Jesus. (See Galatians 5:22–23; Romans 8:29.)

Soon we trust God more deeply, beyond the limits we previously imposed by our human reasonings. Our thinking becomes deeper as we ponder, study, reflect on, and analyze current issues and events in light of biblical truth. We gain a deeper understanding of the Bible, receiving new, refreshing insights from passages we've read and studied for years. We gain a deeper knowledge of and trust in God's ways, never again relying on any methods, programs, or plans that, however popular, are not His. A deeper fear of God grasps and guides us, urging us forward in obedience and restraining us from anything that displeases God. The habit of self-examination is more deeply formed in us, as we confess our internal and external sins and failures quickly and consistently—and let God examine and correct others! As a result, the Holy Spirit establishes new depths of purity in us, cleansing us not only from wrong behavior but also from wrong being; not only from wrong acts and words but also from wrong thoughts, motives and attitudes. Thus our sanctification becomes not only positional but also profound, pervasive, and permanent.

What has happened to us? "Deep waters," deep truths, and deep commitment have remade us in their own image: now *we* are deep!

And we're proponents of deep Christianity! Our new depths of character will command attention, especially in shallow churches: "Now when they saw the boldness of Peter and John…they marveled; and they took knowledge of them, that they had been with Jesus" (Acts 4:13). This will give us new opportunities to make known and honor the Lord of "the deep" and His ways. How? The same shallow Christians who ignored, criticized, or condemned us in our "deepwater" trials will turn to us for instruction, counsel, and fellowship when they enter their own "deep waters" in these last days.

New depths of power in ministry

"Deep waters" call forth, or create, new depths of power in our ministry. Why is this?

"Deepwater" trials create not only deeper character in us, but also deeper spiritual "soul-wells" for the Holy Spirit to fill: "Blessed is the man…who, passing through the [deep] valley of Baca [weeping or sorrow], make it a well [soul-well]; the rain [of the Holy Spirit] also filleth the pools [soul-reservoirs]" (Ps. 84:5–6). And that means more of the Spirit's life and power is present in our enlarged soul-wells, ready to "spring up" and flow out to bless others in need: "The water that I shall give him shall be in him a well of water *springing up* into everlasting life" (John 4:14).

Or, to change the illustration, Jesus taught that if we believe on Him and receive the fullness of the Holy Spirit, a "river of life" constantly flows out of our innermost being to bless others: "he that believeth on me…out of his heart shall flow *rivers of living water*" (John 7:38). Our deeper character increases the depth, or flowing power, of this spiritual river. Like the millennial river of God described by Ezekiel, when "the waters [are] risen" in our souls, their power is truly supernatural, so great that they create spiritual life and fruitfulness in people, families, churches, cities, and nations previously spiritually dead and barren: "Every thing shall live where the river cometh" (Ezek. 47:5, 9); or "Life will flourish wherever this water flows" (NLT).

This power doesn't flow from shallow ministers. However sincere, they simply *can't* help believers struggling in deepwater trials. Why? Though saved, baptized, educated, ordained, earnest, and friendly, they have little or no understanding of "the deep." Only veterans of "the deep"—deeply Spirit-taught, deeply tested, and deeply transformed men and women of God—can speak a deeply powerful word to their powerless peers. They alone have a "word in season" to give "to him who is weary" (Isa. 50:4). They alone can speak a message that lifts the oppressed above the people, problems, and pressures presently overwhelming them. Why?

It is a case of "the deep" in one soul calling "the deep" in another. Only those who seek and live in the deeper truths of God can pass them on to others with authority. When these authorities of "the deep" teach others, their insightful, weighty words *call* (draw, appeal to, minister to) others who are in some way familiar with "deep waters," who either have experienced or are experiencing them. So "the deep" calls unto "the deep"—deep messages speak and minister to deeply tried souls.

Amazingly, this spiritual "call" is not limited by years, distance, or customs. No matter how many centuries, continents, or cultures separate deeply tried souls from spiritually deep teachers, their souls respond to their teachings quickly and affirmatively. Why? The Spirit bears witness to their Christlike accuracy and authority: "The people were astonished at [gripped by] his doctrine [teaching]; for he taught them *as one having authority*, and not as the scribes" (Matt. 7:28–29).

Charles H. Spurgeon's many sermons and books, published well over a century ago, are yet alive with Christ's authority. A still powerful and life-giving call from "the deep," they were born in Spurgeon's own "deepwater" trials, which came early and often in his ministry.

Early in his prolonged and prolific London pastorate (1854–1891), Spurgeon experienced troublesome waves of caustic criticism from the local clergy and press. And only two years into his pastorate, while over twelve thousand were gathered at the Royal Surrey Gardens Music Hall to hear him preach, someone cried, "Fire," causing panic. Seven people were trampled to death and twenty-eight seriously injured in the subsequent chaos. Only twenty-two at the time, Spurgeon was emotionally devastated and unable to preach for weeks. When thirty-five, he began experiencing recurring bouts of various painful illnesses, mainly gout. These continued for the remainder of his life. And late in his life and ministry, a controversy arose when Spurgeon's monthly periodical, *The Sword and the Trowel*, began publishing articles warning his fellow Baptists over the encroaching dangers of liberalism. So bitter was the backlash that Spurgeon resigned from the Baptist Union, which then officially censured him.[3]

Of his many passages through such "deep waters," Spurgeon said:

> I would go into the deeps a hundred times to cheer a downcast spirit. It is good for me to have been afflicted, that I might know how to speak a word in season to one that is weary.[4]

And speak words in season he did! With power from the deeps!

Conversely, the curse of much modern Christianity is its refusal to even hear, much less heed, the call of "the deep." Our desire to conform to the world has made us a glaring contradiction to the uncompromising spirit of the early church and its martyrs. To grow deeper in membership, collections, and public favor, we've grown shallower in devotion, righteousness, and faithfulness to biblical truth. Our zeal to become seeker-friendly has made us truth-hostile. The Spirit foresaw this: "And [in the last days] they shall turn away their ears from [especially] the [sound and deeper] truth[s of true, biblical Christianity]" (2 Tim. 4:4). This has led to our present tragic shallowness. Despite our rich spiritual heritages, broad educations, and excellent organizations, many churches today have pitifully few specialists of "the deep." Many who could become authorities on deepwater trials cling to the safe "shores" of culture conformity when Jesus is calling them to "launch out" into the deep ways of God. This writer's humble rhetoric cannot adequately express how earnestly God seeks, and how urgently we need, ministers who think, teach, counsel, and write with depths of power.

My friend, will *you* endure your "deeps" so He may create in you new depths of insight and power in ministry? The very depths of God's heart—His deepest desires to help His confused, struggling people in these crucial final years of the church age—is calling to the depths of your heart. He is asking, "Whatever the depth of your present walk or ministry, will you let Me take you *deeper*? Make you a *deeper* minister?"

～

The longer we endure the rough and tumble cataracts of life in faith and obedience, the deeper we go in God's truth, in our Christian commitments, in our characters, and in the power of our ministries.

So don't rebel, complain, or pity yourself as you descend the turbulent watercourse of your testing process or bob and swirl in its pools. When you feel overwhelmed by your seemingly unending "white-water" challenges, remember and hold fast the God of Upper Jordan! "Hope thou in God," knowing that, if you endure them, your deepwater trials will make you a much-needed authority, a specialist, an expert on "the deep." And here's one more comforting and golden truth: one day, like the Upper Jordan, your rough river of testing will calm down and flow gently and peacefully into a "Galilee" of fulfillment.

So go into your prayer closet and stand by the river of God's Spirit as it flows through your life today. Be very still and quiet. Listen for the noise of God's waterfalls, "upstream" in your past and "downstream" in your near future. That's the voice of "the deep" calling. It's God's voice. And it's calling *you*:

Launch out into the deep...

—LUKE 5:4

If you can pass through deep rivers, you can also walk through the fire.

Chapter Twenty-Four

THE BENEFITS OF TRIAL BY FIRE

Then these men were . . . cast into the midst of the
burning fiery furnace.

—DANIEL 3:21

*A*s stated in the preface, Jesus' message to the Laodicean church is not only historic but also prophetic. (See Revelation 3:14–22.) It is addressed not only to first-century Laodiceans but also to last-day Christians in this materialistic, lukewarm, "Laodicean," terminal period of the church age. His challenge to us—"I counsel thee to *buy* of me *gold tried* in the *fire*, that thou mayest be rich" (Rev. 3:18)—implies that we will pass through fiery tests in these last days. How else can we "buy," or possess by costly obedience, spiritual "gold," or the precious faith and truth of God, that has been "tried," or tested and proven, in the "fire" of demanding, purifying trials?

Therefore, any work entitled *Gold Tried in the Fire* would be woefully incomplete without describing fiery testing. So, lest I be guilty of a misnomer, this and the next chapter will expound key lessons from the chief biblical passage on "trial by fire," Daniel 3.

Deeply offended by the refusal of Shadrach, Meshach, and Abednego to bow to his "divine" image, and further enraged by their blunt rejection of his rare offer of a second chance, King Nebuchadnezzar of Babylon immediately had a diabolical idea: *I'll cremate these Jews!* (See Daniel 3:1–30.) The livid monarch then hastily ordered his furnace heated far beyond its

281

normal maximum degree...and, moments later, into the blazing inferno they went! Their past trials and triumphs aside (Dan. 1–2), suddenly these three Hebrew youths found themselves confronted by a new and far more daunting challenge—trial by fire.

But as unfair, cruel, and deadly as it was, the three Jews' fiery challenge was also beneficial—very beneficial. In fact, it was absolutely necessary to their full spiritual development. No less than seven spiritual benefits resulted from their fiery ordeal.

They are:

1. Purification
2. Liberation
3. Knowledge of God
4. Glory to God
5. Salvation
6. Reward
7. Establishment

Let's examine more closely the verses and phrases that reveal these wonderful benefits.

BENEFITS OF TRIAL BY FIRE

Purification

In Scripture, God uses three primary purifiers: blood, water, and fire. Also, seven is the biblical number of perfection. Therefore, in Jewish law (the Torah), people or materials were purified perfectly by being sprinkled, washed, or fired seven times. This pattern of *perfect purification by seven cleansings* persists throughout Scripture.

For example, the Jewish priests were purified, or consecrated for office, by being washed with water, and sprinkled with oil and water, once daily for seven days. Once healed, lepers were cleansed, or restored to congregational worship, by being sprinkled with sacrificial blood seven times. God purged King Nebuchadnezzar's pride by putting him through extreme discipline seven years: "*seven times* [years] shall pass over thee, till thou know that the Most High ruleth" (Dan. 4:25). Naaman, the Syrian, was purified from leprosy by washing in the river Jordan seven times. This present world system will be purged of its unbelief and rebellion toward God during a seven-year period of judgment (the Tribulation). David said God's Word is as pure as ancient silver, which was purified in earthen furnaces not once but "seven times." "The words of the LORD are pure...like silver tried in a furnace of earth, *purified seven times*" (Ps. 12:6, KJV).

Like an ancient silversmith, the heavenly Smith purified His choice silver[1] instruments, the "three Jews" (Shadrach, Meshach, and Abednego), seven times. When they were thrust into Nebuchadnezzar's earthen furnace, it was "seven times" hotter than usual: "Nebuchadnezzar...commanded that they should heat the furnace *seven times more* than it was usually heated" (Dan. 3:19). While from a natural viewpoint this reveals Nebuchadnezzar's exceptional fury and lethal intent, from the spiritual perspective it speaks of God using the furnace's power to perfectly purify those who passed through it.

He does the same when we go through "fiery trials," or exceptionally pressurized tests of faith, patience, and loyalty to God. As fire softens and melts precious metals, so God uses the pressure of fiery trials to melt our pride and stubbornness and render us soft and pliable toward Him—willing to forsake long-held wrong attitudes, bad habits, and other impurities untouched by less pressurized trials. Why are we willing at last to abandon these sins?

The pressure of our new, hotter trial is so great that we can't afford to disobey God any longer. It's time to obey or burn, comply or die. Only by living in full surrender to God—complete trust and holiness—can we survive the fire unharmed. As we abandon the last remnants of these stubborn sins, we "mortify," or deaden, their power in our lives and emerge purer in thought, word, and deed: "*Mortify*...fornication, uncleanness, inordinate affection, evil desire, and covetousness (which is idolatry)" (Col. 3:5).

Not content with purging our conscious sins, trial by fire goes further. It exposes unconscious sins—faults we never knew we had.

When a silversmith's fires melt unrefined silver, suddenly, for the first time, its latent (present but hidden) internal impurity (dross) is exposed. Lighter than pure silver, dross rises to the top of the molten mixture, no longer hidden. Then the smith removes this waste material, leaving the silver purer, more valuable, and more useful.

Like the silversmith's refining fires, Job's fiery trials enabled him to see sins previously hidden deep within his nature. In Elihu's inspired address, he told Job that he should be willing to see his unconscious sins and faults:

Surely it is fitting to be said unto God...That which I see not, teach thou me...

—JOB 34:31–32

And he should also be ready to change them:

...If I have done iniquity, I will do no more.

—JOB 34:32

Elihu's words proved to be prophetic. By trial's end, Job clearly recognized one sinful attitude he had never seen in himself before—the pride and strife of self-vindication (or the strife and self-vindication of pride)—and promptly changed it. Job's fiery trial brought this sin, a prideful reaction to his closest friends' false, cruel, and relentless accusations, to the surface of his conscious mind. Without all the "heat"—his friends' shocking disloyalty and pitiless condemnation of him in his time of intense pain and anguish—this potential reaction would never have manifested. The Scripture plainly declares Job's blamelessness *before* his ordeal (Job 1:1, 8) and *after* Satan's first and second major assaults against him (Job 1:22; 2:10), yet makes no such assertion after Job began heatedly complaining to and arguing with his friends (Job 3:1, forward). This implies his sin arose during his long, hot debate with them, not previously. When Job finally confessed his sin (Job 40:3–5; 42:1–6), God removed his "dross" of pride. Then Job's purification process was complete and his rewards forthcoming (Job 42:10–17).

Similarly, trial by fire manifests our latent faults. The sustained, God-ordered pressures of our seven-times-hotter "fires" forces our "dross"—wrong motives, desires, attitudes, and especially our wrong reactions to adversity and adversaries—to the surface of our conscious lives. We then see sins and faults in our lives that would otherwise remain hidden indefinitely. When, as Job did, we humbly confess these sins and firmly turn from them, the Lord cleanses us, by the fiery cleansing power of the Holy Spirit.

He did this for the prophet Isaiah. When under fiery conviction Isaiah confessed, "Woe is me!…I am a man of unclean lips" (Isa. 6:5), the Lord responded through his angel, "Lo…thine iniquity is taken away, and thy sin purged" (v. 7). John the Baptist referred to this deep-cleaning process as the Messiah's fiery purgation of our soul's "chaff," and hinted that it is one of the primary reasons we receive the baptism with the Holy Spirit: "He shall baptize you with the Holy Spirit, and with fire…and…[subsequently] *thoroughly purge* his [threshing] floor, and…*burn up the chaff with unquenchable fire*" [Matt. 3:11–12].

When we emerge from our fiery trials, we are not only more pure but also more prepared to answer the Lord's call, as Isaiah did: "Also I heard the voice of the Lord, saying, Whom shall I send, and who will go for us? Then said I, Here am I; send me" (Isa. 6:8).

Liberation

Just before entering the furnace, the three Jews' hands and feet were "bound," no doubt with the strongest Babylonian rope: "Then these men were *bound*" (Dan. 3:21; see vv. 23–24).

Besides their obvious, immediate purpose of preventing the three Jews from escaping, these physical restraints, albeit briefly, also limited them from doing Jehovah's will, which would have required the use of their hands and feet. Once "bound," they could do nothing but fall headlong into Nebuchadnezzar's blazing furnace: "These three men…*fell down bound* into the midst of the burning fiery furnace" (v. 23). Yet when the king saw them moments later, they were no longer bound but "loose," and no longer falling but "walking" freely in the middle of the furnace (v. 25). He was stunned.

And no wonder! Marvelous multiple miracles had occurred simultaneously in the furnace. The intense flames had not killed the three, or even burned them. To the contrary, they were perfectly uninjured in the king's crematorium. Nebuchadnezzar exclaimed, "They have no hurt" (v. 25) and lauded them before his counselors as "these men, upon whose bodies the fire had no power" (v. 27). Even their hair was unharmed: "nor was an hair of their head singed." Furthermore, though their executioners had put extra clothes on them to act as a natural accelerant (v. 21), their clothes were not burned, or soiled with soot: "nor [were] their coats changed" (v. 27). They didn't even smell as if they had been near a fire, much less in one! "Nor [had even] the smell of fire…passed on them" (v. 27). (Any fireman will tell you that thick, black soot is everywhere after even a small house fire. And the distinctive pungent smell of fire permeates every surviving article of furniture, clothing, or drapery. This powerful stench alone ruins most items.) Despite these wonders of divine preservation, one change was noted: the three Jews were now "loose" from their bindings.

This implies that the furnace destroyed only one thing: the three Jews' bindings. So God turned something very harmful into something very helpful. Or as Deuteronomy puts it, He turned a curse into a blessing: "The LORD thy God turned the curse into a blessing unto thee" (Deut. 23:5). Instead of terminating the three Jews, the fiery furnace *liberated* them from their former limitations.

Before experiencing trial by fire, Christians are in a spiritual condition that parallels the three Jews' physical condition. Just as the three were redeemed yet bound with ropes, so we are saved yet bound with various kinds of fears. Legally, the Savior has freed us from Satan's control, yet in actual day-to-day situations, we still have fears that, like strong Babylonian cords, limit our obedience to and service for our Savior.

Like Gideon, we want to speak out against deceptive idols, sins, and errors in the church, yet we fear being reproached and hated for doing so. We desire to abandon all worldliness hindering us, but we worry we'll be mocked as fanatics. We feel gifted and called by God to start a particular business, yet we fail to start it for fear it will fail. We want to give generously to God's work, but we withhold our gifts or give sparingly because we're unsure God will provide. We sense God's call to ministry, but we fail to answer the call for fear friends and relatives will disapprove. Such trepidations—fear of rejection, fear of reproach, fear of lack, fear of failure—are the prime Babylonian "ropes" that bind us with timidity and limit our ability to serve and glorify God.

Then one day, after we've experienced preliminary trials, God leads us into trial by fire, where we experience *deliverance by controlled exposure*. In our "furnace," or hot trouble, God frees us from our fears, oddly, by bringing them upon us—but always with Him by our side.

He did this with the three Jews. Surely one of their greatest concerns was that their loyalty to God's Word might cause Nebuchadnezzar, their powerful and famously stormy "boss," to reject and punish them. (This had already put them at odds with his wishes once, as we read in Daniel 1:5–16.) So what did God permit? This very thing! The king demanded they bow to his idol (forbidden by God's commandments; see Exod. 20:3, 4–6), they refused, and he promptly flew into one of his patented rages and did his worst! Yet, to their surprise, they survived the worst—and benefited from it! There they discovered the Lord sufficient not only to keep them from trouble but also to help and improve them *in* it: "God is…a very present help [helper] *in* trouble" (Ps. 46:1).

Similarly, God at times delivers us from our dreads, worries, or fears by letting them (to some degree) happen—all the while standing by us, speaking to and guiding us by His Word, comforting us by His Spirit, protecting us by His angels, and eventually delivering us. Somewhere in this "furnace" we learn a vital spiritual lesson: if we abide in God's will, there is nothing to fear, because if we are with God, God is with us, and nothing can overpower Him, or us in Him. This is the thought that inspired the apostle Paul to write, "What shall we then say to these things? If God be for us, who can be against us?" (Rom. 8:31).

After trial by fire, our outlook on life is permanently altered. Whenever doing God's will brings daunting prospects, we quietly press through our dreads and obey God, knowing He will see us through. Why? Like the three Jews, we are now "loose" and "walking," liberated from all our former limitations. Fears of rejection, reproach, lack, failure, etc.—these no longer stop us from doing what God wants. We shout triumphantly with David, "I sought the LORD, and he heard me, and [through trial by fire] delivered me from all my fears" (Ps. 34:4).

Knowledge of God

Their collegiate studies complete (Dan. 1:3–6), the three Jews received further education in the furnace. This postgraduate curriculum was not academic but experiential, a course of learning set, taught, and evaluated by God's Spirit in His school of fiery conflict and contradiction. In the hardest season of their lives, they gained the surest, deepest knowledge of God attainable in life. Let's consider five of its divisions.

First, they learned the closest intimacy with Jesus. In the furnace, they were closer to Jesus—the "form of the fourth...like the Son of God" (Dan. 3:25, NKJV)—than at any other time described in the Book of Daniel. Before entering the fire they believed in and prayed to God and saw Him answer prayer in crucial situations (Dan. 2:17–19, 23), but they never saw *Him*. Now they saw and spoke with Him face-to-face, as Moses did. God had always been present with them in Babylon, but now, in great trouble, He was "a *very present* help *in trouble*" (Ps. 46:1). Thus they discovered this stabilizing spiritual law: when they were specially tried, God drew specially near! And His comforting presence kept them cool and calm in the hottest, most terrifying test imaginable.

Second, they learned that God's protection is truly supernatural. In the fire He kept the deadly flames from harming them, while they killed others exposed to them, even Babylon's "most mighty men" (Dan. 3:20, 22). There is no natural explanation for this; it was a supernatural act of divine protection. So the three Jews concluded that if God kept them unharmed in the very worst circumstances conceivable—Babylon's cruel crematorium—He could keep them safe and sound anywhere, provided they keep trusting and obeying Him.

Third, they learned how to walk with God in the fire. At the beginning of their test they "fell down" (v. 23), obviously unable to walk with the Lord in the furnace. But by trial's end they were "walking in the midst of the fire" (v. 25), with "the Son of God" close by their side. Amazingly, in the worst possible scenario, they were calmly, stably following the Lamb of God, step for step, wherever He went! Clearly, then, at some point during their fiery trial they learned first to stand, and then to walk, and finally to "walk, and not faint" (Isa. 40:31).

Fourth, they learned that God "causes all things" (Rom. 8:28, NAS), even the fieriest crises, to ultimately work for the good of those who faithfully love and follow Him. Considering how their trial began, its end was most surprising. Nebuchadnezzar, who initially put them into the fire in a demonic rage (Dan. 3:19), ultimately called them out with divine respect: "Ye servants of the Most High God, come forth…" (v. 26). Then he, who only moments earlier had opposed their faith and mocked God's saving power—"Who is that God, that shall deliver you out of my hands" (v. 15), praised them for their faith and God for His unique ability to deliver: "Shadrach, Meshach, and Abednego…his servants who *trusted in him*…there is *no other God* that can deliver after this sort" (vv. 28–29). This was another miracle for us to marvel at. The worker of all things had transformed the three Jews' greatest persecutor into their greatest promoter. Nebuchadnezzar, the livid adversary, was now Nebuchadnezzar, the loving advocate.

Fifth, they learned the greatest lesson of all: God is faithful! He faithfully creates escape routes for His faithful ones. Nebuchadnezzar's furnace had no way of escape, only a "mouth" (v. 26) into which objects and persons were thrown and through which it was impossible to return. Yet God released the three anyway. How? As at the Red Sea, God made a way where there was no way. That proud, stubborn, sovereign, answerable-to-no-man King Nebuchadnezzar would change his mind was unthinkable. Yet God made this very thing happen to release His captives. Besides burning away the Jews' bindings, then, the flames seared into their hearts forever the words: "God is faithful, who will…make the way to escape" from every trial, even the fieriest (1 Cor. 10:13).

We learn all these branches of the profound knowledge of God in our fiery tests. In this most unlikely "school," we learn how to draw very close to God daily and how "very present" He is with us in our very worst times. There we discover that God's protecting power is truly supernatural. There we begin walking steadily with God without stumbling or fainting. There we become convinced that He causes not some or most, but all our circumstances to work for us. And there we see more clearly than ever God's amazing ability to release us from life's most impossible circumstances—and thereafter we rest deeply in His unfailing faithfulness.

Glory to God

By overcoming their fiery trials, the three Jews caused God to be honored throughout the Babylonian world in five identifiable ways.

289

First, the king spontaneously acknowledged God's supremacy audibly: "Ye servants of the *Most High God*" (Dan. 3:26). Second, he praised God publicly: "*Blessed be the God*...who hath sent his angel and delivered his servants" (v. 28). Third, as previously stated, his official decree hailed Jehovah's delivering power above all other deities: "*There is no other God that can deliver after this sort*" (v. 29); this was no small laudation in a polytheistic culture. Fourth, his decree also forbade anyone from even speaking against Jehovah...on pain of death! "Every people...who speak anything amiss against the God of Shadrach...shall be *cut in pieces*" (v. 29). Fifth, God's honors continued reverberating throughout the Mesopotamian world for months as the king's decree was read publicly in every city, village, and hamlet in Babylonia. So the only living and intelligent God was set apart from His dead, dumb rivals—Bel, Nebo, and all other false gods—because three humble believers endured trial by fire.

These remarkable honors are even more remarkable when we consider their context. The king had appointed that day as a kind of "Image Day," a national festival and convocation to dedicate the ninety-foot gilded image he had erected. (See Daniel 3:1.) The date had been fixed and publicized months earlier, giving Babylonia's many government officials, provincial leaders, and prominent citizens time to plan their lengthy trips to the capital (vv. 2–3). All Babylon was abuzz with preparation. In modern America, this would be comparable to the extensive preparations for Inauguration Day and all its festivities. But the bold resistance and shocking deliverance of the three Jews changed all these carefully laid plans. By them, God intervened and stole the day—and all its impressive sights, sounds, and honors—from the cold, metallic hands of the king's image. By day's end, the Immortal, not the image, held the land's highest honors firmly in hand.

The same glorious end awaits us at the close of our fiery tests. The God who has seen us through will be seen through us—and recognized, lauded, and loved by many. Christ crucified will be exalted above all supposed saviors, prophets, messiahs, and deities. Christianity will be confirmed as true and its religious rivals false. The Bible will be shown to be God's very Word and wisdom, and all other holy writings of dubious inspiration and intelligence. Everywhere we go the message will be broadcast, written, or rumored that *there is none like Jesus*—because we endured the heat victoriously.

Salvation

The three Jews' fiery trial put a heavenly spotlight on the Savior. When the "form of the fourth...like the Son of God" (Dan. 3:25, NKJV) appeared in the furnace, everyone present witnessed a rare event: a divine visitation. Though briefly, God manifested and dwelt among them to save His loyal servants. Babylon's stunned king, leaders, and citizens, who had come to view the great image, beheld instead the greater One and His saving power fully illuminated at Babylon's center stage. The king quickly called the three out: "Come forth, and come here" (v. 26). His act was over; the next act was God's. As in all God's visitations, conversions followed.

The Bible states that the king professed faith in Israel's God. As stated earlier, he called Jehovah the "Most High God" (v. 26), putting Him above all other deities, including his dazzling golden image. And he worshiped God, calling Him "blessed" (v. 28). Also he acclaimed that God's delivering power was greater than that of any other deity (v. 29). Thus the three Jews' salvation converted their sovereign.

Scripture intimates other conversions. It is unthinkable that the king's counselors and officials, who saw Jesus walking in the fire, touched and smelled the three Jews' clothes, and heard the king's confession of faith, were unaffected. It's also incredible that the rumors of this miracle, racing through the huge crowds like wildfire, plus the many public readings of the king's decree, had no effect on the common people. Surely many hearts turned to Jehovah, just as when, years later, God's judgment of Haman and His raising of Mordecai were reported throughout Persia: "Many of the people of the land became Jews; for the fear of the Jews fell upon them" (Esther 8:17).

The exalting of Jesus confirms these conversions. The three Jews' obedience in the fire enabled God to manifest Jesus in Babylon very prominently—at the center of a convocation in its capital. When Jesus was thus "lifted up" before Babylon's citizens, the Holy Spirit surely drew many of them to personal faith in Him. Jesus taught, "If I be *lifted up*...[I] will draw all men unto me" (John 12:32).

Will you also "lift up" Jesus in your furnace? "Glorify [honor] the

LORD in the fires, even the name of the LORD" (Isa. 24:15). If you endure, He will visit and save you: "He that shall endure unto the end, the same shall be saved" (Matt. 24:13). Then your exemplary trust in and loyalty to God through it all will win many "Babylonians," or worldlings, to the Savior of the furnace. Drawn by the Spirit, they will come asking, "Sirs, what must I do to be saved?" (Acts 16:30). As you exit the flames, they will enter the kingdom.

Reward

For their extraordinary loyalty, confession, and trust in Him, God gave the three Jews three excellent rewards at trial's end: deliverance, honor, and promotion.

As described above, deliverance (salvation) came in the form of God's personal visitation, which prompted their release from the raging fire. Their honor came from Babylon's king—the world's most renowned ruler—who praised their abandonment and service to God in the hearing of his clustered national leaders. They were also distinguished by the king's decree, read publicly throughout the empire, which mentioned them by name: "the God of *Shadrach, Meshach, and Abednego*" (Dan. 3:29). Promotion came when the king awarded them higher government jobs: "Then the king *promoted* Shadrach, Meshach, and Abednego in the province" (v. 30). These enviable prizes underscore the truths, "Verily, there is a reward for the righteous" (Ps. 58:11), and "He is a rewarder of them that diligently seek [and obey] him" (Heb. 11:6).

Equally wonderful rewards await us after trial by fire. For faithfully serving Him in the furnace, God will faithfully save us from it. For honoring Him by our faith, He will honor us for our faith. And for promoting Him, He will promote us—to higher places of more effective service or ministry: "Friend, go up higher" (Luke 14:10).

Establishment

After a potter forms a clay pot as he wishes, he decorates and glazes it, and then "fires" it in a kiln. This firing hardens, strengthens, and establishes his completed work. Its shape, color (glaze), and finish (flat or glossy) are permanently fixed, never to be changed.

Similarly, during the three Jews' former training and trials (Dan. 1–2),

God the heavenly Potter formed their characters according to His desire. Then He placed them in His "kiln," Nebuchadnezzar's furnace, to "fire" them. There the heat the king designed to cremate them instead cemented in them the very virtues he despised and God delighted in—uncompromising obedience and loyalty to God and utter trust in His faithfulness. As a result, their spiritual characters were established, or permanentized. These character qualities remained in them for the rest of their lives.

Thereafter God knew their faith would never waiver. He could count on them to be loyal, courageous, and, if necessary, sacrificially obedient, whatever the situation. He knew no person, however close or powerful, and no threat, however dangerous or deadly, could turn them from doing His will, in His way, and in His time. Thanks to trial by fire, the three Jews were fully and exclusively *His*—finished vessels "unto honor," unchanging servants fit and ready to serve their unchanging God.

Their establishment in the faith strengthened the faith of other Jews. Wherever the king's decree was proclaimed, Jews were encouraged. Not since their nation had fallen to the Babylonians had they felt so good about Jehovah or so secure in Babylonia. There was rejoicing in every Jewish home and synagogue. Shame was gone; being Jewish was honorable again! The king's decree was a powerful religious toleration order. If the empire's inhabitants could not even *speak* against Jehovah without risking deprivation of property and death (Dan. 3:29), they certainly had to be tolerant of His people! So Jews everywhere experienced a reprieve from prejudice, injustice, and persecution. This was most refreshing, a kind of religious revival, an intermission of joy and rest in an otherwise long captivity to sorrow and weariness. The shock and misery of their exile had made the Jews feel abandoned by God. The three Jews' victory made them realize anew that God was still with them, still working, and still sovereign. Thus their faith was revived, confirmed, and strengthened...because three of their kind overcame trial by fire!

The same results will follow if we overcome trial by fire. God will establish our characters, as the apostle Peter envisioned: "But the God of all grace...after ye have suffered awhile [in trial by fire], make you perfect, *establish*, strengthen, settle you" (1 Pet. 5:10). "Fired" in utter reliance on God's faithfulness, our faith will be permanentized. Thereafter, we'll remain "vessels unto honor...fit for the master's use" (2 Tim. 2:21). Possessing "gold tried in the fire" (Rev. 3:18)—faith and knowledge proven in fiery conflicts and contradictions—we'll be spiritually rich in this life and ready for the next when Jesus appears.

Moreover, like the king's decree, our testimony will confirm and strengthen the faith of other Christians. Challenged by our courage, they will face their difficulties with more courage. Stirred by our bold confession, they will speak their faith more readily. Aroused by our loyalty to biblical truth, they will stand with God's Word more firmly. Impressed by our total reliance on God, they will lean on the everlasting arms more fully. Inspired by our victory, they will anticipate theirs more hopefully.

~

There's one more thing we must realize. In trial by fire, we have one enemy that's more dangerous than either our "furnaces" or the people who ignite them. That ultimate nemesis is *unspiritual thinking*—thinking and reacting to life as any "carnal," or biblically unenlightened, person would: "Ye are yet carnal...and walk [think, live] as [unsaved, untaught] men" (1 Cor. 3:3). This is deadly to our faith. The apostle Paul warned, "For to be carnally minded is death, but to be spiritually minded is life and peace" (Rom. 8:6).

Mull these translations:

> If people's thinking is controlled by the sinful self, there is death. But if their thinking is controlled by the Spirit, there is life and peace.
> —ROMANS 8:6, NCV

> Letting your sinful nature control your mind leads to death. But letting the Spirit control your mind leads to life and peace.
> —ROMANS 8:6, NLT

It is vital that we think from a spiritual, or *scriptural*, viewpoint. We must see every situation, especially our fiery trials, through the Spirit-inspired viewfinder of God's Word. Since the Spirit inspired the Word, the Word is spiritual. So to be Word-minded is to be Spirit-minded, and steadily refilled with and refreshed by the Spirit's "life" in even our fieriest trials. We become spiritually minded generally by meditating on God's Word and specifically by pondering the benefits of trial by fire as opened in this chapter and similar teachings. To fail to do this means "death"—our faith and knowledge will end, not be established, in our "furnaces"!

To be spiritually minded, we must also refuse typically human unspiritual reactions.

For example, don't focus on the heat—"This pressure is too intense. It's destructive!" Seek God's grace, which is always sufficient. Don't fret at the unfairness—"Why am I suffering for *obeying* God?" Believe in God's unfailing ultimate justice. Don't be shocked by your enemies' cruel intentions—"They're trying to destroy my faith…and me!" You're not wrestling with flesh and blood only but with the influence of evil spirits. Don't be offended with God for letting evil people triumph over you temporarily—"How can my loving heavenly Father stand by idly while they do this to me?" He's humbling you now so He can later give you an honorable and permanent victory. If instead of correcting your unspiritual thinking you indulge it, you'll burn. Your confidence in God, fellowship with Him, and fruitfulness for Him will be reduced to ashes.

Or you'll crack. You'll rebel and take the easiest, quickest way out of your trouble, righteous or not, God's will or not. Then, like a pot plucked from the kiln and suddenly exposed to cool air, you'll fall apart. Your Christian character will quickly break up and you'll return to your old life. Instead of being a useful, honorable vessel in God's house, you'll be a useless dishonorable, "crackpot" Christian. Saved by grace but broken by trial, you'll be a big disappointment to the heavenly Potter and His people.

To avoid this abysmal end, don't just think spiritually, talk spiritually! Before the three Jews entered the king's furnace, they made a bold confession of faith: "*Our God, whom we serve, is able to deliver us…and he will deliver us*" (Dan. 3:17). Delighted, God quickly and powerfully confirmed their confession. With this in mind, make your own bold confession of faith, confidently declaring the benefits you expect to gain in your furnace!

O Lord, praise You! I believe this fiery trial will develop me, not destroy me. It will purify and liberate me and give me a surer, deeper knowledge of You. Enduring it, I will honor You, and You will establish my character and faith and reward me richly. I'll be spiritually, eternally rich, with "gold tried in the fire!" And my testimony will save the lost and strengthen the saved!

Then focus on God's goal and go for it!

Chapter Twenty-Five

THE GOAL OF TRIAL BY FIRE

Lo, I see four men loose, walking in the midst of the fire,
and they have no hurt...

—DANIEL 3:25

esides revealing the benefits of trial by fire, Daniel 3 also discloses its goal. That divine objective is encapsulated in the words King Nebuchadnezzar spoke when he realized the three Jews had survived his attempt to incinerate them.

Stunned, he described them as:

> ...loose, walking in the midst of the fire, and they have no
> hurt...

—DANIEL 3:25

It was *at this moment* that he called them out of the fire: "Then Nebuchadnezzar came near to the mouth of the burning fiery furnace, and spoke...come forth" (Dan. 3:26). After being enraged at them only minutes earlier, why did the king now abruptly end their harrowing trial?

There were two reasons for this remarkable royal reversal. First, the king saw for himself that, much to his chagrin, the three Jews had bested the worst punishment he could devise. What else, then, could he do but release them? When your best plan fails, why continue? Second, and far more importantly, though the king didn't know it, *God's* goal had been reached in the three Jews. So He "turned" the shaken king's heart to stop persecuting them and start promoting them: "The king's heart is in the hand of the LORD, like the rivers of water; *he turneth it* whithersoever he will" (Prov. 21:1). And, heathen though he was, the king of Babylon promptly obeyed the King of heaven, releasing his three captives (Dan. 3:26–30).

Indeed, the three Jews' physical condition at the moment they were called out of the fire portrays precisely God's target in testing Christians with fiery trials. *He will release us from our fiery trials when our spiritual condition parallels their physical condition at the time of their release.*

To clearly and fully understand God's aim in subjecting us to trial by fire, let's probe these key words: "...loose, walking in the midst of the fire, and they have no hurt" (Dan. 3:25).

THE GOAL OF TRIAL BY FIRE

Free indeed

Stated first is that the three Jews were "loose." Their former restrictions—the ropes they had been bound with—were gone, burned off by the flames. So even though they were still detained in the furnace, they were free men, "free indeed."

Their fully liberated bodies represent *the full spiritual liberty of overcoming Christians.* Jesus promised that we can be "free indeed," or truly free from all limitations of sin and self: "The Son...shall make you *free...free indeed*" (John 8:36). This full liberty is necessary if we are to do God's will without hindrance or diversion. The three Jews' physical liberty in the furnace is a symbolic demonstration of Jesus' promise.

For us to experience the reality of living "free indeed," we need to understand what our "ropes" are, how we get free from them, and what this results in.

As stated in the previous chapter, our primary "ropes" are *fears*—of reproach, rejection, failure, lack of provisions, disaster, death, or the failure of God's promises. Other ropes are *evil thoughts*—of unbelief, carnal reasoning, malice, immorality, vain imaginations, or illusions of grandeur. Others are *bad attitudes*—misjudging, condemning, insubordination, self-pity, doubt, contempt, discontentment, unmercifulness, stubbornness, prejudice, despising correction, or rejecting adversity. Others are *root sins*—covetousness, pride, envy, worldly ambition, anger, or vengeance. Others are *sinful or undisciplined behavior*—immorality, lying, stealing, complaining, arguing, rage, mocking, and bad habits (drunkenness, smoking, overeating, laziness, and so forth). *Anything God dislikes* that we permit in our lives is also a binding. As long as it remains, it limits what God can do in us and through us to help others.

God liberates us by our obedience in the fire. *If* we continue studying and obeying God's Word and obeying His guidance in our intense difficulties, we're on the way to full spiritual liberty: "*If ye continue* in my word...the truth shall make you *free...free indeed*" (John 8:31–32, 36). If we stop short in obedience, we cut short our liberation. If we persist, it persists.

Steady obedience in the fire leads to full liberty and fruitfulness in the fire. Eventually we become thoroughly "loosed"—released motivationally, emotionally, mentally, and behaviorally—from all our sin- and self-bonds. Our feet now free, we can walk closely with Jesus. Our hands now free, we can work closely with Him. Our soul now "free indeed," we can be "fruitful indeed"—in the fire!

Stable

Peering through the flames, the king noticed only one activity in which the three Jews were engaged: "walking" (Dan. 3:25). Walking is a steady, or evenly paced, human action. The use of this term implies their actions were not erratic—walking, stumbling, falling, lying, rising and stumbling again, and so forth—but stable, fixed in a steady pattern of positive action.

Their physical stability represents our spiritual stability. So often Christians suffer spiritual instability. One day we're in the Spirit, and three days we're out. One morning we seek the Lord, and for two weeks we forget the morning watch. One month we draw closer to Christ, and three months we draw back. We're inconsistent, up and down, on and off, walking and stumbling. Trial by fire ends this because, as we soon learn, we can't survive if we remain inconsistent. The strong difficulties surrounding us goad or force us to get our act together, to practice the self-discipline of true disciples of Christ.

So we begin forming a personal spiritual regimen. We seek the Lord first every morning and do all the things necessary to walk closely with Him daily—screening our thoughts, forgiving offenders, meditating on God's Word, praying often, giving thanks in all situations, choosing to trust God at all times, avoiding overindulgence, discharging our duties faithfully, and so forth.

And somewhere in this learning process we discover the great secret of spiritual stability: we must *never* get down on ourselves! As discussed in chapter one, when we fail or sin, we must quickly confess this to God and put it behind us, completely trusting His promise, "If we confess our sins, he is faithful and just to forgive us our sins, and to cleanse us from all unrighteousness" (1 John 1:9). And regardless of our feelings, we must rise and reset our feet on the path of obedience. The more quickly we do this, the less spiritual "down time" we experience, and the more our spiritual consistency grows until, eventually, we're stable.

Soon God and people alike see that, like the three Jews, we've learned to "walk, and not faint" (Isa. 40:31) every day—in the fire!

Upright

Unlike other creatures, human beings walk in a fully upright position. That the three Jews were "walking" in the fire implies they were upright.

Their physical uprightness speaks of our moral uprightness—honesty in speech, faithfulness in relationships, sexual purity, and financial integrity.

Many Christians today are forgetful of the fact that we are called to live not by the world's standards of what is right, but by "his righteousness" (Matt. 6:33). As a result, they let streaks of unfaithful, immoral, unethical, or illegal conduct remain in their lives. In money matters, they cut corners, break laws or regulations, or abandon accountability. In conversations, they omit, invent, or distort information to favor themselves or their friends or to misrepresent adversaries. In relationships, they think nothing of breaking vows, promises, or commitments. In business or professional life, they practice and excuse unethical methods of achieving their ends. In private life, they view pornography or pursue extramarital flirtations and affairs.

Trial by fire comes to eliminate these and other areas of unrighteousness and hypocrisy. In the fire, the heat of the Spirit's conviction intensifies. We hear His call to holiness clearer, stronger, more urgently: "As he who hath called you is holy, *so be ye holy in all manner of life*" (1 Pet. 1:15). When God chastens us for disobedience, we recognize it more distinctly. The fear of the Lord grips us as we realize that even though God forgives us, we can't sin with impunity. His judgments against sin are predictable and inescapable. Sin always harms someone or something; if not openly, then privately; if not immediately, then eventually. Freshly impressed with this fact, we begin taking Christ's righteousness much more seriously. Aware that loving but holy divine eyes are watching, we begin being much more careful about everything we watch, say, and do, publicly and privately. Why? We "fear," or deeply respect, the Lord and His righteousness.

Simultaneously, a new desire to please the Lord is born in us. This springs from the conviction that, just as surely as disobedience brings punishment, *uprightness brings rewards*: "*No good thing will he withhold* from them that walk uprightly" (Ps. 84:11). This implies, "*Every good thing will He give* to them that walk uprightly."

In this new holy fear and hopeful faith, we begin walking uprightly with much greater consistency—in the fire!

Steadily moving forward

By "walking" in the furnace, the three Jews neither went back nor stood still but steadily moved forward. Always they went onward, advancing straight ahead. One step. Then another. And another.

Their steady forward movement symbolizes perfectly our steady spiritual progress in walking and working with God as "forward-moving Christians." (See chapter one.)

To walk consistently with God, we must spend time with Him every day in the "secret place" of private fellowship, praying, worshiping Him, and feeding on His Word (Ps. 91:1). We must also obey Him, examine ourselves, avoid emotional extremes, and control our zeal.

Failure to seek the Lord shuts down all spiritual progress—and we stand still. Delaying to obey the Spirit's guidance causes us to wobble—and we stumble. Rebelling against God's Word or correction causes us to revert to carnal thinking and living—and we backslide. Excessive rejoicing over blessings and successes, or self-condemnation over sins and failures, stops our advance—while we leap with excitement or lie down in depression. If we zealously rush ahead of God in presumptuous, undisciplined haste—*running* in the furnace—we break fellowship with "the form of the fourth," who always *walks* at a steady pace, even in fiery tribulation or persecution. (See Luke 13:31–33.) Any of these things may keep us from moving steadily forward in our walk.

And that keeps us from moving steadily forward in our work. Our ministry for Jesus advances only as our relationship with Him advances. It is closeness to the Lord that gives us the strength and courage to keep working when our labor is hard and its results few. In the fire, the Spirit repeatedly reminds us of God's promises to reward steady, faithful work:

> Be ye steadfast, unmovable, always abounding in the work of the Lord, forasmuch as ye know that your labor is not in vain in the Lord.
> —1 CORINTHIANS 15:58

> God is not unrighteous to forget your work and labor of love…in that ye have ministered to the saints, and do minister.
> —HEBREWS 6:10

> Be ye strong…let not your hands be weak, for your work shall be rewarded.
> —2 CHRONICLES 15:7

Contemplated in faith, these biblical confidence boosters prod us to steadily move on with our work or calling every day, regardless of our difficulties or results. Soon we're "diligent in season, out of season" (2 Tim. 4:2)—in the fire!

Unoffended

Even more amazing than the three Jews' survival was their perfect preservation. In shock and frustration the king exclaimed, "…they have no hurt [injury]" (Dan. 3:25). His counselors' thorough inspection confirmed that, indeed, his most injurious treatment had failed to injure them: "...these men, upon whose bodies the fire had no power" (v. 27). Not even one hair in their thick Hebrew beards was singed: "Nor was an hair of their head singed" (v. 27). Despite the holocaust, or *whole burning*, the three Jews were wholly well and blessed.

Chiefly, their absence of physical injury symbolizes overcomers being without soul injury or spiritual offense. They are not offended by malicious offenses, and they are not bitter at God or people, including the very ones who create their fiery tests and thrust them into them with relish! Why? They want the blessing of Jesus, who taught, "Blessed is he, whosoever shall *not be offended in [or at] me*" (Luke 7:23). A free translation of this is, "God specially blesses those who refuse to get angry with Him, no matter how bad their circumstances!"

When the three Jews emerged, there is no evidence that they were disillusioned with Jehovah or chaffed at the king. To the contrary, they completely accepted their mistreatment as being divinely permitted and continued relying confidently on God. When called out, they humbly exited the king's furnace, received his honors, accepted his promotion, and continued working faithfully in his administration without a single complaint, threat, or act of retaliation (Dan. 3:30)! Surely, the grace of Jesus Christ—who drew near them in the furnace, always trusted His heavenly Father, forgave and prayed for His enemies, and taught us to do so—was upon them. His grace is sufficient for us also.

If we stay close to Christ in our fiery tests, we will emerge with "no hurt"—without a trace of anger, ill will, or rancor. Our spiritual life will not be worse for our enemies having done, and our God permitted, their worst. How is this possible? The Holy Spirit gives us His grace (divine ability imparted to the believer) as we steadily obey Jesus' command to forgive all offenders all offenses, even the cruelest: "And when ye stand praying, *forgive*, if ye have *anything against any*" (Mark 11:25). No matter how much our enemies wish to harm our souls, we must forgive them quickly and completely, refusing to harbor any anger or vengeance. Why? Jesus commands this. When we consistently forgive even our worst offenders and are willing to reconcile if they repent (as Nebuchadnezzar), we're like the three Jews—and ready for release from the furnace.

This "unoffendable" attitude will also bring us another great blessing: our bodies will suffer "no hurt" in our fiery trials. As we consistently obey God's Word—including His orders to, as needed, take physical rest (Ps. 23:2) and spiritual rest (time in His presence; see Matt. 11:28–30)—the Word's supernatural healing power is released to benefit our bodies. Believing God's promises to preserve, deliver, and reward us tranquilizes our nerves and so protects our bodies from the numerous harmful effects of excessive stress. Thus as we consistently believe and obey God's "words" and "sayings," they steadily minister "life" and "healing and health" to all our "flesh":

> My son, attend to *my words*; consent and submit to *my say-ings*…for they are *life* to those who find them, *healing and health to all their flesh.*
> —PROVERBS 4:20, 22, AMP

After his "fiery," or intense, experience in the lion's den, Daniel emerged with "no manner of hurt," not only because he obeyed but also because "he believed in his God" (Dan. 6:23). If we follow his example, we too will pass through our "flames" of lethal stress without any stress-induced (psychosomatic) illnesses or ailments. To our amazement and God's glory, both our souls and our bodies will have "no hurt"—in the fire!

Unaffected

Upon closer examination, the king discovered that not only were the three Jews' bodies uninjured, their clothing was also unaffected by his ferocious, roaring, fiery furnace: "…neither were their coats changed" (Dan. 3:27). Their cloaks were not burned, nor their stockings, nor their turbans. No char! No smudges! Not even a whiff of the fire's stench was detectible! "Nor the smell of fire had passed on them" (v. 27). Except for their former rope bindings, the three Jews' clothes were exactly the same as when they entered the fire.

Their unaffected garments represent overcomers' unchanged character traits, especially their faith, loyalty, and courage. God wants these traits—the chief traits of the three Jews—to remain in us not only before and during but also *after* our trials. Because we've taken a courageous stand of faith once for loyalty to God, His Word, or His calling doesn't mean we'll do it again.

After emerging from an adverse situation, our human tendency is to build a wall of protection to ensure that we will never encounter that particular adversity again. After an airliner crashes, new safety procedures are begun to avoid future accidents. After an auto accident, drivers increase their insurance coverage. After divorce, divorcees sometimes avoid remarriage. After a heart attack, a victim studies and adopts a heart-healthy diet. Christians don't like to be "burned" twice either, if we can avoid it.

So when we emerge from fiery trials, the devil immediately offers us his pseudo-wisdom. He plants the seemingly harmless, tiny seed-thought, "You don't have to go through this fiery trouble again. All you have to do to avoid it is just compromise a little. Loosen up! Don't insist on biblical standards. Don't focus so much on your calling. Just go with the flow of the times. You'll do this the next time your faith gets you into trouble…if you're smart!"

But mature Christians learn true wisdom: "If God sustained me through the fiery trial once, He'll do it again, if necessary." And while they're not foolishly eager to do so (as they perhaps were before their fiery trial!), they're soberly ready and willing to take yet another stand on their biblical beliefs or practices, if God requires it. That's the mind-set of a perfectly unaffected overcomer—and it's pure "gold tried in the fire." The devil's worst scare tactics or bullying can't move him. Why? He's too rich in proven faith, loyalty, and courage: "He shall not be afraid of evil tidings [prospects or threats of trouble]; his heart is fixed, trusting in the LORD" (Ps. 112:7). He's already learned how to live unaffected—in the fire!

Closer to Jesus daily

As previously stated, Jesus walked closely with the three Jews in the fire. The king cried, "I see four men…walking…[with] the Son of God" (Dan. 3:25, KJV). And, as already noted, this was the closest they ever walked with Him. So when their fiery trial ended, they were *drawing closer* to Jesus.

Bad as it sounds, many Christians don't want to draw closer to

Jesus. Slow to believe His saying, "Apart from Me you can do nothing" (John 15:5, NAS), they seek Him rarely instead of regularly. Rather than walk as close to Him as possible, they stay as far from Him as possible, as Peter did on one occasion: "Peter followed him afar off" (Mark 14:54). These seek the Lord's face very few times, if any, in their lifetime. Others believe Christ's dictum and draw near Him steadily for a season—one month, one year, several years—but then stop drawing near. Still others, driven by an inspired sense of need, seek Him with greater regularity. These devoted seekers draw near the Lord habitually every day, every circumstance, every season.

Whatever our prior devotion, trial by fire urges us to adopt the mindset of passionate pursuers of God. The law of spiritual supply and demand is at work here. To survive the constant pressure of our fiery trials, we must have constant spiritual nourishment. To meet this new demand, we must seek the Lord more consistently: "Seek the LORD, and his strength; seek his face *evermore*" (Ps. 105:4). As we seek Him and His strength "evermore," we find ourselves growing *ever closer* to Him. When this habit is deeply formed, we're ready to exit the furnace—much closer to Him than when we entered it!

Thereafter, we continue drawing very close to Jesus daily, regardless of our situation or season. Why? Necessity has seared this discipline into our hearts—in the fire!

Content

Amazingly, the three Jews grew content in the fire, so much that they didn't even try to escape! When the king looked, they were calmly "walking" (Dan. 3:25) in the furnace—not climbing its walls, groping wildly for an opening, franticly running around, or calling for help. They seem to have forgotten where they were, because the king had to *call* to prompt them to leave the furnace: "Nebuchadnezzar came near...and spoke...*come forth*" (v. 26). Why were they so at ease?

Apparently, *who* was with them overruled *where* they were. The permeating comfort of Jesus' presence compensated for the distressing cruelty of their persecution. Another reason is that they were spiritually minded.

They reasoned that God was with them, "a very present help in trouble"

(Ps. 46:1), so why panic? In His presence (even in a furnace!) was "fullness of joy" (Ps. 16:11), so why worry or strive for better circumstances? Their reliable Deliverer, who is "faithful... [to] make a way to escape" (1 Cor. 10:13), was present, so why rack their brains for an escape plan? The living Word was speaking to them steadily, so He would surely speak a word to release them in His time. Meanwhile they would satisfy their souls with sweet, sustaining fellowship with Him and with one another. Thus they learned, as never before, to be content—satisfied enough with what they had—in "whatever" state they were in. They also realized, more than ever, that "my grace is sufficient for thee" *anywhere!* This spiritual thinking enabled them to walk in heavenly contentment in a hellish trial.

Without question, theirs was an extraordinary contentment. There are four levels, or degrees, of contentment. They are:

1. *In prosperity and success.* To be content while we are successful, prosperous, healthy, and loved by everyone requires little or no grace. Even sinners and carnal Christians are content when everything goes their way.

2. *In mundane circumstances.* To be content when life consists of ordinary days and monotonous duties demands God's grace. When the mundane rules, the agitation of sin robs most people of their peace. But Christians need not loathe quiet, ordinary times. If mindful of Jesus, we can find the richest life, purpose, and joy in the dullest days. "Thou wilt keep him in perfect peace, whose mind is stayed on thee" (Isa. 26:3).

3. *In adversity.* The ability to be content in adversity is rarer still, and evidence that the Spirit is strengthening us. When people and events conspire against us and we continue steadily seeking and serving the Lord, the grace of contentment is thriving in us.

4. *In great adversity.* To be content in extreme adversities (deep waters, fiery trials) is the rarest of wonders. It proves that extraordinary divine grace, like that Jesus demonstrated in His sufferings, is sustaining us. When every work fails,

every path is blocked, every hope is quenched, every kind of trouble visits, all our friends turn away, and yet we continue walking contentedly with Jesus in the "fire," our contentment is fully mature.

Undeniably, the three Jews displayed the fourth, or highest, kind of contentment. Their satisfaction in God was impervious, untouchable, of the highest order—just what God wants us to have!

Many Christians before us have had it: Peter sleeping peacefully in prison on the eve of his execution, John "in the Spirit" in exile on Patmos, Paul praising God while wrongly jailed and injured, and so forth. These strongly satisfied ones formed the habit of cultivating God's presence long before their fiery trials visited. When they came, they merely held fast their habit of finding contentment in their fellowship with Jesus. And as they held it fast, it held them fast and firm...until they exited the fire.

Their examples challenge us. Are we learning to "be content with such things as ye have," knowing that, whatever our circumstances, Jesus is there to satisfy us with His fellowship? "He hath said, I will never leave thee, nor forsake thee" (Heb. 13:5). If so, we'll find that His presence, peace, strength, guidance, and insight into the Word can keep us calm and content in even the fieriest trials: unjust legal action, loss of property, serious illness, betrayal, bereavement, family conflicts, slander, oppressive or abusive authorities, and so forth. As we grow in this understanding, we stop urgently seeking escape.

Still human, we request and anticipate release. But, spiritually minded now, we're no longer hasty or desperate to have it. Why? The all-powerful, unchanging, faithful, and merciful God is with us and we know it. Every time we meditate in His Word, He strengthens and speaks to us. Every time we worship, we sense His presence. Every time we pray, He revives and answers us. Every time we long for release we remember: He released the three Jews, He'll release us too! So we abide in faith-driven contentment day by day—in the fire!

GOD STANDS BY OUR FURNACES

Nebuchadnezzar, the lord of Babylon's furnace, stood by hoping to see the three Jews suffer. But when he saw them "loose, walking in the midst of the fire, and … [having] no hurt," he released them.

Jesus, the Lord of our fiery trials, stands by our afflictions, hoping to see us overcome them. Why? He finds His choicest servants, and forges His strongest instruments, in the fire: "I have chosen thee in the furnace of affliction" (Isa. 48:10). He reserves His fullest approval for those who reach the goal of trial by fire. Like the three Jews, they're free indeed, stable, upright, steadily moving forward, unoffended, unaffected, drawing closer to Jesus daily, and content—in the fire!

This advanced state of spiritual development is described in different terms throughout the Bible. It is Christlikeness, or the "fruit of the Spirit" in fullest manifestation. (See Galatians 5:22–23.) It is the highest "good" toward which God is working "all things" (Rom. 8:28) together in our lives, namely, that we be fully conformed to the image of Jesus' character (v. 29). It is the fully developed Christianity the apostle Paul (and the Holy Spirit) envisioned for Christians and churches when he prayed that we might "walk worthy of the Lord … strengthened with all might … unto all patience and long-suffering with joyfulness, giving thanks" (Col. 1:10, 12); and that we might "stand perfect and complete in all the will of God" (4:12); and that "Christ may dwell in your hearts by faith … that ye might be filled with all the fullness of God" (Eph. 3:17, 19). And, as this book has repeatedly and variously described and recommended, the goal of trial by fire is "gold tried in the fire."

When the Lord of our fiery trials sees His goal—and gold—in us, He will release us just as Nebuchadnezzar did the three Jews.

Then we'll not only *have* "gold tried in the fire"—a fully mature, fully proven faith and knowledge of God; we'll also *be* "gold tried in the fire" in God's sight.

And we'll be spiritually rich beyond our wildest dreams. We'll be rich in unshakable confidence in God in these increasingly unstable last days. We'll be rich in God's unfailing truth, when so many are searching frantically to buy truth from religions, philosophies, psychics, politicians, and pundits, only to discover they've purchased falsehood. We'll be rich in this world, having every monetary need met by our Good Shepherd and resting in a soul-contentment money can't buy. We'll be rich in the next world, ruling and rejoicing with Christ during His thousand-year kingdom. We'll be rich in eternity, enjoying perpetual residence in an indescribably fabulous golden city and rapturous fellowship with One worth far more than gold! And finally, we'll be forever rich in the satisfying memory that we answered Jesus' challenge to our generation: "I counsel thee to buy of me gold tried in the fire, that thou mayest be rich" (Rev. 3:18). For these reasons Christ, our Judge, will reward us with tokens of our spiritual wealth—large golden crowns and lustrous gold chains like those given to David, Joseph, and Daniel after their fiery trials—when He judges the church.

Informed of these facts and inspired with this faith, why not make Job's confession of faith your own?

When he hath tested me, *I shall come forth as gold.*

—JOB 23:10

My friend, in these last days, seek God's gold, study His gold, and show Him gold!

Notes

CHAPTER 1
THE FORWARD-MOVING CHRISTIAN

1. James Strong, *Strong's Exhaustive Concordance of the Bible* (Iowa Falls, IA: Riverside Book and Bible House, n.d.); James Strong, *The Enhanced Strong's Lexicon* (Ontario: Woodside Bible Fellowship, 1995).

2. E. Sifton, *The Serenity Prayer* (New York, NY; W.W. Norton & Co., 2003).

CHAPTER 7
THE TEN IMPLICATIONS

1. Strong, *Strong's Exhaustive Concordance of the Bible.* Also, W. E. Vine, *Vine's Complete Expository Dictionary of Old and New Testament Words* (Nashville: Thomas Nelson Publishers, 1996).

2. Vine, *Vine's Complete Expository Dictionary of Old and New Testament Words.*

3. L. Richards, *The Bible Reader's Companion* (Wheaton, IL: Victor Books, 1991).

CHAPTER 8
SPIRITUAL ABORTION

1. National Right to Life Committee (NRLC), "Abortion Statistics: United States Data and Trends," http://www.nrlc.org/Factsheets/FS03_AbortionintheUS.pdf (accessed January 10, 2008). The NRLC bases its estimated annual abortion count on data provided by the Centers for Disease Control (CDC) and the Allen Guttmacher Institute (AGI), Planned Parenthood's designated research affiliate that tracks abortion industry data and trends.

2. Ibid.

3. National Highway Traffic Safety Administration, "2006 Traffic Safety Annual Assessment—a Preview," July 2007, http://www-nrd.nhtsa.dot.gov/Pubs/810791.PDF (accessed January 10, 2008).

4. Based on statistics obtained from The History Place, "Statistics of the Holocaust," http://www.historyplace.com/worldwar2/holocaust/h-statistics.htm (accessed February 23, 2008).

CHAPTER 9
SODOM REVISITED: A SIGN

1. MSNBC.com, "General Regrets Remarks on Homosexuality," March 13, 2007, http://www.msnbc.msn.com/id/17590518/ (accessed January 10, 2008).

2. Ibid.

3. Ibid.

4. R. Albert Mohler Jr., "Ministry Is Stranger Than It Used to Be," *Brush Arbor Quarterly*, issue 4, Spring 2007 (Covert, MI: Wisdom's Gate Publishers, 2007).

5. CNN.com, "Episcopalians Approve Gay Bishop," August 6, 2003, http://www.cnn.com/2003/US/08/05/bishop/ (accessed January 10, 2008).

6. CNN.com, "Evangelical Confesses to 'Sexual Immorality' in Letter," November 6, 2006, http://www.cnn.com/2006/US/11/05/haggard.allegations/index.html (accessed May 3, 2007).

7. *Webster's New World College Dictionary*, fourth edition (Cleveland, OH: MacMillan, 1999), s.v. "high time."

CHAPTER 10
THE LIE STOPPER

1. *Webster's Encyclopedic Unabridged Dictionary of the English Language* (New York, NY: Random House, 1996), s.v. "lie."

2. Ibid.

3. New Jerusalem, the capital city of the new earth, as described in the Book of Revelation 21:1–22:5, esp. 21:27.

4. Ibid.

CHAPTER 11
QUENCHING THE HOLY SPIRIT

1. Strong, *Strong's Exhaustive Concordance of the Bible.*

2. Vine, *Vine's Complete Expository Dictionary of Old and New Testament Words.*

3. Ibid.

4. A. W. Tozer, *Man: The Dwelling Place of God* (Harrisburg, PA: Christian Publications, 1966).

CHAPTER 12
SEEK MEEKNESS!

1. Strong, *Strong's Exhaustive Concordance of the Bible.*

2. Vine, *Vine's Complete Expository Dictionary of Old and New Testament Words.*

3. Ibid.

4. Strong, *Strong's Exhaustive Concordance of the Bible.*

CHAPTER 13
HOW TO HUMBLE YOURSELF

1. American Standard Version; English Standard Version; New American Standard Version; New King James Version; The Bible: A New Translation, by James Moffatt; Young's Literal Translation.

CHAPTER 15
MAY I RECOMMEND THE PSALMS?

1. *The Life Application Study Bible* (Wheaton, IL: Tyndale House Publishers, 2004).

2. *Christian History*, "John Knox: The Thundering Scot," issue 46, vol. 14, no. 2, 1995. James Kirk, "Worship Before and After," *Christian History*, May 1995, 30-23.

3. *Christian History*, "A Devoted Life: Benedict and the Rise of Western Monasticism," issue 93, Winter 2007. Hugh Feiss, "A Life of Listening," *Christian History and Biography*, Winter 2007.

4. Ibid.

5. *The Spirit-Filled Life Bible* (Nashville, TN: Thomas Nelson Publishers, 1991).

6. *The New Analytical Bible* (Chicago, IL: John A. Dickson Publishing, 1973).

7. Ibid.

CHAPTER 17
ON LEADING WORSHIP

1. A. W. Tozer, *Of God and Men* (Camp Hill, PA: Christian Publications, 1960, renewed 1987 by the Tozer Children). Used by permission of WingSpread Publishers, a division of Zur Ltd., 800.884.4571.

2. I certainly do not recommend tattooing, because it's a defacing of the body, graffiti on the temple of the Holy Spirit. But we must not condemn

Christians who tattoo themselves, especially before conversion. Instead, we should look beyond body markings, as Christ does, who looks not on the "outward appearance," but "on the heart" (1 Sam. 16:7).

Chapter 18
The Highest Ministry

1. *Webster's Encyclopedic Unabridged Dictionary of the English Language*, s.v. "intercede."

2. Ibid.

3. A. Kenneth Curtis, J. Stephen Lang, and Randy Peterson, *The 100 Most Important Events in Christian History* (Grand Rapids, MI; Fleming H. Revell, 1991).

4. Ibid.

5. Lewis A. Drummond, "The Secrets of Spurgeon's Preaching," *Christian History*, issue 29, vol, 10, no. 1, 1991.

6. Oswald Chambers, *My Utmost for His Highest* (New York, NY: Dodd, Mead, & Company, 1935).

Chapter 19
To the Pastors and People of Small Churches

1. Oswald Chambers Publications Assoc., *Oswald Chambers: His Life and Work* (London: Marshall, Morgan and Scott, Ltd., 1959).

2. Charles F. Pfeiffer, Howard F. Vos, and John Rea, *Wycliffe Bible Encyclopedia*, vol. 2 (Chicago, IL: Moody Press, 1975).

Chapter 20
Hope for the Parents of Captive Children

1. Pfeiffer, Vos, and Rea, *Wycliffe Bible Encyclopedia*, vol. 1.

2. Strong, *Strong's Exhaustive Concordance of the Bible*.

3. *The World Book Encyclopedia*, deluxe edition CD (Chicago, IL: World Book, Inc., 2003).

4. Herodotus of Halicarnassus, *The History of Herodotus*, George Rawlinson, trans., Manuel Komroff, ed. (New York: Tudor Publishing Co., 1939).

CHAPTER 21
ABOUT LOYALTY TO GOD

1. *Webster's Encyclopedic Unabridged Dictionary of the English Language*, s.v. "loyalty."

CHAPTER 23
THE DEEP IS CALLING

1. Merrill C. Tenney, *The Zondervan Pictorial Bible Dictionary* (Grand Rapids, MI: Zondervan Publishing House, 1967). Also, Pfeiffer, Vos, and Rea, *Wycliffe Bible Encyclopedia*, vol. 1.

2. Charles Caldwell Ryrie, *The Ryrie Study Bible* (Chicago, IL: Moody Press, 1978).

3. Patricia Stallings Kruppa, "The Life and Times of Charles H. Spurgeon," *Christian History Magazine*, issue 29, vol. 10, no. 1, 1991. Also, Mark Hopkins, "The Down-Grade Controversy."

4. Darrel W. Amundsen, "The Anguish and Agonies of Charles Spurgeon," *Christian History Magazine*, issue 29, vol. 10, no. 1, 1991.

CHAPTER 24
THE BENEFITS OF TRIAL BY FIRE

1. In this section silver, not gold, is used to describe the purifying effects of "trial by fire." Though not gold, silver is its most closely related, or "sister," precious metal. (Platinum wasn't discovered until the sixteenth century.) In ancient times, fire played a key role in the processes by which both silver and gold were smelted and purified. Through Malachi God parallels His work of refining Levites' characters through testing to that of a refiner who purges both "gold and silver" in fiery crucibles: "He [the Lord] is like a refiner's fire...he shall sit like a refiner and purifier...he shall purify the sons of Levi, and purge them like *gold and silver*... " (Mal. 3:2–3).

OTHER BOOKS BY THIS AUTHOR

Walking in His Ways
0-88419-758-1

Walking on Water
0-88419-875-8

Precious Pearls From the Proverbs
1-59185-900-x

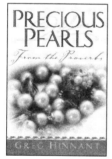

*Word Portraits: Five Illustrations
of the Mature Christian*
978-1-59979-087-9

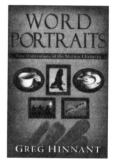

*DanielNotes: An Inspirational Com-
mentary on the Book of Daniel*
1-59185-169-6

*Key New Testament Passages
on Divorce and Remarriage*
1-931527-49-0

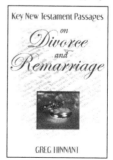

About This Ministry

Mission Statement

GREG HINNANT MINISTRIES exists to train believers to walk in New Testament discipleship by teaching the timeless, priceless, and unfailing principles of the Word of God. In this way we are contributing to the spiritual preparation of the bride of Christ in anticipation of the appearing of Jesus Christ.

Our slogan is, "Prepare ye the way of the LORD" (Isa. 40:3).

Ministries Available

We presently offer a free *devotional message*, the Weekly Word, posted weekly to our Web site. To view this, or to browse our books, cassette tapes, or CDs, please visit our Web site at: www.greghinnantministries.org.

To Contact This Ministry:

Greg Hinnant Ministries
P. O. Box 788
High Point, NC 27261

Web site: www.greghinnantministries.org
E-mail: rghministries@aol.com
Telephone: (336) 882-1645
Fax: (336) 886-7227

NOTES